COME
to win

COME to win.

Business Leaders, Artists, Doctors, and Other
Visionaries on How Sports Can Help You Top
Your Profession

VENUS WILLIAMS

with Kelly E. Carter

Amistad

Amistad

An Imprint of HarperCollins*Publishers*

HarperCollins books may be purchased for educational, business, or sales promotional use. For information, please write: Special Markets Department, HarperCollins Publishers, 10 East 53rd Street, New York, NY 10022.

FIRST EDITION

Designed by Lisa Stokes

Library of Congress Cataloging-in-Publication Data

Come to win: business leaders, artists, doctors, and other visionaries on how sports can help you top your profession / [compiled] by Venus Williams; with Kelly E. Carter. — 1st ed.
  p. cm.
Summary: "From multiple Grand Slam tennis champion and entrepreneur Venus Williams comes a book of wisdom—on how the principles of competitive athletics translate into business success. Full of insight and knowledge from an A-list cast of politicians, CEOs, and media figures."—Provided by publisher.
Includes index.
ISBN 978-0-06-171825-0
1. Sports. 2. Success. 3. Success in business. 4. Conduct of life. I. Williams, Venus, 1980– II. Carter, Kelly E.
GV706.55.C66 2010
796—dc22   2010011263

10 11 12 13 14   ov/rrd   10 9 8 7 6 5 4 3 2 1

This book is dedicated to my sisters, Yetunde, Isha, Lyndrea, and Serena. You are my best friends and give meaning to my life. I love you.

Contents

Preface
by *Venus Williams*

T HE ARC OF AN ATHLETE'S life is funny. Just when other young professionals are peaking, hitting their stride, and consolidating their skills, we're starting, if we're smart, to think of our future, one that doesn't depend on our athleticism and our injury-prone bodies to pay the rent. Let's be clear: I'm not retiring anytime soon. At thirty, I still have game and can think of nothing more gratifying than traveling the world to play tennis. But I am putting into practice something my mother, Oracene, and father, Richard, who once owned a security-guard company, told me and my sisters, Lyndrea, Yetunde, Isha, and Serena: Think entrepreneurially.

When we were growing up in Compton, California, the whole family would have these sit-down meetings led by my dad, who is a philosopher type. He'd ask questions such as, "Why is it that the poor person stays in the ghetto and the rich person gets richer?" or "Why is it that when you do something for someone it doesn't work as well as when you help them help themselves?" We wouldn't always have an answer, but that was, in a way, beside the point. He was training us early on to be independent thinkers. Of course, he was also training us to be financially independent. I remember him talking to us about the mechanics of buying properties out of foreclosure. While I was too young to absorb the details, the basic ideas seeped through. And if he was teaching us about real estate when we were young, you can only imagine how much my parents stressed the importance of education.

I coveted getting a degree as much as I did having my own business. After enrolling in an interior design program through the London-based Rhodec International correspondence school, I launched V Starr Interiors, a commercial and residential interior design company, in April 2002. I received my associate's degree in Fashion Design in 2007, the same year I debuted my clothing line, EleVen. And last year Serena and I bought a minority stake in the Miami Dolphins NFL team, a wonderful way to become even more entrenched in the business world. Let's say my parents' advice made a lasting impression.

A multitasker, I wanted to play tennis *and* study, *and* I also wanted to launch my first businesses while I was still playing rather than wait until after my career was over. There are a few benefits to starting a business early. The obvious one is I get to use my name to help market my endeavors; but, just as important, I gain experience and credibility now so that when I do retire, I'll already have industry knowledge as well as a client base. As Earvin "Magic" Johnson points out in the pages that follow, it's harder than it looks for athletes to start businesses because many people will take meetings with us just to get a ball or jersey signed with no intention of taking our proposals seriously. Like Roger Staubach, whose story also follows, I want to log in the hours that lead to credibility in the businesses while I continue to play professionally rather than get in after the fact, when it will be more difficult to be taken seriously.

With the launch of V Starr, I immediately realized that although tennis and design couldn't be further apart, I was bringing lessons learned on the court into the meetings, whether they were with potential clients, my team, or suppliers. My curiosity piqued, I began to compile a list of former athletes (not all of whom played professionally) who are now at the top of their professions. If I could talk to each one I'd ask them if their sports background was of any use in their professional life. And that curiosity led to this book. Along with my co-author, Kelly E. Carter, I did get to talk with this impressive and varied group of former athletes, and their responses comprise this book. I was encouraged and pleasantly surprised by their contributions. Though they come from a variety of fields—there are actors, designers, CEOs, chefs, doctors, editors, financiers, reporters, and politicians, as well as former professional athletes—the drive and discipline they bring into their work mirrors what they gave on the field, rink, and court or in the pool.

I loved working on this book, and I hope you too take something away—whether you're an aspiring visionary, an established or ascending executive, a burgeoning designer or actor. I hope you'll see how sports gives you a foundation that is transferrable, and how if you've played sports (at any level, professional or amateur), you are carrying around knowledge that you can use effectively in other fields. Reading the experiences of others made me cognizant of the benefits from sports I didn't even realize I had received—character, strength of body and mind, confidence, a sense of value and validation. Sarina Bratton, an entrepreneur who started a cruise line, perhaps sums it up best: "All of the training, the discipline, the determination, the good attitude and hard work that you're putting into your sport now are inherent values that you will carry with you through life, and you can apply those same values and disciplines to anything that you choose in your life. Recognize that and never be afraid to use them in your career or whatever you choose to do."

Not only did this book validate my sense that sports will benefit my post-sports career, but the stories also moved me. I get teary-eyed every time I read about former secretary of defense William Cohen's dad standing in the snow, peeking in through the window to watch his son play basketball, or how Vera Wang's figure skating not only bonded her to her family but may have extended her mother's life when illness struck.

More than move me, these essays motivated me. They have given me words of wisdom I'll take with me on the court *and* in the proverbial boardroom. In fact, I've already started putting some of these inspirational thoughts into my notebook—another idea I picked up from my father. He would prepare notebooks for us and fill up the pages with thoughts—sometimes even stories—about improving our tennis and attitudes. Everything was typed out, and the pages were laminated. Sometimes he'd hand us just a couple of pages, and sometimes a laminated binder folder. Some of them were even made into signs with sayings like "Believe It. Achieve It"; or "If you fail to plan, you plan to fail"; or "Perfect practice makes perfect," which he'd hang around the tennis court and in the house. There's still one hanging in the bathroom that reads: "Always try to be the most polite person in the world."

I'll use ideas from the contributors in *Come to Win* to inspire my next generation of signs. I can see the first one already; it simply says, "Extreme Effort." It will remind me that just as I have to work my tail off as an athlete, I'll have to put in the hours at EleVen and V Starr to make them work. As a little girl I practiced no fewer than five hours a day, every single day of the year. The only time we got a break was when it rained, which is why, to this day, I still find the rain comforting. Every athlete in this book somehow acquired a similar work ethic. Dr. Keith L. Black got up at five to swim laps before school, and Wang trained twelve hours each day. Richie Rich puts it in context: "Practice was an hour and twenty minutes away. I would go to the rink and skate for about four hours and then drive an hour to school, then after school, go to the local mall, Vallco, and skate, and then do my homework. And I loved it. Looking back at how hard I worked, it was so crazy." Crazy, yes. But just as the focus helped him launch his business, having a similar work ethic has already served me in my schoolwork and in playing professionally, in preparing designs for my clients, and in training for a major tournament. It goes back to what Bratton calls "Extreme Effort"—hence the sign. As she explains, "One of the greatest lessons I learned from sports that has helped me in business is to never be afraid to put extreme effort in. If you don't do your absolute best, then you can't expect to achieve anything different from what anybody else has done."

There are so many more lessons that are transferrable, so many more "signs," some related to teamwork, some related to visualizing success before you even start a challenge, others related to leadership or the notion of consistent improvement. It inspires me to know that the more I design, the better at it I'll become. The most surprising takeaway I gained from working on this book, however, is that people who've walked the path I want to walk have found that they learned more from losing than from winning. I was brought up to respect my parents, so I could relate to Jack Welch's respect for his mother, Grace, and the influence she had on his development. He recounts a time when she runs into the boys' locker room after a loss in which he ungraciously threw his hockey stick across the ice in anguished defeat. Suddenly his mother appears in a floral print dress, yelling at him in front of all his teammates. Embarrassing, I'm sure. But the lesson stayed with him: "If you don't know how to lose, you'll never know how to win," she insisted. I'm not sure if that's a slogan I'll laminate anytime soon, though intellectually I can see how she might be right. For me, losing is still emotional.

When I lose, the pain is so intense, and the emotions roll through me. Facing a loss where I know I could have done better is even harder. When I do think about the losses, I'm more inclined to side with Susan Mersereau, who says that "one of the things that helped me later on in my business career was not seeing failure or losing as a bad thing so much as something you can learn from. . . . Losing never felt good emotionally, but how we handled failure was almost more important than the failure itself." My loss to Martina Hingis in the semifinals at the 1999 U.S. Open later benefited me in the way Mersereau notes. In that match, I had a lot of opportunities. Hingis was very good, but I believed I was the better player. Yet I didn't win, which was upsetting. I thought, from now on I'm going to do whatever it takes to win. (Well, not whatever it takes—certainly not cheating.) So going forward, if a ball lands short and I can get to the ball and come to the net, I'm going to get there. I'm not going to sit back and hit the short ball and be scared on the baseline. If the court is open, I'm going to take my shot. I'm not going to miss it. From that loss, my mind-set changed. I played a few more tournaments that year and then had an injury. I was off four months in the beginning of the next year but was determined to win a major at that point. When I played Wimbledon that year, I was the most determined in the draw. That was my tournament and no one else's. I think that loss to Hingis helped me to make sure I did what it took to win my first Grand Slam tournament.

And, boy, do I love to win; everything is right in the world when I do. I go to tournaments with that goal in mind. From my perspective, you learn a lot from winning and putting yourself in a position to win. There have been times when I've woken up after Wimbledon thinking, "Ah-ha, I'm the Wimbledon champ." There's a complete feeling of satisfaction. Senator Bill Bradley, who won two championships with the New York Knicks, writes about the memories of reaching the mountaintop. I've been there, too. Once you're there, you take a deep breath and look down, with a deep feeling of satisfaction, though it doesn't last forever because there's always something new to conquer, another tournament to play. But it's amazing, and nothing in my interior design business, no matter how much I love design, compares to holding something like the Venus Rosewater Dish, awarded to the ladies' singles champion at Wimbledon.

And yet, since so many of this book's contributors—people I look up to, from Robin Roberts, Phil Knight, and Irene Rosenfeld to Mersereau, Ken Chenault, and others—talk about the value of losing,

I guess I'll have to give some more thought to the idea that losses can be beneficial; it certainly seems to be the case in business. Already, EleVen has had some distribution challenges in its young life, and while I could see these as setbacks, I'm going to try to internalize what Donny Deutsch says: "You don't grow from the wins. You grow from the defeats."

It would be a mistake to think that the rich material here is just for established and budding creative and business executives. I hope coaches, parents, and young athletes are inspired as well. An obvious benefit for our youth, as President Bill Clinton writes, is that active children are less likely to be obese. I, too, encourage parents to get their children involved in sports, not only for the physical benefits but also because it teaches them to set and reach goals, and gives them that sense of pride and self-worth that goes along with it. As the oft-repeated story goes, my father once heard tennis commentator Bud Collins say to Romanian tennis player Virginia Ruzici, the 1978 French Open champion, "Forty thousand dollars isn't bad for four days' work." My dad thought it was a joke, but the next day he read it in the paper. He told my mother they were going to have two kids and get them into tennis. My dad learned how to play by looking at tennis magazines and watching videotapes, but for the most part he taught himself his own theories. My mother learned to hit very well, as did all of my sisters. Isha, the second oldest, could have been a great but for the intense back spasms she experienced. I was born in June 1980 and Serena followed fifteen months later. Because I was probably about three years old at the time, I don't remember the first time I picked up a racquet. Later, my father said that when he took us to the public courts to practice, I was the only kid who wanted to hit all of the balls in the shopping cart. I wasn't happy until I did it, and if I had to stop before the cart was empty, I'd start crying. On the last ball I always wanted to say, "Last one," and that was very special to me because it signified reaching a goal, though I most likely wouldn't have articulated it that way as a young girl. Whacking a basket of tennis balls and not stopping until I could say "last one" was probably my first experience with goal setting, and I haven't stopped setting goals since. (Incidentally, that was something I continued to say up until just a few years ago.)

Then there's the obvious. Sports show you how to work on a team, an invaluable trait if ever there is one. I couldn't run my business without my team, which includes my family. Sports also teaches humility—for every time you hit the game-winning hit, you just might strike out. And it keeps kids out of trouble, as Denzel Washington and others remind us: "It wears them out. I've heard that the most dangerous time for kids is after school between the hours of three and six, because the parents usually are still working. When you're young, you want to fit in somewhere. You're going to fit in with jocks, or you're going to fit in with the geeks, or you're going to fit in with the stars, the handsome people, the Goths, the drug heads. I just felt it was important for my children to stay busy"—and so he made sure they fit in with the athletes. Sports are, as Betsy Bernard says, an awesome enabler of success.

Advocacy in women's tennis has long been a concern of mine. Picking up where Billie Jean King left off, I, along with others, have fought hard for equal prize money for women at Wimbledon. Many people point to an essay I wrote that appeared in *The Times* of London in 2006, before the fortnight began, as a major turning point in the battle for equal pay. So I was particularly heartened when I read what a positive experience sports has had on the women in this book. I started playing tennis after Title IX, so I never realized what an advantage I'd had as a result of having played competitive sports and having my competitive fire lit early on until I read passages from the successful women in this book. Debra Lee eloquently speaks to what an advantage athletic girls have out in the world: "One of the advantages that men had over women is that they learned at an early age to compete and that it's okay to lose and keep going. Girls missed out on that for a long time because we didn't have team sports. I see what my kids have gone through recently and it's a whole different world. . . . The more girls grow up competing and learning how tough it is and that you've just got to get back up and keep going when you lose, the better off we are." I've always wanted to compete, and not just for the sake of competing, but to gain against the big guys. When I first went pro, I didn't understand the seeding of players in tournaments. In my first breakthrough tournament, a player asked me, "So, what part of the draw are you in?" I said, "Oh, in the middle." She said, "There's no middle." I didn't get it. We weren't taught draw. We were taught, "Go out there and play. It doesn't matter who you play. Play your game, then you're the better one." Back then, you got "quality points," so if you beat a higher-ranked player, you would get more points. If you beat the number one, you got one hundred points, and if you beat the number one hundred, you got one point, or five points. When we drew a higher-ranked player, we said, "Yeah! Now I can get all those points." The other players had the attitude of, "Oh shoot! I drew this higher-ranked player. Bad luck for me." My mentality was totally different. Back in the day, if someone asked me whom I would rather play, I said, "Well, whoever is ranked higher," because I wanted the points. I didn't want to labor against someone lower-ranked and not even get any points. Once a generation of women finally got to play organized sports in college, it's no wonder they made the strides they did in the marketplace.

Yet more than learning how to be competitive early on, sports can give girls healthy attitudes about their bodies, attitudes that if nourished can last a lifetime. Soledad O'Brien expresses it best: "One of the reasons I wanted my kids to play sports is I just love the idea of thinking of your body as something positive as opposed to thinking, 'I'm fat.' . . . I want my girls to feel like they're strong. To think, 'I can do a backflip. I can stand on my hands. I can jump a fence with my pony. I can run faster than somebody.' To think of your body in those terms for girls is a really empowering thing." I'll take that.

We have had some proud moments at V Starr, which designed the set for the *Tavis Smiley Show* on the PBS network, and the Olympic athletes' apartments used by the city of New York in its proposal to host the 2012 Olympic Games. When I designed my first large residential interior, I can't say the client was the easiest to work with. I had to convince them that it would look good. And when the work was completed and they were happy, it was more than satisfying for me not only because I delivered but because I knew then that I was able to trust my team. On the final walk-through, I nodded to myself and thought, "Yeah, this is my work." That's how I feel about this book, which is a labor of love, taking what so many of us love—sports—and seeing how we can utilize its benefits in other ways.

PART 1

The Business Executives (Part I)

THOMAS BARRACK, JR.

A real team effort involves utilizing tremendous strength and tremendous ego for the benefit of the team. You can have great individual efforts but an individual effort is only as good as you are. You can't get exponential power. The practice in business is doing all of the little things and doing them perfectly.

Thomas Barrack, Jr., is the founder, chairman, and CEO of Colony Capital, LLC, a private equity firm. He previously was a principal with the Robert M. Bass Group, president of Oxford Development Ventures, Inc., and a senior vice president of E.F. Hutton & Co. He served in the Reagan administration as deputy undersecretary of the Department of the Interior. He grew up in Culver City, California, and earned his B.A. at the University of Southern California. He attended law school at the University of San Diego and USC, where he was an editor of the Law Review and received a J.D. from the University of San Diego.

Pushing Through Comfort Barriers

I COME FROM A MODEST background. I wasn't driven by a powerful, athletic father the way many athletes are. Amazingly, it's the opposite. My father had nothing to do with sports. He owned a shop and worked from five-thirty in the morning until eleven at night. He never had any sports in his background, since he started working when he was thirteen. It was my mom, Mamie, who encouraged me to get involved in everything. I always loved sports, and my mom provided the confidence and the opportunity for me to do it. She was always positive. No matter how mediocre I may have thought my own talents were, she encouraged me to push through the pain, participate, get to the end, and do my best.

When I was in the sixth grade I started working at the Red Riding Stable in Culver City, and in exchange for cleaning stalls we could ride on the horses. Horses were a passion and my sports were split between Junior Rodeo Cowboys Association and football, basketball, and baseball. My mother's view was that team sports produced great human beings and individual sports produced a different kind of a human being. I didn't take up tennis or golf until I was out of college.

I was one of those guys who was good at a lot of things and not great at any. To become great I had to work twice as hard as everybody else. What I learned along the way was that I could outwork people who had better talent than me, and so that's where I had to find my competitive edge. That held true throughout everything. The kind of preparation and discipline is what I had to rely on rather than just God-given unbelievable talent.

I went to Loyola High School my freshman year and had a tough time when I showed up. I thought I was so hot coming out of grammar school, and I knew the football coach, Jack Boyle, who had been a coach at a rival school. During the summer I didn't train or work out. I thought, "This is a piece of cake. I know the coach. He knows me." I was surprised when he cut me from the freshman football team, which was one of the most traumatic and probably one of the best experiences and greatest lessons in my life. It created a rage, a dedication, and a motivation that then spurred me on not to have that happen again. When I went into JVs the next year I was ready. I was motivated. But I was an average athlete through high school.

Still, I wanted to play football at USC. John McKay was the football coach at the time. A good friend of mine's father was the athletic director, and he said, "Why don't you try and see John McKay as a walk-on." I went out one day in the fall. McKay watched me and said, "Look, you're a good kid. You've got talent. You've got a lot of fire. But you're never going to make it as a starter at USC. Either go to another school where you can play or try rugby, which is a varsity sport at USC and is a great game for your kind of talent." At that time, the football players were all playing rugby in the off season. He said, "Go play rugby for a year or two. Get more experience, and then come back to me." I knew nothing about rugby. It was not a game in my high school but having him say that to me spurred me on and that became my sport. I had found my footing and excelled for the next few years at USC in that sport. I never had any desire to go back to football.

My rugby coach, an exceptional guy named John Callahan, was unbelievably motivational and encouraging. He knew how to find the key inside of you to open it up. I loved him. He was sensational. He gave me leadership roles when things really got tough and always believed that I had the ability to pull it out. He was all about pushing through the pain, and that resonates for me with everything. Push through comfort barriers and get to the other side. I was an all-American and for two years in a row got Most Inspirational, which was the greatest award that I could have received. I didn't have the most talent, but for sure I had the most drive. The first year the reason I got it was in the finals against Stanford I had started with a broken nose. By the end of the game I had a broken nose, a separated shoulder, torn cartilage in my right knee, and a broken left ankle. It was the epitome of pushing through comfort barriers.

What drives me today still is this unquenchable thirst to push through comfort barriers. I get satisfaction out of motivating people to do things that they feel are beyond their means. At work this comes into play because the private equity business, or the opportunity fund business, is based on arbitrary things, so it's all about investing at a moment when no one wants to invest and seeing things that others don't see. The consequence is you can never operate through your rearview mirror. You're always a first mover, and in that comes lots of danger because there's tremendous comfort with a herd and that herd mentality. Most of what we do is to always move into a new type of business and a new geographical region where others have not gone before.

The greatest lesson I learned in sports that helps me run my business is there's no *I* in *team*. That's the hardest lesson for people to learn. A real team effort involves utilizing tremendous strength and tremendous ego for the benefit of the team. You can have great individual efforts, but an individual effort is only as good as you are. You can't get exponential power. The practice in business is doing all of the little things and doing them perfectly. A typo on a letter, a grumpy answer on a phone call, a slovenly look when I walk in the office, my own lack of preparation on a simple issue, a dirty or messy desk—all of these things that seem insignificant build over time to create a culture that is then manifested in the big things. Every player has to push through his or her comfort barriers by practice and bettering him- or herself to overcome their weaknesses. I'm not saying it's easy. In sports we have a beginning, middle, and end. You can always tell how well you're doing in sports because you have a result. Lots of people in business get lost because sometimes they can't find the beginning, middle, and end.

As managers we can help by figuring out where each team member is best utilized. Some people think that they're a tight end and they're really a center. Others want to be a quarterback and they're a halfback. In sports, the coaches who do the best are not the ones that necessarily have the star players. It's the ones who know how to utilize every player they have on the field and get those players to play over their handicap.

When I'm looking at hiring a senior executive, I look to see if they have a sports background. It's directly proportional to their ability to participate in a team. You find golfers and tennis players are not often great team business people. That ability to be great at an individual sport sometimes runs contrary to the ability to operate on a team. They can be tremendous entrepreneurs but not so great when they're immersed in an environment where their colleagues, who have participated in team sports, have learned to tamp down their own ego for the greater good.

One of the biggest things I learned in sports was how to deal with frustration. Some of the frustrating moments were also some of the most educational ones. For example, we had a rugby tournament called the Monterey Tournament. You played three games a day. Our biggest rival at that time was Cal, and we were in the second half against Cal. We were losing. I was out of my mind trying to do everything when Coach Callahan pulled me out of the game and sat me on the bench. I went crazy! It's my senior year and we've got to win this tournament. We have everything turning to crap on us and then he pulls me out when I'm working three times as hard to do the best I could. I couldn't see through that. It's like being a lawyer and arguing before a judge who's already rendered the decision. What Callahan knew was, we had already lost that game. Had I kept playing, I was going to get injured. I was going to wear myself out, and then for the next two games, which were critical to us winning the tournament, I would have been useless. But at the moment, I didn't want to hear it, didn't want to see it. I was so irate that I couldn't even speak to him. Three days later, when I realized what was going on, I was pretty humbled. We won the tournament, which was huge.

It goes to an idea of winning the war rather that the battle. There is a huge difference between winning a match or a battle and *winning*. The way that I look at life, it's not about winning a match. It's not about winning a battle. It's about winning the war, which may necessarily require that you lose matches and battles. But you win the war strategically by taking those lost battles, or those lost matches, into your lives appropriately. And in business, like sports, if you concentrate on the score you're going to do really badly. If you concentrate on the season, it's very difficult. You concentrate play by play, inch by inch, foot by foot. You move down the field, and as you do so, eventually, you get to the goal line. If you're thinking about the goal line every second, you're going to drop the ball. That's pretty much the way business is.

I still surf and play polo today; both take you to the edge. Polo is a complicated game. Just like in business, ninety percent of the game is won off the field. It's bringing a whole series of talents and things together, which starts with the horses. You've got to buy, breed, and train the right horses. Then you have to take care of those horses like athletes. You have to pick a team, which is very strategic, and understand that the team won't stay together for longer than the tournament. You have four disparate players. Sometimes they get along. Sometimes they don't. And then there's the physical demands of the game. You're on a 1,200-pound animal running at forty miles an hour with the other 1,200-pound animals running forty miles an hour, trying to run you over and kill you, and you're trying to hit this ball while standing in the irons as you're running down the field at full speed. Knowing your envelope is what it's all about in polo. In other words, if you don't push hard enough, you're going to lose. If you push too hard, if you go outside of your technical envelope, you'll die. That balance of learning where that envelope is and how to push it is exactly the same to me as what we do in business.

The same holds true in surfing. Ninety percent of surfing is preparation and wave selection. You have the wind and the sea, and you have to calculate everything in a split instant. It's knowing where to be when the waves get there. It's not necessarily riding the wave at the moment. It's staying out of the way of "gremmies"—you don't go where there are novices. You go where there are other people that you trust. Business is exactly the same way. Sometimes it's intriguing to get involved in something with a bunch of amateurs, but usually you all pay the price. Surfer Laird Hamilton could have been the CEO of a Fortune 500 company. We had him as a speaker at our investor conference in 2008. He's an individual surfer, but with his ability as one of the greatest big-wave riders in the world to analyze risk, to prepare, to discharge fear, and to approach it as a team sport, which he does with tow-in surfing, he could run a Fortune 500 company. The time for him to be fearful is not the time that he's dropping down the face of a thirty-five-foot wave. It's during the seven months of preparation before that.

Success is based on pushing through comfort barriers and shattering fear of failure and fear of success. In business, I was never taken by these fears because I had gotten prepared for them during two previous decades of sports. Discipline, perseverance, commitment, teamwork, and pushing through pain were all attributes that I trained for most of my life. Consequently, when obstacles presented themselves in business, I was prepared. I am sure that I would never have achieved whatever modicum of success I have today if it weren't for the emotional, mental, and physical lessons I learned from sports.

BETSY BERNARD

I wouldn't have wanted to try to succeed in business without sports. It would be as if someone were to ask me, would you want to face the world without a college degree? A lot of people do great without one, but it's such a positive enabler for success. I look at sports for kids in that regard— an enabler for success. Why wouldn't you want to have that advantage?

Betsy Bernard served as president of AT&T from 2002 to 2004. She received a B.A. from St. Lawrence University, an M.B.A. from Fairleigh Dickinson University, and an M.S. degree in management from Stanford University's Sloan Fellowship Program. She grew up in Holyoke, Massachusetts.

Make the Practice Harder Than the Game

WHEN I WAS FIVE YEARS old, a ski area called Mount Tom Ski Area opened in our town of Holyoke, Massachusetts. My entire family, which is my parents and my sister, who is three years older, got skis. It became my absolute passion. I loved the speed, the fresh air, the movement, everything about it. Once the ski season started, that was where you would find me. If I wasn't in school, I was skiing. Until I went to college, skiing was the most important thing in my life. If you didn't ski, we probably couldn't hang.

I lived on this mountain and would participate in any races they were having. They had this thing called the Powder Puff Derby, arranged by age group. My mother loves to tell the story about the first Powder Puff Derby. I'm five years old, so I'm pretty close to the ground. I take off. I fell, picked myself up, fell again. She said, "I think you came in last, but when you came through the finish line you were yelling, 'I finished. I finished.'" I always enjoyed whatever it was, whether it was swimming or tennis, another sport I played competitively through high school. Obviously one always wants to win, but if I didn't, my world didn't fall apart either. I always had fun doing it whether I came in first, second, or last, and no matter how many times I fell down.

Being competitive was reinforced and encouraged in my family. But I look at my sister, Nancy. We're from the same environment yet she was just not competitive. That was not her personality type. I really think part of it is how you pop out. I can turn anything into a competition. That's just who I am. My partner said, "Yoga is not a competitive sport," and I said, "Who says it's not?" Corporate events used to be centered around golf, but in 2001 I started getting invited to winter ski events. There was a race at one event and it took me about half a nanosecond of being in the starting gate to get all those competitive juices back. My partner likes to joke that a CEO's daughter, who was truly a top racer in college, was the only one that beat me.

I went to MacDuffie, a girls' prep school. It was a day school and they had a ski team. That was my first involvement with more formal racing. I was on the alpine ski team at St. Lawrence University in Canton, New York. I was always enthusiastic, always passionate, but never the top skier on the team. I didn't have a car in college so, quite frankly, by sticking with the team I could get a ride on the team bus to the mountain that the school owned. It was a practical way to continue skiing while I was in college, which I did until I graduated.

My college ski coach, Margie Strait, went on to run the entire athletics program at St. Lawrence University. If you look at who is running the athletics programs of men's sports and women's sports at most colleges, there are not a lot of women in there. Here was a woman, along with my entrepreneurial mother, who was a major influence in my life. She was nice, fun, successful, and professional. She was a good role model who said figure out what it is that you want to do, put your passion behind it, and you can do it.

One memory I have of her is at a meet where multiple schools were competing at Johnson State College in Vermont. She didn't have enough skiers to front the cross-country team. Because she knew I cross-country skied for fun, she convinced me to participate in the race so that the real cross-country racers could compete. That stands out as the most memorable ski experience I had. First, it gave me a whole new respect for the cross-country folks. What a difference between what I had been doing for fun versus racing. I was a pretty solid downhill skier, but in that cross-country experience I was down as much as I was up. I think I came in last. But I finished, which was what they needed me to do. And it was fun. Hopefully, I added value to the larger goal, which was to allow the team to compete. My ego was still intact even though I had made a pretty pathetic showing.

Out of that cross-country experience I adopted the spirit of "What's the worst that can happen?" There are so many people who freeze when they have to make decisions because they're fearful something is going to happen. I think back to that race. "What's the worst that's going to happen? I come in last? I'm not trying to make my living at this. The team will be better off. The team will get to compete." That spirit and belief have been valuable to me whenever I've been at a crossroads or whenever I analyze something a little too much, whether it's making certain career decisions or just everyday business choices.

From that experience also comes the lesson of "just do it." I know, technically it's Nike's phrase, but that idea has been huge for me, from the first Powder Puff Derby to some of my big presentations and big opportunities, which might have caused people to say, "Oh, I'm not prepared for that," or "I don't have enough experience for that." That's just not part of my DNA. "Just do it" *is*. And "have fun." I always have fun, whether it is sports or work, this job or that job. If I'm not having fun I've got to change something. I have fun skiing. I have fun working. I fall down, I pick myself up. The confidence to be able to fail, to fall, to trip, and to know I'm human and will pick myself up and learn from the experience and get on with it is invaluable. All those beliefs and traits that I look at as the real drivers of my business success are what came out of that whole skiing experience.

There's an expression that goes "Make the practice harder than the game," and I absolutely always believed that. I probably applied it more forcefully in my career than in my skiing days, but I definitely believe if you make the practice harder than the game, the game is a whole lot more enjoyable. Whether it's an earnings call, a town hall meeting, customer presentations, road shows, or keynote speeches, I am always prepared, and I like to make sure people know that. When people say, "Oh, you make it look so easy," or "Oh, you're such a natural," or "Oh, you're so lucky"—well, luck is the intersection of a lot of hard work and opportunity.

Sports also definitely helped me as a female in the workplace. I had a lot of jobs at a lot of companies and never had a female boss. People say, "It's not feminine to be competitive," or "I don't want people to look at me as too aggressive or cutthroat." All those little voices that can be in the heads of some girls, and then women, based on how they were socialized, are not factors when you grow up in an environment where competition is natural. I never had any of that in my head. The voices that got developed in my head through my skiing and tennis said: Go for it. Have fun. Be competitive. What's the worst that can happen? Practice, practice, practice, and just do it.

I started working for AT&T before I even graduated because I had finished all of my course work early. When I was twenty-four, I was put in charge of a central office at AT&T. My employees were both supervisors, who were management, and union-represented employees. It was a 24/7 operation, meaning it ran twenty-four hours a day, seven days a week. If it wasn't operating perfectly, I'd be one of the first to know it. I remember a friend who was living with me at the time to save money saying, "My God, it's like you're a fireman. You get called at two or three o'clock in the morning. God, this is crazy."

Twenty-four is a young age to be in that position. I dealt with it the same way I raced in the Powder Puff Derby at age five, having barely had skis on for three days. I just did it. I was not afraid of failing. If you don't have a fear of failing, then it frees you up to just go for it and learn along the way. I think one of the things that I was pretty good at then, and really got good at later in life, is the ability to say, "I don't get it. I don't understand that." I developed a confidence that said, "Okay, I work hard, study hard, and practice really hard, and so if I don't know something, that's okay," though it's not okay to then not go and learn it.

I developed phrases like "fall forward fast," to know how valuable it is to be outside your comfort zone. I literally spent almost my entire career outside my comfort zone. I mean, who is comfortable walking in to be the president of AT&T the first day on the job? You just aren't. I was fortunate because I kept getting one big wonderful wild challenge after another, such that being outside my comfort zone became a very comfortable place for me to be.

I wouldn't have wanted to try to succeed in business without sports. It would be as if someone were to ask me, would you want to face the world without a college degree? A lot of people do great without one, but it's such a positive enabler for success. I look at sports for kids in that regard—an enabler for success. Why wouldn't you want to have that advantage?

SIR RICHARD BRANSON

Adventure sports aren't like playing sports in school, where you're pretty well guaranteed to come off the football pitch at the end of the game. Doing something that man hasn't done before has major elements of risk and is more comparable to business. If I'm building a business or entertaining a new business venture, I have to try to think of all the things that can go wrong. I have to make sure that it's not going to make all the other companies I've built come crashing down because of one stupid mistake.

Sir Richard Branson is a British entrepreneur and founder of the Virgin Group, which now includes approximately three hundred companies in over thirty countries and has expanded into leisure, travel, tourism, mobile communications, broadband, television, radio, music festivals, finance, and health.

More Fun in Saying Yes Than No

B ECAUSE I WAS DYSLEXIC, I didn't excel at normal schooling and concentrated on sports. I loved playing football and became captain of the team at a very early age. I also captained the rugby and cricket teams. As an English public school boy [public schools in England are actually private], you're brought up to be competitive in sports. I enjoyed the constant cut and thrust of it, and it was a hell of a lot more pleasant than sitting in a classroom, learning French or Latin, which was completely above my head. It was nice to be good at something.

I was a natural sportsperson and at my prep school, Scaitcliffe, in Windsor Great Park, there was one embarrassing sports day when I ended up winning every cup there was to win—running, jumping, long jump, high jump. There must have been an element of determination about it, but I was born with the right genes to perform well. Then, one day I was playing football when I suddenly heard this almighty scream. I realized that the scream had come from my own mouth. I think I had done too much sports too young and had ripped the ligaments and cartilage in my knee. For a while, that was the end of my sporting exploits.

I turned my attention to the Vietnam War, which was a terribly unnecessary war. I was fifteen years old and decided to launch a magazine, *Student*, to campaign to help stop the war. As it turned out, I ended up leaving school, which I never would have done if I had still been doing sports. The magazine captivated people and became the clarion call for the young generation in England to try to stop unnecessary wars, and it was a forum for them to talk about their grievances.

During the few years when I wasn't competing in sports, I focused on *Student* and in 1970 wondered whether we could advertise and sell cheap mail-order records through the magazine. That's when I started Virgin Mail Order, the first Virgin company. *Student* died a quiet death and we switched all our attention to Virgin Records. In 1984 I launched a very small airline across the Atlantic, called Virgin Atlantic, with one plane. I didn't have any advertising money. The mid-1980s was the period when I had to put myself forward to promote Virgin. In 1985 I tried to bring the Blue Riband back to England. For some time America had held the cup, which goes to the fastest boat to cross the Atlantic. We built the *Virgin Atlantic Challenger*, to try to be the quickest boat. During the first crossing we sank and had to be rescued by a banana boat—and at the same time I learned about the birth of my child. The second year we were successful with *Virgin Atlantic Challenger II*. It was tremendously exciting and captivated the attention of people across Britain. Because we were flying the Virgin flag, it helped put Virgin on the map as an airline that was exciting and adventurous and not boring like our rival, British Airways.

We couldn't compete with British Airways in advertising so we competed with them on the sports field. Promotion was one of the keys to our growth. If nobody knew about us, nobody would fly us. We decided to see whether we could be the first to cross the Atlantic in a hot air balloon. There were seven people that had attempted it, and five of those had died. We thought that if we could build a balloon that could fly high in the jet stream that would propel us across the Atlantic very quickly. We'd be way above the clouds and therefore we'd have an upward chance. However, everything went wrong that could go wrong. I ended up flying the balloon on my own (my co-pilot bailed out) and had only just learned to fly a balloon. Still, we became the first in 1987 to cross the Atlantic. After that I thought that sporting activities were not such a good idea and that I should go back to work.

But I'm driven to try new adventures. Having gotten the record for the first hot air balloon crossing of the Atlantic in *Virgin Atlantic Flyer*, the following year we decided to see if we could be the first to cross the Pacific in a hot air balloon. Right at takeoff, with five thousand people gathered in Japan to watch, we were forced to abort after discovering holes in the balloon where the lamination had peeled off. We came back in 1991 and successfully ballooned from Japan to Arctic Canada. We made many attempts to be the first around the world in a balloon. I'm motivated by the sporting and competitive element. They'll never be able to take it away from us in the Guinness Book of Records that we were the first to cross the Atlantic and Pacific. We failed to be the first to go around the world, but we had fantastic adventures in attempting it. We crossed the Himalayas, Mount Everest, and K2. We were flying in places that balloonists had never dreamt of flying before and developed a wonderful camaraderie with our fellow balloonists.

Interestingly, it's not so much about being the first to do something that matters for me. It's training for it and trying to see what your body is capable of, whether you mentally can cope with it and work with a good team of people who are helping you to achieve it. You're going to countries that you never would have visited otherwise. You're having incredible experiences. The main thing I've learned from all of this is that there's much more fun in saying yes than in saying no. My nickname on my board at Virgin Group is Dr. Yes. I love to say yes. I think if you're lucky enough and have the wish to push yourself to the limit, then what a waste to say no.

Adventure sports aren't like playing sports in school, where you're pretty well guaranteed to come off the football pitch at the end of the game. Doing something that man hasn't done before has major elements of risk and is more comparable to business. If I'm building a business or entertaining a new business venture, I have to try to think of all the things that can go wrong. I have to make sure that it's not going to make all the other companies I've built come crashing down because of one stupid mistake. And in adventure sports, I have to make sure that, even if I don't succeed in what I'm setting out to do, that I come home to tell the tale. That's making sure that the capsule that I've built can float in water, or making sure that I've had my sky diving lessons and am doing everything I can to avoid absolute disaster. Sadly, a lot of the great challenges have now been conquered, and therefore for young people today, trying to be the first at something is quite difficult. We're building underwater "planes" to explore the depths of the ocean, which is going to be tremendously exciting. Submarines have not been below twenty thousand feet. We want to go down to thirty-five thousand feet, right to the bottom of the Pacific and Atlantic trenches. The kinds of adventurers that want to go up in our spaceship program, Virgin Galactic, also want to go down in our Virgin Oceanic submarines.

When it comes to managing people, I run the Virgin Group the same way I played. From a very young age, if I ever criticized somebody, my parents would send me straight to the bathroom and tell me to look in the mirror. Their attitude was that criticizing somebody is a terribly bad reflection on yourself, and having had to look in the mirror for ten minutes on a number of occasions (which wasn't much fun) I stopped criticizing people. I learned from a young age that praise gets the best out of people. It's like watering plants, but it's watering people. You get people's encouragement up with praise. It doesn't matter who they are in my life. People don't need to be criticized. They know when they've done wrong. I must have written hundreds of letters to my staff over the years. There's never been one paragraph of criticism in any of them. Instead, I search out the best in people, praise them, and encourage them.

If I don't accomplish what I set out to do, I'm the kind of person who will rebound straightaway if I've done everything I can to succeed. I have great difficulty remembering bad moments. I'm quite lucky that way. I know I've had an incredible life. I think it's counterproductive to dwell on falling short. Learn from your failures, but for God's sake don't dwell on them. I was the same way in sports. I would try hard but if we didn't win the match, I would move on to the next match. I'm not the sort of person who gets upset very easily. When people lose their temper it's counterproductive. As long as you've tried hard to succeed at something in life, if you have failure, you pick yourself up, learn from it, and move on.

The positive thing about setbacks is they set you on a different path. If I hadn't had my knee injury, I likely would have been an average sportsperson and never would have started the magazine or Virgin. I never would have had the incredible life I've had. So setbacks in sports will lead you in other directions and are as likely to be more positive than negative. The same applies to business. In 1992 I had to sell my record company because British Airways was trying to put our airline out of business. After we announced to the Virgin Music staff that they would become a part of Thorn EMI, I left the room. I went outside, took off in a sprint, and was running down the street past a billboard of the *Evening Standard* newspaper that read, "Branson Sells for £510 Million Cash." I had tears streaming down my face. I felt very uncomfortable about selling a company—and about the people who worked there—that we'd started from scratch. By the next day I had moved on positively. We picked ourselves up again and moved in a whole lot of different fascinating areas. We wouldn't have moved into space, for instance, if we hadn't had the billion dollars we got from selling Virgin Records. When you have certain setbacks or obstacles in life, just think positively about the new road ahead. It may be a different road, but it can be just as rewarding and exciting.

The challenge of going up against big companies never intimidated me. David managed to bring Goliath down. I always thought the biggest guys would fall harder, but it hasn't always been the case. Coca-Cola still seems to be standing strong, but it's been a lot of fun trying with Virgin Cola. Sometimes we succeeded. We have taken on some of the biggest airlines in the world, whether it's internationally, domestically now in the United States with Virgin America, or in Australia with Virgin Blue. The Virgin brand is generally renowned for being the best quality airline in the world. We've had some major battles with British Airways and other airlines and we've survived them. I think when you do take on the biggest obstacles and the biggest guys, you find that the most successful begin to become slightly overweight and slightly complacent. They let their overheads grow and therefore you have a chance to be successful against them, and certainly that applies to sports as well as business.

My sporting adventures in my later years played a major part in my career path. Perhaps people wouldn't know Virgin if I hadn't become an adventure sportsperson because that helped propel our airline to international fame. It's made the Virgin brand one of the top brands in the world and a much bigger brand than we are in reality. We're nowhere as big as Google in profits or turnover, but the brand is up there with the best brands of the world.

SARINA BRATTON

I liken starting a new business to diving. When you start a new business it is very high risk, and I oftentimes think or reflect on the fact that if you consider that you're diving off a ten-meter platform and you're going to do a dive for the first time in your life, it's very, very scary. But before you go and you take that leap of faith in your own capability, you've practiced, you've done all of the preparatory work, you can see visually in your own mind what needs to be done, how to achieve it, what technique needs to be deployed to achieve it.

Sarina Bratton is founder and managing director of Orion Expedition Cruises, a five-star, Australian-based cruise line. She previously was founder and managing director of Norwegian Capricorn Line, and spent fourteen years at Cunard Line, where she served as vice president and general manager for Asia Pacific. She was born in Sydney and held Australian national sporting titles in gymnastics, diving, and trampoline.

Extreme Effort

I COULD SWIM BEFORE I could walk. My mom had a flower shop right on Bondi Beach and we lived not far from there. My mother always talked about the difficulty she used to have when she had me and my sister—in particular me—down on the beach. I always wanted to be in the water and never get out. My sister, who is four years older than me, would try different sports, and I'd get dragged along and try things as well. We did floor gymnastics and display gymnastics, and then we used to swim at the Bondi Ladies Swimming Club. My sister decided to stop swimming and take up diving because they had a diving board down at the club.

When I would finish training, I'd get up onto the diving board and just throw these backflips and frontflips and land on my face, my head, or any which way. When I was about seven or eight, Jack Barnett, who was one of Australia's Olympic diving coaches, was down at the pool and saw me. He went up to my mom and said, "That young girl should be diving." And that was the start of me getting into both diving and trampolining. I'd never had any lessons about how to dive headfirst, apart from the racing dive for swimming. To me, all the fun was spinning around in the air. I think he saw the aerial skills in me.

Because we didn't have indoor diving pools, you couldn't train throughout the whole year. A lot of the divers did trampolining in the winter because there are a lot of very similar aerial skills involved in the two sports. I would do diving in the summer and trampolining in the winter competitively. My physical education teacher at high school was an Eastern European gymnastics coach. Because I had learned to tumble at a very young age, she thought that I would be quite good at gymnastics and got me involved in that as well through school.

One year in diving I won the Australian Junior Elite A Grade Platform event and the Junior Elite A Grade one-meter event, and I was runner-up on the three-meter in the Australian championships. In the same year I was the Australian Junior Trampoline Champion and the Australian Open Trampoline Champion. And in gymnastics I won a silver medal in the Australian Junior in the independent apparatus on vault. At the time I had to make a decision about which sport to follow because I was sixteen. It's interesting nowadays that junior sports cut off at eighteen. No Australian diver at that point had ever really done well at the Olympics. No Australian gymnast had done well at the Olympics. My scores were in the world rankings for trampoline and I was both a Junior and Open champion, which was quite an accomplishment. I spoke to my coach and decided that if I got the world ranking for trampoline maybe that's what I should pursue. So I made a mental decision to give up diving and gymnastics.

But stupid me—I went into the New South Wales gymnastics championships and was selected for the team to go to the Australian championships again. Prior to the event, my trampoline coach said, "Oh, please don't go. I'm worried something is going to happen." I said, "Nothing will happen. It's fun." In the middle of my floor routine I had an accident. I was one of the first women in Australia to ever do a back somersault with a full twist in the middle of a floor routine. I lost concentration and very badly damaged my left ankle and foot on landing. I was carried off on a stretcher. I had a lot of physiotherapy every day but after six months we realized that I was never really going to get back a lot of that natural spring I had, which was a real advantage to me. I was then seventeen and realized that there were other things in the world apart from training thirty hours a week—boys, parties, movies, and all those activities that I hadn't been exposed to. So that's when my sporting career as an athlete fully evaporated. I was finished when I was about seventeen.

I had done what I loved to do and didn't have any problem getting up at five in the morning every day except for Sundays. I didn't mind training late at night. I somehow seemed to accomplish getting my schoolwork done. My whole life was sports, and the people that I mixed with were heavily involved in sports. I didn't know or understand that any other life was going to be better than the way I was living, which quite frankly it wasn't. When I looked around at what other teenagers were doing, I didn't feel as if I was missing out on anything.

When you realize that you've got ability and opportunity to be one of the best at something, it really is quite a motivating force. And one of the things I learned at a very young age is that I wasn't afraid of putting the effort in to achieve the desired outcome. That's something that has stayed with me for life. The development and starting up of new businesses takes an enormous amount of energy, discipline, and determination to get through because most businesses fail within the first eighteen months to three years. I oftentimes advise people whom I speak to or mentor to be prepared that when you start your own business you will work harder than you've ever worked in your entire life for at least the first three years.

One of the greatest lessons I learned from sports that has helped me in business is to never be afraid to put extreme effort in. If you don't do your absolute best, then you can't expect to achieve anything different from what anybody else has done.

If you think about it, as a young person in sports, you're doing thirty hours of training a week and you're also going to school, which is another six hours per day, so there's another thirty. You've committed sixty hours before you start to do anything else. I've never counted the hours that I work because I'd probably scare myself if I did. They would be excessive, but the industry I'm in—cruise lines—is one that operates twenty-four hours a day, seven days a week. If there's ever an issue that anybody needs to talk to me about, they can call me any time, day or night, and over the years I have had calls at three and four in the morning.

In 1997, when I started Norwegian Capricorn Line, which was a joint venture with Norwegian Cruise Line of Miami, my company Capricorn Cruise Line, and another Australian investor, I had one hundred people in the office and four hundred on the ship. When you're available to five hundred people, it is fairly demanding. Orion, which I founded in 2004, is a much smaller operation. We have only fifteen to twenty, including the part-timers, in the office, and seventy-five on the ship. But there's all the same issues that you need to deal with, and the ship is operating twenty-four hours a day, seven days a week. There's no getting away from that—but that doesn't worry me because I love what I do. Just as I didn't begrudge putting in the hours in sports. That was what I did. And because I did it, I was achieving certain personal goals and recognition in sports.

Also, it's very good to have the recognition within your school environment as an elite sportsperson, and I thoroughly enjoyed that. And it made my parents very, very proud. My parents are proud of my various achievements in the sporting arena and business. They know it has been through hard work and perseverance that I have been able to achieve at the highest level. They didn't ever push me in sports—it was always up to me.

The other thing I learned through sports was to make sure to look at all angles of business. I liken starting a new business to diving. When you start a new business, it is very high risk, and I often reflect on the fact that if you consider that when you're diving off a ten-meter platform, and doing a dive for the first time in your life, it's very, very scary. But before you go and take that leap of faith in your own capability, you've practiced, you've done all of the preparatory work, you can visualize in your own mind what needs to be done, what technique needs to be deployed to achieve it. It's so clear in your mind how it needs to be executed. So before you go leaping off the ten-meter platform trying a new dive where, potentially, you could land flat and seriously hurt yourself, you've qualified the risk. And I brought that same discipline to bear when I started up businesses. I don't proceed on a whim, like "this seems like a good thing to do." When I launch I use extreme discipline, analysis, preparation, and planning of what needs to be done to achieve the final goal of getting the business up and running. Going into any business, obviously, one needs to have a business plan, but the clarity of the vision rests with you. In terms of starting a business, you have to be able to articulate that vision and get other people to share it, to understand it, so they can come along with you on the ride.

When you do a dive for the first time, you're virtually outside of your comfort zone, and this happens on a regular basis. And when you do start a business for the first time, you're virtually outside of your own comfort zone every day. You are doing things that are difficult, that require a lot of skill, and if you don't get it right, or if you lose concentration, you will end up hurting yourself. So to be outside one's comfort zone is not a state that I'm afraid of.

When I was being interviewed for the 2006 Veuve Clicquot award for Australia's businesswoman of the year, I was asked, "What would you have done if this was a failure?" I'd never been asked that question before. I said, "If I started Orion and it was a failure, I would know that the model is not sustainable, because I had the ability, I had the management team, I had the right ship, I had the right destinations to embark on this particular adventure, and I am convinced that if I wasn't able to do it, it probably was not a sustainable business model and I would then have to walk away." I remember afterward one of the heads of one of the major banks in Australia saying, "That was absolutely the right answer to that question," because oftentimes so many people, particularly entrepreneurs who start businesses, will never admit that something is a failure. They'll keep going and keep sinking money into it, thinking they'll get there eventually.

One of the things I particularly spend a lot of time on now is trying to coach and mentor my own people. It's very important that the business is sustainable. Therefore, I need to make sure that I've got really good people behind me coming through and that at any given time, should something happen to me, the business can continue and prosper. I hold weekly management meetings with the senior management where I get to talk to them in depth about all aspects of business, about what we're doing, what we need to do. I emphasize not to be afraid of trying something new because if we don't have new ideas we'll be dead in the water, that not every new idea will be successful or will be a good idea, but if we don't have new, creative ideas, then we may as well pack up shop. But many people aren't comfortable in trying new things. Many people are afraid of failure, which is a natural instinct for us as human beings. But what we do is learn from it. Taking it back to the ten-meter platform, if you do land very short or flat and hurt yourself, that doesn't mean that you don't get back up there and do it again. It means that what you did wrong you will never do again. You learn from your mistakes.

In 2009 I gave the address at the closing dinner of the Australian Elite Junior Diving Championships, which I was refereeing and judging. I sit on the board of Diving Australia as well. One of the things that I said to these young athletes—and a number of them will be competing at the Olympics in 2012, and some of them will compete in 2010 at the Commonwealth Games in Delhi, India—is that no matter what you're doing, all of the training, the discipline, the determination, the good attitude and hard work that you're putting into your sport now are inherent values that you will carry with you through life, and you can apply those same values and disciplines to anything that you choose in your life. Recognize that and never be afraid to use them in your career or whatever you choose to do. Afterward, the head of gymnastics came up to introduce himself and said, "Oh, thank you so much for saying that, because, number one, the kids don't understand it. But, number two, it's just as important for the parents to understand. There are so few who ever make it to the top but what they do learn along the way is so important for them as individuals. Thank you for expressing and articulating it."

KEN CHENAULT

My background in sports has played a role in my success. There are a lot of forces at work and sports isn't the only force, but you learn how to be a competitor and, if you have the right coaches, to be a competitor with honor. That's important in business. I'm very competitive. I want to win, but I want to do it with honor.

Ken Chenault is the chairman and CEO of American Express. Prior to joining American Express, he was a management consultant with Bain & Company and an attorney with Rogers & Wells. He holds a J.D. from Harvard Law School and a B.A. in history from Bowdoin College. He was raised in Hempstead, New York.

Sharing the Credit and Taking the Blame

WHEN I WAS FIVE YEARS old, a teacher at the Waldorf School of Garden City lined up all the kids on the playground for a race and I won. Even at a very young age, I wanted to win. I enjoyed not only the contest itself but what came afterwards: all my classmates coming up to me and congratulating me on winning. I developed at track, which I participated in through college, but it was really that first race that inspired me.

I started playing basketball when I was six and developed a very strong interest in the sport while I was at Waldorf. I was fortunate to grow up in a neighborhood with Julius Erving and a number of other sports folks. I remember most weekends, and particularly in the summer months, going to the park for pickup games. The experience of being one of the first people picked and moving up the hierarchy of the playground from a pretty good to a very good player was particularly meaningful. I was also very involved in Little League, and we played in a lot of tournaments. Between the ages of ten and thirteen I decided to try to learn every position on the baseball field.

I also played soccer from the age of five, which was unusual for kids in the United States at the time. We had the longest winning streak in the country when I was in high school, but we ended up losing the last game of my senior year. It was devastating. It didn't take long to get over, but we learned a number of life lessons. One, it was obviously a stinging defeat. We had taken winning for granted. We were playing a good but not great team, and it didn't have our true level of skill. As our coach told us after the game, we thought we were entitled to win because of our record.

Our goalie, a terrific person who had played very well through the season, missed an easy save. There were some players who initially sought to blame him. One of the things that I felt strongly about as captain of the team is that we had all contributed to that loss. I made sure to attend to his needs and also explain to the team that we shared ownership in the loss and accountability. That second lesson is very important in business. You want to build a team, but you also want its members to share in the successes and to take ownership for the failures.

What I like about sports is it requires you to really stretch yourself both mentally and physically. When everything is clicking, either for the team or for you individually, you almost have a rush. You get in the zone, an incredibly unique and exhilarating feeling. I experienced it my freshman year of high school when we were in a holiday basketball tournament. We were a very small school playing one of the top schools in the league, a team that was heavily favored. The game went into overtime. We had four seniors on the team and I was starting as a freshman guard. The coach called my number for an outside shot. I was a little bit taken aback that he was running the play for me. Fortunately, I made the shot. It was at the top of the key and the crowd went wild. The game was in the opposing team's gym, but we had some of our fans there. It was a terrific feeling. But what also impressed me is that our other guard, who was a senior and a really good player, had the maturity to call me at home that night. I'll never forget this. He said, "You were the right person to take that shot." I knew how much pride he had in his ability, but the fact that he could subjugate his ego for the sake of the team left an indelible impression on me.

My view is that top leaders should share the credit, and then in certain situations take the blame. You're always better off, without being sycophantic or patronizing, sharing the credit. People appreciate the recognition of their contributions, and that, frankly, makes them want to work ever harder for the organization and for you.

In high school I started to apply myself more in the classroom. The headmaster, Peter Curran, who also taught history, motivated me to do so, along with other teachers. He coached me in basketball in my early years. Peter believed I had strong leadership potential, and he pushed me both academically and athletically. He was one of the first people to start to talk to me about the correlation between sports and leadership. He thought I could be a leader in business or politics. Because I loved to read and applied myself in the subjects that I liked, his view was, "I think you're very bright. You've got all of the core skills. You've got to apply yourself, and in fact you're someone who I think could be a really outstanding leader. You don't want to waste that talent."

I earned an athletic scholarship to Springfield College, where I played soccer, and as I recall we had a very good team. But after my freshman year I decided that I wanted an institution that had a very strong reputation in the liberal arts and transferred to Bowdoin, which was Peter's alma mater. At Bowdoin, I played soccer and ran track.

I was a good athlete and captain of most of my teams; but what I learned—probably because of the coaches that I had, and through my involvement in soccer, baseball, and basketball in particular—is that it's not enough to be a natural athlete. You have to continually improve your skills and capabilities or else you won't be able to maintain your position; you are going to fall behind. A point I often make in business is that if you stand still, you're going to fall back. There is no truth to the view that you can simply keep your position. You really have to go forward. That's something I realized as a result of my involvement in sports.

Another thing that I found—probably more through playing soccer, but also through basketball—is that as I played with people from a range of nationalities, each brought a different perspective on life and issues. In business, I think the need for our company to act globally but think locally is important. At Bowdoin we had a team that was representative of a very diverse group of nationalities and races. That was an important, formative experience for me, because I learned from it how to get people galvanized around some common objectives despite some very different perspectives and cultural backgrounds.

The terrific thing about sports is that it is played out in the open field. Everyone can see the behavior, and the definition of the objective is very clear. In business you have to be more conscious of establishing what the vision is. Sometimes you even have to determine what the game is, set some very specific objectives, and then make sure that people understand what their different roles and responsibilities are and that they need to be accountable for that.

I think the reason I captained so many of my sports teams is that people trusted me. One of the key attributes of leadership is integrity, and for me that means consistency in words and action. Growing up, I wouldn't have characterized it as integrity. But I think my teammates believed I was someone they could trust and who had the best interests of the team overall in mind, someone who would be willing to sacrifice some of his personal objectives for what was best for the team.

In business, people need time to assess your consistency and see whether you're adhering to the values you are espousing. But I think from day one in any situation you can exhibit those attributes and qualities and start to build a reputation. What will be enduring is how you behave and act over time and how people see you in a variety of situations. One thing I emphasize to our leaders is that you can have an impact on day one, but what's going to be critical is how you are perceived two or three years later.

When I became CEO of American Express, I had been with the company for a significant period of time. It was very important for me to reinforce to people that my core values were not changing because I had become CEO. I was going to stand for integrity. I was going to stand for supporting people who were willing to take courageous actions and who had the willingness to take some risks that showed a level of caring and compassion for employees and for business in general but who also were willing to be decisive on the issues. Just as in a sports contest, when you hesitate to make an important move, you can really be hurt. While you want to be prudent and careful in business, you've got to be decisive in taking action or else you're going to lose out. One of the things I've observed when looking at a sporting event is that those athletes who move with clear purpose and decisiveness are generally going to be successful. Those who hesitate, are unsure, and are overly careful are generally not going to win.

· I took risks in sports, but I would calculate the odds and practice before doing so. For example, at the end of soccer practice, I continued to practice what's called a scissor kick thirty or forty times and I calibrated its use. I didn't use it until the last seconds of this one game when an opportunity presented itself. Some of it was instinct based on preparation. It was a risky move for a shot on goal, but it went in. Afterward the coach said to me, "It was a big risk, but I saw you practice that move every single day, and that was the right time to take that risk."

I've taken risks in business as well. In the early '90s, the credit card business was going through a set of challenges. I devised a strategy that had the company focus on broadening the card product line as far as coming out with different types of products or different segments, but also we came out with a rewards loyalty program that's now called "Membership Rewards" that turned out to be one of the most successful loyalty programs in the card industry. I think it is the largest and most successful program today. Another business idea was partnering with banks to issue American Express–branded cards. Both of those moves at the time were viewed as controversial within the company. But the risks, in my view, were based on an analysis and understanding of the market opportunities and challenges. I thought it was worthwhile taking those risks.

I'm very competitive, and I don't like to lose, period, whether it's a pickup game in a playground or an organized game in high school or college. But what is important about dealing with losing is building resilience, so if you lose that you know it's not the end of the world and that you can come back. It also gives you perspective on what's important. What have you gained? What have you learned? Is it the most important event in your life? And it helps you set priorities. There's nothing wrong with being highly competitive and wanting to win all the time. The key is—and this is particularly true in business—*how* you win, *how* you behave, and *how* you deal with adversity. That is what's most important.

You learn through a range of childhood experiences, and if sports are a part of your background, you are used to dealing with the challenges of trying to excel. You recognize that you can't use excuses because they don't change the outcome. You either win or lose. The question is how you deal and overcome the losses.

The events of 9/11 occurred during my first year as CEO, a very challenging time, obviously. In addition to losing eleven employees, the businesses in which we competed all suffered a great deal. We had to create a set of strategies and build morale within the organization such that our employees would recognize that we could come out of that challenge stronger. This idea of being resilient—which we're being called to draw upon now in the most challenging economic times since the 1930s—resonated with what I experienced as an athlete. In sports you learn the harsh reality of losing, but you also learn that to be a strong athlete, you have to have aspirations, dreams, and a hope that there'll be a better day, as well as the willingness to work to ensure that that will be the case. So I would certainly say 9/11 and the economic downturn are two major events where my background in sports—while certainly not the only contributing factor—did help me manage.

My background in sports has played a role in my success. There are a lot of forces at work, of course, and sports isn't the only one, but through sports you learn how to be a competitor, and, if you have the right coaches, to be a competitor with honor. That's important in business. I'm very competitive. I want to win, but I want to do it with honor. The second valuable trait is resilience, the need to recover from a loss quickly and move on to try to win the next game. And the third is the understanding that in a successful enterprise it's important that you ensure that you have the right people in the right roles. Often in organizations people are not always placed in the right roles, they're not given the right support, and they are not motivated to operate as a team. The focus on team unity is important. The concept of the blend of individual excellence and teamwork is an enduring life lesson.

I think I got everything out of sports that I wanted to. I would have loved to have won more races, won more events, more games, but I got invaluable life lessons. And I had the opportunity to get in the zone.

LYNN ELSENHANS

*You can't get overconfident when you're ahead. Like-
wise, when you're behind you can't throw in the towel. You
give it everything you've got and make the best of the situation to pull out the win. That's just as true in business as
it is in sports.*

Lynn Elsenhans is chairman, CEO, and president of
Sunoco, Inc. She previously served as executive vice president of global manufacturing for Royal Dutch Shell. She
earned a master's of business administration from Harvard Business School before joining Shell Oil Company in
Houston. She was born in Rahway, New Jersey, and was
raised in Texas, New Jersey, and Connecticut.

Confidence

ISTARTED PLAYING SOFTBALL AS a natural offshoot from my brother's interest in baseball. Al is three and a half years younger and a naturally gifted athlete in many sports. When we were growing up, my dad, Albert Laverty, coached some of his teams, in particular his baseball teams. I was recruited to help with his practice and would typically play first base because I'm left-handed. Al was a shortstop. My dad would hit grounders and my brother would throw them over to first. I negotiated to have my dad pitch to me and I would hit to my brother. I wasn't very good at that, but I really enjoyed it.

One of the few organized sports for girls in school where we lived in Houston was softball, which I played from the age of eight. Our high school team won the state softball championship and subsequently I was asked to play on a team called the Raybestos Brakettes. Raybestos was an auto brake company in Bridgeport, Connecticut, and it had a very sophisticated women's summer league. When the workers went on vacation, they were always looking for high school students to fill in. That was a lot of fun. People actually paid to go to those games. No one ever paid to go to our high school games.

When I first started playing softball I was a pretty poor hitter and struck out a lot. I was determined to get better, and Mr. Stabler, who was my coach from when I was nine until high school, worked with me a lot. I finally had a breakthrough and ended up becoming a really good hitter. The lessons around that were perseverance and continuous improvement. Don't give up. Keep going at it even when things are looking down. And even when you start to have some success, don't sit on that. He had a lot of faith in me, and patience. Sticking with somebody and having faith and patience is something that I hearken back to when I'm dealing with employees who are going through a rough patch. Emulating Mr. Stabler is something that helps me remember to be a better coach, a better leader in business.

My dad, who worked at Exxon USA—now ExxonMobil—never coached me, but he was a great role model when it came to integrity and honoring commitment. He used to say to me, "The most important thing you own is your name"—meaning, protect it at all costs. I experienced a lesson in commitment when I was twelve or thirteen. I had agreed to go to an amusement park with a friend who was a musician in a band with me but not an athlete. On the way back home we got caught in traffic. As a result, I was late for my softball game that night. My father was furious with me and wasn't even going to take me to the game, the lesson being "You've made a commitment to your team and you're letting them down by not showing up." My response to that argument was to say, "Well, Dad, we're late, but we should at least show up." We went, and my dad talked to the coach. He told the coach to bench me, which the coach did. I had never missed playing in an inning unless we were way ahead. That was really painful, to have to sit on the bench, but I learned from that to do what you say you're going to do, honor your commitments, and don't let your team down. To this day I'm pretty punctual.

We moved to Connecticut when I was a junior in high school, and my new school offered sports for girls. Because I'm five-foot-ten, the coach of the basketball team came to me and said, "You're very tall. Have you ever tried basketball?" I said, "Well, other than playing horse in the driveway with my brother, no." That's the first competitive basketball I played, and I went on to play basketball at Rice University. There was no varsity softball team in college, but I played intramural softball and powder puff football.

I was much better at softball than basketball and really had to persevere when I played basketball my freshman year at Rice. This was pre–Title IX, a law passed in 1972 and applied to college athletics in 1975 that requires gender equity for boys and girls in every educational program that receives federal funding, so schools did not have to give scholarships to women. They didn't actually have to field teams of any sport if they didn't want to, but Rice did field a basketball team and I was on the first one that they put forward at the varsity level. None of the Rice women had scholarships. We were all walk-ons. But teams we played such as the University of Texas and Texas A&M did have women athletes on scholarship, so we lost every game that year. We never gave up. We stuck with it and said, "We are going to win one of these games." We were motivated by the prospect of winning and beating one of these teams that had much more talented athletes. It never happened that year. But that Rice team got better and better and in recent years has done really well in Conference USA, and before that the Western Athletic Conference.

I started to have a lot of problems with my engineering courses and the laboratories. I was faced with a choice: either play basketball or change my major. There was no way I could concentrate on both. I knew I was never going to make money playing basketball, so I stuck with my major. Because I was a very good student all through school, I had one set of friends that were kind of intellectual. Sports helped me meet a broader spectrum of students and some folks that I would say were "more normal." That helped my socialization process a great deal. It also helped me develop time-management skills. When you play a sport, have a demanding academic schedule, and are involved in other things like I was, such as a band, you learn how to manage your time and keep track of multiple commitments.

One of the things I say often in business is: "It isn't over until it's over." I didn't see that so much in those basketball games at Rice, because we would get behind and stay behind. But in general you have many twists and turns in competition. You can get ahead, but if you let your guard down your competition keeps after you and before you know it you're not ahead anymore. Likewise, there's times when you're behind, but you have faith in the team and know that you can pull it out, and it happens. There are a lot of situations in business that are just like that. You can't get overconfident when you're ahead. Likewise, when you're behind you can't throw in the towel. You give it everything you've got and make the best of the situation to pull out the win. That's just as true in business as it is in sports.

One thing about sports which helped me later in life and I think is a really big deal for women is you get a certain confidence that you can do it and that you're capable in something. You can build upon that confidence. I always enjoyed practicing and preparing in sports and in a way found it relaxing. But the game? It didn't matter how many times I'd done it, I always got butterflies in every single game. It's similar in the business world. If I have something big, like a major presentation or speech to make, I get butterflies until I get rolling. That fear of failure grips me. But then confidence sets in and I per-form as required. For sports it was always the first hit or the first play. In business it is when I start to see some positive body language from the audience, then I can start to relax and feel like I've connected with them.

I'll never forget how sports helped me in one tough situation. I had just gotten promoted into the senior executive ranks at Shell, which at the time meant you gained access to the executive dining room. Before I opened the door, the very first time I went to dine there, I could hear people talking. I walked in and there was dead silence. I get my soup and sit down; it's a very uncomfortable feeling. There's still no one talking. I'm the only woman in there, and it occurs to me that these guys don't know what to say to me. I've always enjoyed sports. I usually keep up with teams so I started talking about sports. That was the best icebreaker. Any time I find myself in a situation where men don't really know what to say, sports have been a great icebreaker and a way to help them feel comfortable.

Women tend not to gravitate toward the team sports quite as much as men do, and I think playing team sports is a bit of an advantage for men. When I speak to young women, I often encourage them to get involved in team sports early on. It has to do with working toward an objective that you can't do by yourself, learning the power of the team. Learning how, if you are one of the better players, to behave in a way that still lets the rest of the team shine; and then, when you are one of the poorer players, just how thrilling it is to be a part of a winning team. That winning spirit is something that I look for in business and try to re-create. How do you achieve the best results where the team's effort is more than the sum of the parts?

So much of business is getting things done through other people. It's not all about yourself and what you can do. It's almost always about what you can achieve through others on the team. If you have practiced that on the playing field, you are more likely to know how to behave in order to get those kinds of results.

I'm a competitive person, and sports provided an outlet for that. Competing at a pretty high level within the boundaries of what was available to me as a young athlete has helped me in business, in that I developed confidence and a sense of perseverance. The combination of sports and intellect helped me arrive at where I am today. It's a good package. The time management and the discipline that go with sports, the idea of continuing to work at something and work at it for continuous improvement—that's incredibly beneficial for success in business.

BRIAN P. KELLEY

Often people make the mistake of thinking leadership is about getting a bunch of followers behind you. The job of a leader is to create more leaders. My way of defining whether I won or not will be how many great leaders came after me that I had a role in developing. Ultimately, that is the measurement. There will be lots of wins and losses along the way, as there are in every business, but the real key is what you did to develop people and give them the capability to win and to lead a whole group of others to win.

Brian P. Kelley is president and general manager of the Still Beverages and Supply Chain Business Unit at Coca-Cola North America. He served as president and CEO of SIRVA from 2002 to 2007 after serving as Ford's vice president of global marketing and consumer services, COO of the Ford Investment Company, and president of Lincoln Mercury. He began his career in 1983 at Procter & Gamble, where he had a number of brand-management, marketing, and sales assignments.

The Contrasting Skills

I GREW UP ON THE west side of Cincinnati, where sports are huge. My parents had six boys and a girl, and we played everything. We had a hoop in the backyard and had a built-in starting five. The whole street was filled with kids with families of five or six kids, and both the girls and guys played sports. We grew up in the gyms and on the fields and went to everybody else's games. We had a terrific childhood, growing up with sports and academics. That's what was pushed and we loved it.

At Archbishop Elder High School, I played basketball and football all four years and was captain of the basketball team. I was also a high jumper my freshman and sophomore years, played tennis my junior and senior years. I earned a football scholarship to Holy Cross, where I played all four years and became the captain as well. When I played at Holy Cross, my father, Tom Kelley, didn't miss a game in four years. He didn't have the money to fly each week from Cincinnati, but he'd drive to every game, whether it was at West Point, Boston College, Rutgers, Harvard, or Yale.

I didn't realize it then, but everything I would learn and need today in business, I did on the field or court. Sports taught me five key things. Everybody is going to tell you sports teach you discipline, teamwork, and leadership, and I agree. But it's what I see as the contrasting skills that are important.

First, you need to learn how to lead *and* follow, and know when each is appropriate. There are many times you're called upon as a leader. Some of us do it naturally, some of us don't. But you need to know when to lead and when to follow. Sports teach you that.

Second, you need to learn to both compete *and* collaborate. You've got to be mentally tough to compete and win, but you have to have the ability to work as part of a team. You have to collaborate with other people because you can never get it done by yourself. Ever. That's important, as we discover later in life.

Third, in sports, because so much is done in day-to-day practice, you have to know about execution. You do something well because you've practiced it fifteen hundred times before you ever get on the field or on the court. But execution isn't enough. You also have to be strong at strategy. When do you employ which plays? And what's the plan to beat this team? Strategy *and* execution are core contrasts that you learn in sports.

Next, you learn how to win *and* how to lose. You don't ever like losing, but you learn from it. You're going to do both in life, and so you need the ability to manage both, well and productively.

The final one is balancing confidence *and* humility. You have to be ultimately confident when you go out there. Confidence wins, always. That's one of the things Jack Welch taught us at General Electric. But that confidence has to be laced with enough humility, because there are others out there that could beat you if you're not on your game, and others that are better at certain areas. And if you don't compensate for their strengths, you're not going to win.

Every one of those five core contrasts can be used to overcome adversity and make you stronger and victorious. You do them naturally in sports, where they are critical, and then you learn to apply them in the business world.

At Holy Cross, it was a real honor to be team captain because physically I clearly wasn't the best player on the team. There were guys with much better skills. As the captain, you're coach on the field, and you represent the players to the coach, to the administration, and to the outside world. You have to both inspire and drive the team, but also to make sure the coaches understand what's going on and what isn't. You learn to listen, be mentally tough, and to get an intuitive feel. You can't lead without doing. You can't lead without being in the game. If I weren't playing, there's no way I could lead a group of guys. You have to have credibility with them. Likewise, you can't lead in a business from afar. If you don't get your hands in the game and be seen as somebody who knows what your people are going through, knows what their issues are, you'll never be an effective leader.

At Coca-Cola, I oversee our Still Beverages and Supply Chain in North America. Still Beverages includes juice, water, sports and energy drinks, tea, and coffee. The sales force needs to know that I know what it does. I started as a sales rep. I was out in the field, selling to retailers, when I was twenty-two years old. With retailers, you need to understand the operations of the store, the personnel in the stores, what their issues are, what makes people buy and pass on your brands, what makes them embrace your brands. It's very hard to do it if you can't talk the language of your teammates. You can't just come in and artificially lead; it never works. It has to be organic. It has to be natural. The only way that happens is if you know what they do.

Organizations move when things are simple and clear and there's a very clear competitor. In sports that's easy to identify because you're out there competing. You're practicing with that preparation in mind every day. Sometimes in the business world, the enemy is not so clear because the enemy could be a market shift, a change in technology, a competitor, or a number of other factors. We have a portfolio strategy and individual brand strategies. The portfolio strategy determines where each brand plays in the marketplace and how it relates to all of our other brands; but then, importantly, each brand has to compete with a competitor out there that offers a similar benefit to the consumer. We take our Smartwater, Dasani, Vitaminwater, and Powerade, and our juice brands, Minute Maid, Simply, Fuze, and Odwalla, and strategically position the portfolio; but then Minute Maid and Simply have to work together to beat Tropicana in the market. Vitaminwater and Powerade have to work together to win against Gatorade in the market. It's like any other sport, we face very tough competitors in our business and have to be on top of our game constantly from a strategic and from an execution standpoint.

I loved competing, and it's what drives me. I despise losing. If you have this mind-set that you have to win, it forces you to continually rethink everything you're doing. It forces you to make sure that your competition doesn't have a step on you in any area of the business. It's no different than when we were at Elder High School playing our rival Moeller High School. We had to make sure we were better than them in every single element—on the offensive line, in the backfield, on the defensive line, in the defensive backfield. It's this tension between humility and confidence. You're constantly fearful that the competitor is going to get a step ahead. And it's not a debilitating fear. You can't let it be. It's an energizing fear that keeps you pushing to win.

I learned this through experience. My senior year in high school we were playing basketball in the district championships, and had we won we would have gone on to regionals, and then the state championships, which we had won in the past. We were up seventeen points at the half against Withrow High School, which at the time had a six-foot-eleven center named LaSalle Thompson, who went on to play in the pros. We had an excellent strategy on how to contain him, and it worked in the first half. They came out after halftime, adjusted, and we didn't. They beat us. It was crushing because it was our senior year and we were convinced we were going to go on and win the state title. My co-captain, Mike Finley, who is a good buddy of mine, and I were cocky. We got overconfident at the half. We thought we had it, and so we continued to do what we were doing. We completely missed that they were going to adjust. You learn humility at times like that. You learn that you're not always as smart as you think, and if you don't constantly reassess where you are versus your competition, you don't win. I remember my dad saying to me after the game, "You guys didn't change a thing at halftime. They changed everything." Of course I didn't really see that as a player then.

A similar thing occurred when I was at GE's appliance business. We sold to retailers, like Sears and Best Buy, and we also sold to builders who build homes. We had a very large share of the builder business because we had a very good service infrastructure that we had built over the years which allowed us to serve them better than anybody else. The retail business was tough and competitive. Because of the need to put more time and effort into the retail business, we overinvested in retail and underinvested in our builder business. The business was worse off for it because winning in retail is not a very profitable proposition. We ended up with an imbalance in our investment. I guess I have to constantly learn the same lessons over and over, like we all do. Both of these examples go back to the same five basic concepts. You have to learn to do all of them, and you have to do them well, and you have to do it in adversity. That's the thing, because I think you get to see the heart and soul of a person in times of adversity.

Being a president of a unit in business is similar to being a coach. A coach has to pick the best talent and then fully utilize it. In the business world it's even more important. Developing talent is the single most important thing a coach does, and it's the single most important thing I do every day, because I can't ever be in a position to make all the decisions. But I have to be able to have people that can, and I have to train, develop, and empower them to win in the market. It's what a great coach does.

Often people make the mistake of thinking leadership is about getting a bunch of followers behind you. The job of a leader is to create more leaders. My way of defining whether I won or not will be how many great leaders came after me that I had a role in developing. Ultimately, that is the measurement. There will be lots of wins and losses along the way, as there are in every business, but the real key is what you did to develop people and give them the capability to win and to lead a whole group of others to win.

PART 2

The Creative Executives

HILL HARPER

I wish that more of life was like athletic competition, which is much more meritocratic than most any other things in life. At the end of the day, if you're the best, you win. Now, officiating can sometimes screw things up. But for the most part, no matter if it's a team sport or an individual sport, if you're the best, you tend to win. Whereas in life, the person who is the best doesn't always win. That meritocracy is something I love about athletics.

Hill Harper is an award-winning film, television, and stage actor, and bestselling author. He graduated magna cum laude from Brown University and cum laude from Harvard Law School and holds a master's degree with honors from Harvard's Kennedy School of Government. He serves on President Barack Obama's National Finance Committee. Born in Iowa City, he moved with his family to California's Bay Area when he was six, and later to Sacramento.

Meritocracy

I CAN'T REMEMBER NOT PLAYING sports. I loved all sports—football, basketball, baseball, running. When we came to San Francisco my mother put me and my brother in a French bilingual school, where a lot of the students were European. So I played a ton of soccer. Anytime I had a chance, I would play. Even when I was younger, if there was no one to play football with I would be out there by myself with the football. I'd kick it up and catch it. My brother Harry, who is two and a half years older than me, was athletic as well. Because I was always trying to keep up with him I became a better player in everything I did.

In high school I was captain of the track team, and I also played basketball. But football is my true, true love. My goal was to someday play for the Dallas Cowboys or the San Francisco 49ers. The type of offense that my team ran was somewhat nontraditional. We had a wingback position, which is hybrid between a receiver and a running back. That's what I played. I was all-State at Bella Vista High School in Sacramento, California. I was never huge, and it's funny that I chose a sport like football, where size makes a difference. Looking back, if I really wanted to be a professional athlete I probably should have chosen baseball, where size makes less of a difference.

I have a saying: No matter what your goals or dreams are, sometimes rejection is God's protection. The story I tell behind that saying is that when I was in high school, my goal was to get a full ride to the University of California, Berkeley. I wanted to run track and play football there. We had a big game coming up my senior year against Vacaville, which is a big school with a really good football team. Joe Kapp, the head coach from Cal at the time, came to scout me in this particular game. I caught two touchdown passes, ran for a touchdown, and then threw a two-point conversion. I was over the moon. We won the game and he saw this incredible performance.

He called me on Tuesday the next week and my father gave me the phone. I knew he was going to say, "You have a full ride to Cal. We want you to come." I already called him Coach. I answered, "Yeah, Coach." He said, "We want you to come to Cal." A pause before he added, "We've gotten you admittance into the school." I said, "Fantastic, thank you." He said, "But . . ." My heart started to go downward toward my shoes. "But there's some concern on the staff as to whether you're big enough to play Pac-10 football. We got you in, but we want you to walk on your first year, and if you make the team we'll give you scholarship money the next three years. But we're not going to guarantee you a full ride." My heart sank into my shoes; I went from this high of excitement to this low of rejection. There's nothing I could do about how big I was.

In retrospect, that was the greatest thing that ever happened to me because it sent me back east to go to Brown University to play football where there's a different mind-set and mentality. Pac-10 football is all about football, whereas at Brown I was introduced to people who were into things that at a big football school I may very well not have been introduced to. I have friends that played at these big schools, and they were watching tapes in early-morning meetings before breakfast. The program sort of pushed them toward taking classes that were more centered around physical education and the like so that they were available as early as two o'clock to start practice, which goes all the way to seven o'clock. And then they ate with the team. So they were not really necessarily meeting a lot of the other students.

The first time I saw Brown or set foot on campus was the day I showed up for the first day of football practice, a couple of weeks before all the students arrived. At that point *U.S. News & World Report* had listed Brown as one of its top schools. Its reputation was progressive and cool. John F. Kennedy, Jr., had graduated right before I got there. Amy Carter came when I was still there. It was the place where people really wanted to go.

I met some really good friends on the football team, and I was exposed to all of these different things. My overall focus on sports began to decrease. Although I still loved athletic competition and was going to continue to play sports, I found other things that were just as, if not more, interesting to me, such as the arts, theater, politics, sociology, and economics. I wasn't going to the gym every waking hour, although there were guys at Brown who still had dreams of playing professional football. My dreams started drifting away from wanting to be a professional athlete toward things that to me seemed significantly more important—the status of disadvantaged people in the world, arts, and theater.

In many ways we are all products of our environment. In certain ways I'm an environmental determinist. That's why when I talk to people I stress that who they surround themselves with and what they do is important because no matter who you are, who you've surrounded yourself with or what you're surrounded by is going to have an effect on you. As I began to be around all these other new people, places, and ideas, I became interested in all these other things.

Still, there are so many wonderful aspects of athletic competition that are vital and serve me to this day. Things like perseverance, hard work, training, and having faith that the training is going to pay off. When it comes to team sports, are you the type of person who is about making the team better or are you more about your own glory? The success of a team is dependent on people working together and encouraging each other and figuring out ways to make every person better. All of those things I still use to this day.

I miss athletic competition. To be honest, I wish that more of life was like athletic competition, which is much more meritocratic than most any other things in life. At the end of the day, if you're the best, you win. Now, officiating can sometimes screw things up. But for the most part, no matter if it's a team sport or an individual sport, if you're the best, you tend to win. Whereas in life, the person who is the best doesn't always win. That meritocracy is something I love about athletics.

Initially, I really thought a career in acting was going to be very similar to a career in sports, where the best person wins. I really thought that you show up at an audition and the person who's the best actor at the audition gets the job. I thought that must be the way that Paul Robeson, Sidney Poitier, and Denzel Washington became great actors. They auditioned and got the job. I should have done a little more research. It became very clear to me relatively early on that the person who has the best audition in the room does not necessarily get the job, it isn't based on merit. In fact, it's not even close. It was a difficult realization. To use a sports analogy, many athletes think: "I love game day, but everything besides game day I can't stand." Whereas some think: "I love practice day. I love training. I love all that just as much as I love game day." In acting, I experience the former. Every actor will tell you that the actual auditioning element and attempting to get gigs is not fun at all. Once you have the job and the research, acting is a true joy. So you do all the work, even though it's not a meritocracy, to hopefully get a role that you really can sink your teeth into.

One thing that athletics and acting do have in common is that you don't just turn it either on or off. When you're successful you train your body and your mind to operate on a very high level. I felt the same way about acting and getting ready for auditions as I did when I trained my body, really sinking myself into the audition and not worrying about whether or not I made a fool of myself. I remember early on in my career, sometimes at auditions people would look at me funny because I would come dressed as a character. If the character was a country bumpkin, then I would come dressed like that. If he were a doctor I would dress like that. I really wanted to do everything to reflect the character, and I drew upon all aspects of my athletic background for auditions.

It goes back to faith, because that's why you train. That's why you practice. That's why you do all the work, because you have faith that there's going to be a positive result because you put the work in. Then, come game day, every single extra rep you did, every single extra run you did, every single extra bead of sweat that dripped off of you will have an impact on how you perform. And the athletes that I know who would never practice that hard, never quite gave it their all, never did the things that they needed to do.

There's only one Super Bowl champion every year, and all the teams are attempting to be in that game. I guarantee you, when you speak to a team that's finally won it, when they look back at not having won in the other years, they say, "Wow, all of that prepared us to actually win it this year." And I think about life in the same way. My experiences athletically in terms of competition have prepared me to really understand the work I need to put into acting and other of my life goals. This recent presidential election is a good example of the same principles.

When many of us started working hard and campaigning and raising money for then-senator Barack Obama, he was thirty points down in the polls. He talked about it because he has an athletic background. We still had to do the work, educate people about how great a candidate he was and how great a president he would make. Just do the work and then have faith that in doing the work you'll see it start to incrementally move, and that's what happened. We started in Iowa, working for the Iowa caucuses. We started with really small meetings, because no one really knew who he was, and then the meetings started to grow a little bit bigger. And then they started to grow a little bit bigger. And a bit bigger. And that's what athletics teaches you. You're going to get better with every rep. And then if you have faith, if you really started training early enough and do the work, come game time you're going to win.

RICHIE RICH

[My coach Christy Kjarsgaard] taught me how to keep my eye on the prize and block out all the distractions. I think that's really what makes a champion in any field, business, or sport. Don't let people naysay, get you down, or judge you. She really was a big advocate of that. She was great at saying, "It's up to you. It's nobody else. You can't blame everybody else." I have friends in sports, they blame their tennis racquets. They blame their skates. They blame everything but themselves, but at the end of the day it's you. It's your job to make sure you're the best you can be.

Fashion designer Richie Rich co-launched the Heatherette clothing line in 1999 before debuting his eponymous line in 2009. He recently unveiled his new clothing line, A*muse, with Pamela Anderson and Tabloid Hero. He grew up in North Brunswick, New Jersey, and San Jose, California, where he skated competitively as a child.

Blocking Out Distractions

I STARTED ICE-SKATING WHEN I was two years old. There was a pond outside of my house in North Brunswick, New Jersey. I'd go skating with my two older brothers. They played hockey, which I wasn't into. I was a bit more artistic. Once I turned about seven or eight, I was still skating every winter and loving it. I got teased by other boys because I was spinning and jumping. I had no idea what I was doing. I would see it on television and then just teach myself. When I was eight my father transferred jobs and we moved to San Jose, California. I didn't have any friends so my mother took me to the mall to go ice-skating. This coach saw me on the ice and said, "Everything you're doing is wrong but you're actually really good at what you're doing." She started giving me lessons and from there the lessons just kept growing. Eventually, I started getting kind of serious in the small-time competition.

When I was ten or eleven, I was spotted at a competition by a woman named Christy Kjarsgaard. I had a few coaches before I met Christy. When I got to Christy it was as if I had to go through an interview process. She was a badass because she had this neon-green

Porsche Carrera. I thought, "Wow, you're cool." She was very serious. It was always business, business, business. I was scared of her, to be honest. But I also couldn't wait to get out of bed, even though I had to wake up at three-thirty in the morning, to work with her because I learned so much from her.

Christy had a bunch of girls that were really amazing. Kristi Yamaguchi was one of her students. But she had never had a boy. I became her first male student. She was so tough, but she taught me discipline. If I were compiling a dictionary, I'd put Christy's picture next to the word *discipline*.

My father was an assistant sports editor at the *San Jose Mercury News*. He would get off work and then drive me out to practice at three-thirty a.m. every morning, six days a week, except Sundays—I loved Sundays. Practice was an hour and twenty minutes away. I would go to the rink and skate for about four hours and then drive an hour to school, then after school, go to the local mall, Vallco, and skate, and then do my homework. And I loved it. Looking back at how hard I worked, it was so crazy

My father was a night owl. He looked forward to practices because he would have his coffee, read the newspaper, and sit through the entire practice. He was probably my biggest fan. He saw the athletic side of skating and didn't think really about the costumes. He was also a professional umpire and referee for wheelchair basketball. Seeing my father happy that I was learning so much was part of what I liked about skating. Anybody who's in sports looks to their coach or family or mentor when they're doing well. You see their faces light up and you see the belief in you that makes you as an athlete feel great about yourself. It keeps you going. It can be the most horrifying thing for you because of the pressure, but at the same time it can also be incredibly cool because you see yourself accelerating and getting better at what you do.

Christy's practices were demanding. I remember always holding on to the side rail of the rink when I fell after doing a double axel. Christy would smack my hand and say, "You don't need to rest." I'd respond, "All right, I'll do it again. All right, I'll work." She was very strict, but not in an abusive way. She just wanted to make us great champions. That's what my parents worked hard to pay her for, though when I was younger I viewed it differently.

I learned so much from her—ideas I use today. Before we went on the ice there was always a warm-up exercise we would do with our sneakers on. She would say you have to feel the same on the ice as you do on the floor. And now I'm actually more of a klutz on the ground than I am when I'm on the ice. My friends laugh at me. I'm the biggest klutz in the world, but get me on the ice and I'm like a bird. But she was very good at making her students feel really in tune with their bodies, and then when we were on the ice we didn't feel as if it were an out-of-body experience. It's more the same kind of thing. That's what I tell models now: "You're wearing six-inch heels. Whether you're on the ground flat foot or you have the heels on, it should be the same thing."

By the time I was seventeen I thought, "I don't really want to get up at three-thirty in the morning anymore." I started to have a double life. By my senior year in high school I started going out with my girlfriends. They put glitter on me and they'd say things like, "You're so pretty." They would make me up like David Bowie and we'd go to the nightclubs in San Francisco. I never drank because I was skating, but I loved the attention and thought, "Wow, this is amazing." We all had fake IDs, and I think my ID said I was thirty-five years old. There was a club called the Eyebeam on Haight Street we used to go to, and a guy saw me dancing. He gave me about one hundred and twenty dollars a week to jump on the bar and dance. "This is fun," I thought. But then I would stay up all night and go back to my house and sneak back into my bed. My father wasn't home yet and my mother was fast asleep. Then I would pretend I was just waking up. I remember that year, I was about seventeen or eighteen, my coach, Christy, asked, "Are you going to bed at seven p.m.?" I said, "Oh yes."

Meanwhile I probably smelled like cigarette smoke and had glitter all over me, which was stupid. I was falling all over the place. And that's when I made the rational decision that the Olympics weren't going to happen for me because I saw something else out there.

With Christy, whenever you won, you saw no greater sign of satisfaction than her smile. She would beam. You knew you did well. But when I told her I didn't want to compete anymore, that I was "moving along," there was no such smile on her face.

At one point I was ranked twelfth in the nation. I reached the level just before Junior Nationals. I probably could have gone on to Juniors and the Nationals, but it just wasn't my thing. There are eight tests you have to pass for the Olympic level. I passed six, and then I was about to take the seventh. It was kind of make-or-break with Christy. She asked, "Do you want this or not?" I didn't. And I don't regret the decision whatsoever.

As much as I liked sports and skating, I also had this other love for art, fashion, and pop stars—for Madonna in particular because she's a great role model for discipline. Once I graduated high school I was to go to UCLA on a drama scholarship, but at the same time I felt this different kind of artist bug inside of me. A scout spotted me at the rink and told me Ice Capades was having this resurgence of a tour. I snuck out of my house and went to Las Vegas and auditioned for the show. I made my friends drive me there. Tai Babilonia and Randy Gardner, the figure skating champions, were rehearsing, and they stopped and watched my audition. I remember thinking, "Ooh, this isn't real." I got into the show and ended up in Duluth, Minnesota. I stayed in the show for about a year and a half. I volunteered to fly on the wire, and performed in Madison Square Garden and all these big arenas, and met so many great people.

Some of the skaters were twenty years older than me. Some would always ask me for drugs. I never did drugs, and still never have. I worked so hard as an athlete, I never understood why athletes do drugs. I just shied away from that side of it.

Ice Capades really situated me between the competitive world and the professional world. It conditioned me to be in front of people, which I never had a problem with. I actually love it, but I also got more exposure to the discipline of a schedule and touring and the idea of keeping yourself together. I think a lot of people don't realize what all that entails.

I didn't hang out with the older kids in Ice Capades, so I'd hang out in the wardrobe department. There was this blond queen named Jerry. He reminded me of Rip Taylor. He taught me how to sequin and apply rhinestones, so I'd sit there and fix the costumes with him, which really made a big impression on me because I've always been crafty. And I think it influences what I'm doing today. Some people go to Paris and study appliquéing. I learned in the Ice Capades in the wardrobe department.

I made the conscious decision to make a plan, a blueprint, and move to New York. I became one of the Club Kids, a famous group of club personalities back in the late '80s and early '90s. It was our job to draw customers to clubs. To me it was like being Mickey Mouse at Disneyland, where you create the atmosphere at the party. I used the clubs as a launch pad. I didn't know what else to do because I didn't want to go to college. My father even said, "What are you going to do with a degree in drama?" I felt like I have charm, charisma. I like attention. I put skating on the back burner but everything I learned from skating kind of came back to me without me really even realizing it.

I didn't come to New York just to party per se. Michael Alig, who founded the Club Kids, put me in charge of budgets, what the invitations were going to look like, and the artwork. I'd worked from 11 a.m. to 7 p.m., go home for a couple of hours, spend four or five hours getting ready, then go to the club around midnight. I was shameless for sneaking out of the clubs when everybody else was going to after-hours spots. I didn't do after-hours. I had to be up to work the next morning. It was the same kind of discipline as in skating.

My plan was I would do parties and then I'd make clothing. Designer Patricia Field and photographer David LaChapelle played a big role in helping me get started in fashion. People would see my designs, then want me to do something for them. I started dressing Gwen Stefani, Foxy Brown, and Paris Hilton. Once I decided to really make clothing my bread and butter I needed money to make my line and get my brand out there.

Two venture capitalists helped me to find investors in the beginning. I said, "Why do you believe in me so much?" They never were in fashion. Their deals were in other industries. And they said, "To be honest with you, you were a figure skater and we see your discipline. We know you don't do drugs. We've done our research. And it takes a lot for somebody to have a career as an athlete and to make things look so smooth and effortless and fun, but behind the scenes we know how much goes into everything."

Showmanship is probably the biggest thing I took from figure skating into my world as a fashion designer. That part came naturally to me. The discipline comes when you have this goal you have to accomplish. It's like looking at the piñata that you're trying to break. This is my goal, A to Z. You look at the A. You look at the Z. In between you figure out what the steps are to get it accomplished. It's the same thing as a skating routine, a tennis match, or a football game. You know what you're supposed to do, what your goal is, and hopefully you'll obtain it.

Runway shows are like sporting events. It's the same energy because the audience and the crowd go crazy. When I produce my shows I get the same feeling I had when I was skating, I'm excited, electrified. It's the same feeling, I think, when people watch our fashion shows. I want the same energy. Even though I'm selling more chiffon and that kind of thing, it's the spectacle. If runway shows didn't exist, I wouldn't love fashion as much as I do, because it's such a charge and so much fun—at least the shows *I* do are.

The fashion world is totally competitive. But how I act toward my colleagues and my team is something else I learned from Christy. As much as a youngster as I was, I was so scared of her. But I knew she cared about me. She was always very pleasant with people and that's the way I always try to be with people as well. She never had that condescending side to her. In the fashion world, especially, there can be so much arrogance and so much "I'm better than you." But for what? We make clothes. She taught me you're only as good as your last competition in skating.

I haven't talked to Christy in years. She got married and is now Christy Kjarsgaard-Ness. If I saw her today I would say to her, "Thank you so much. You took me under your wing and you taught me so much." She embedded in me a self-confidence when I didn't know I had it in me. And she taught me how not to be intimidated, how to go out there and prove yourself and do what you believe in. How to go out there and be a heavy hitter and make something of yourself. She taught me how to keep my eye on the prize and block out all the distractions. I think that's really what makes a champion in any field, business, or sport. Don't let people naysay, get you down, or judge you. She really was a big advocate of that. She was great at saying, "It's up to you. It's nobody else." I have friends in sports, they blame their tennis racquets. They blame their skates. They blame everything but themselves, but at the end of the day it's you. It's your job to make sure you're the best you can be.

MARCUS SAMUELSSON

Playing soccer is very much like cooking because you're on a team, and within this group you can do amazing stuff if you stick together. In both you've got to work hard, and both are very honest. Whatever you put in is what you're going to get out. You can't cheat in soccer. You can't cheat in cooking.

Marcus Samuelsson is a chef-restaurateur with several restaurants in New York City, Chicago, Tokyo, and Stockholm and a two-time winner of the James Beard Foundation's "Best Chef" award. In 1995, he became the youngest chef to receive a three-star review from the *New York Times* for his restaurant Aquavit. Born in Ethiopia, he was orphaned at the age of three after his parents fell victim to a tuberculosis epidemic that ravaged his homeland. He was adopted by a young Swedish couple from Göteborg and raised in Sweden.

Work Ethic

I'VE PLAYED SOCCER PROBABLY SINCE I was six. I started in a local club in Sweden and will never forget meeting Lars Bengtsson, my coach, when I was twelve. He completely changed how my teammates and I competed. We were used to always winning, and all of a sudden we lost, *a lot*, because he changed how we played the game. He treated us twelve-year-olds as adults. We couldn't just kick up the ball, run, and score. He said, "You can do that, but you can't come here to this club and do that. You have to play properly." Our practices were suddenly serious. He even went so far as to tell us what to eat. "What is this, you guys eating McDonald's? No, no, no, no, no. Really, what energy do you get from that? Check with your parents. How often do you eat pasta? Eat real food. Don't come with candy into the practice." He told us how to run. Before, it was "Let's go and play soccer." He said, "No, no, no. Today, no ball. Today we just run." He changed us as young boys. He also had a big impact on how we behaved toward each other.

We became extremely successful a year and a half later. But at first we thought he was crazy. Our parents, nonetheless, approved.

They all thought, "This is the guy. He's doing the right thing." He was young, no more than twenty-four or twenty-five, but our parents loved him because he was very strict. He also invested in us as soccer players, there was no more just kicking the ball to the tallest guy and everybody runs after the ball. We now had positions, I remember him saying "You're a midfielder" to someone playing a different position. We had real conversations about the game.

It was a rough year, but we liked it. It was fun; we even studied other teams. We watched Brazilians on tape one day. Of course we still thought passing the ball was much more fun to do. It was difficult to break our former mode of play, it was difficult not to cheat—to actually commit to it. But if you did cheat, he'd take you out of the game. We had a reunion with him three or four years ago in Sweden. All of us, now adults, came out for him. We had other coaches after that, but this was a special guy, so everyone came from all over Sweden. I flew from the States because he had such an impact on me. His methods are still the proper way to play soccer.

I didn't realize it at the time because I was too young, but I realize now that he taught me life skills. If I was late to practice, I couldn't practice. I'm still in contact with him by e-mail. I told him that it's funny that the things that he told me at that age were things that I could take with me for the rest of my life. Work hard. Don't cheat. If you want to cheat go ahead, but you won't get away with it.

The principles that he taught are the same ones I use in my kitchen. Have a work ethic. You've got to be a good guy. You can give a lot. You can be hard on people but it's how you treat people, how you relate to people, that matters. Stay true to your character because it doesn't work otherwise. A lot of those lessons were echoed in my household but were probably easier to take from him than from my parents. It's a different relationship. With him, he could teach us through what we treasured most—soccer. If we acted up, all he had to say was, "Okay, no problem. You can't play. Thank you very much. Come back next week."

In many ways I'm like him in the kitchen. The chef-apprentice relationship is almost like a coach-player one. You really listen. I think I have a similar relationship with the cooks that work for me. They're here because they want to be, and they want to go somewhere in their career. And the minute that's broken, we don't have anything. I can't overstep it and they can't overstep it. They won't overstep it. Ever.

I see a lot of different things through sports. I still solve issues through sports. If something doesn't go my way, I very often go out and run six or seven miles and think it through. Running is also, often, the only time when I'm by myself in the whole day. Playing soccer is very much like cooking because you're on a team, and within this group you can do amazing stuff if you stick together. In both you've got to work hard, and both are very honest. Whatever you put in is what you're going to get out. You can't cheat in soccer. You can't cheat in cooking.

I was in the kitchen with my grandmother when I was six. I either played soccer or I was home around food. My dad was the one who started to kick the ball around to whatever friends I had over in the backyard. I played so much at home, my mom finally said, "I'm taking him down to the local club now. Enough of this running around here. It's got to be something organized"—which wasn't easy for me at first. When you run around in your backyard it's your rules. Then all of a sudden there's a coach and it's different. But I loved it right away. It was a Swedish summer, about seventy-five degrees, and there was a beautiful grass pitch. We wore yellow-and-black shirts. I remember being a little bit nervous because I was meeting twenty new kids. When I played in my backyard I knew all of the kids and made all the rules. If I thought you were too tall, you couldn't play. Here I had to listen.

As a young boy it's important to be busy, because if you have too much time—you can go any direction. On a soccer team you have to listen to the coach. You have to be a good teammate. You have to show up on time. Obviously, you have to be focused. You learn how to do your homework on the bus and you juggle a lot of stuff, as you will do later in life. All of these are life skills.

Here in the States sports are very school-related. In Europe they are club-related. You go from your local little community team to the city, and then all of a sudden you're playing against kids from all over. I played in Göteborg and my club was called GAIS. We traveled through Europe. We played in the Dallas Cup in America. I met Pelé in Dallas. I played center midfield. You have the ball. You're in control and make everything go.

Growing up in Sweden, I learned a lot about myself through soccer. Probably the first time I really started to see myself as an African individual, as a Black man, was as a young boy on the field. I knew I was different, that I was from Africa. I could do moves that nobody else could do. I was weaker than guys in certain aspects. Swedish guys are very tall, very Viking-esque, and strong. I could run longer and faster than them. Growing up, you realize there's actually a difference with body structure, pros and cons. All the moves I could do were definitely not Sweden-esque moves. But also as an Ethiopian, my muscles are not the same as those of a Viking, so I'd lose a tackle here and there.

Any sport prepares you for life in many ways. You're going to get injured. You're going to lose some games. You've got to take it, and life is like that. You're going to come into an awkward situation. You're going to get one for free every now and then, and you're going to lose some. It's the same for life situations. Sports can be a fantastic way to see it, especially through the eyes of a twelve-, thirteen-year-old boy.

I always thought I would become a pro soccer player. I was so surprised when the day didn't happen. In Europe, there's a hard-core selection for the development team, ages seventeen to eighteen. It's a buildup with young kids being recruited from all over the country. It's extremely competitive. When I was up for the team, they called all the names, and my name was not called. I can never describe the chill that went through my veins. That is the saddest memory. I thought, "It must be a mistake." All of a sudden, I felt four inches shorter. One minute, you are part of a team, you walk around with your team T-shirt. You have a swagger from being part of it. Everything is tied into that. Then it's gone. It took me a long time to overcome that. A long time.

At the time I learned I wasn't going to become pro, life was very confusing; it seemed unfair. But I had my interest in food right there. That picked me up and, whoosh, I was on this other journey. I'm very happy and lucky that I had this other interest in food because it made me focus on something else.

More often than one would think, a lesson I learned in sports has helped me as a chef. It's worth repeating. Work ethic is something I'm reminded of all of the time, and having a dedicated work ethic is something that was reinforced for me three different ways. I got it from my grandmother, who first kindled my interest in food; from my parents; and I got it through sports. Interestingly, it's through sports that I forged my first relationships outside of my house, which is important. By listening to my coach and watching the results, I got an indication that hard work does lead to results. I could see that it did pay off. It wasn't a bunch of mumbo jumbo. So that gave me the belief that if I worked hard and practiced I could eventually make it as a chef in France. All I had to do was keep at it. At the time I decided I had learned all I could in Sweden, but I didn't speak French. I learned, though. I taught myself French by walking around with a Sony Walkman and a French language tape and taking French classes. Still, I knew I wasn't ready, so when it was time to take my career to the next level, I went to Switzerland first. I didn't speak German, but I felt I could get by with my Swedish. I used my work ethic to get really good skills, both in the kitchen and with additional languages. And I used my vanity—because I was used to winning. I had to be not in a one-star or a two-star Michelin restaurant. I had to be in a three-star. And it's very hard to get into a three-star. It's the hardest. But I knew I would get in. I got thirty-two nos and one yes. Eventually, I got in. Life is a lot of rejection. Then, *boom*, you get it, a yes.

I still play on a team now, called Blatte United. We play on Sundays in Chinatown. It's so interesting to play in New York because the biggest sport in the world is still an underground sport in New York City. We have a game once a week, which I try to make. I do make it for the big games, which is fun because a completely different side of me comes out. It's very much about winning. And I love it.

No matter my record as a chef, I'll always view myself as a failed soccer player. It's good. It keeps you humble.

VERA WANG

I fell at Nationals in 1968. . . . It is a lot of pressure when thirty or forty thousand people are going "Oooh" together and you're sitting on the ice. It's the same with fashion. I've had a show that I thought represented a great effort, and a certain reviewer killed it. . . . It's not unlike sports where one is subjectively judged! . . . It's the ups and downs of it. You have to be passionate to stay in it. If you don't love it, why put yourself through it?

Vera Wang is a fashion designer. She launched her eponymous label in 1990. She served as design director of women's accessories for Ralph Lauren, and spent sixteen years at *Vogue*, where she became the magazine's youngest editor. She was born in New York City and graduated from Sarah Lawrence College with a degree in art history.

The Power of Reinvention

WHEN I WAS SEVEN, MY father, Cheng Ching Wang, who first learned to skate when he lived in China, bought me a pair of ice skates for Christmas. He took me skating that first time at the Seventy-second Street boat pond off Fifth Avenue in Central Park. I still remember where we sat. He strapped on my skates and took me out on the ice. It was just a pond that was frozen over, but it felt magical, sort of like flying. You could feel the wind in your face; there was a kind of freedom.

I started taking lessons and fell in love with it. Eventually, I found the right coaches and wound my way around the skating world. It was always my mother, Florence, who really pushed me. She was at the rink with me every day. It was a huge, huge sacrifice. She had Hodgkin's disease, a blood cancer, but my father never told her or me because he thought that would discourage her. She got cancer when she was in her thirties, but survived to be eighty-nine. I think my skating career is what kept her alive for a very long time because there was a reason for her to get up in the morning. My father used to joke when she'd say things like, "Oh, we landed a double axel," or "We skated perfectly."

Of course it was only me skating, but she would refer to it as "we." That's how much it meant to her, and how much it meant to me, that we did it together. It was a level of intimacy, love, caring, and sacrifice that I'll never forget and that I'm trying to impart to my kids.

Skating is a beautiful and empowering sport. The sad thing is your parents have to give up a lot. They have to try to be able to fund it. You train insane hours on and off the ice and rink time is so expensive. Figure skaters, unlike hockey clinics, get the earliest hours of ice time. I skated at six or seven o'clock in the morning and then we went to school, after which I went back to the rink and skated again until eight o'clock at night. And three days a week I danced, from five-thirty to seven in the evening, at the Balanchine School of American Ballet, which taught me grace, extension, and tremendous core control. I then came home and did homework. It was pretty grueling. In the summer I went to skating camp. By noon I'd already skated seven hours. Then I had lunch, rested, and went back and skated some more. We used to train sometimes up to twelve hours a day. It was intense.

Some days if I didn't want to skate at four in the morning, my mother would say, "You don't have to get up. You're not skating for me." And then, of course, I'd leap out of bed. Through skating my parents instilled in me a sense of discipline, responsibility, wisdom, and good sportsmanship. They stressed all along that it was about the journey. Even though I may not have won Worlds or Olympic gold, it was about what skating taught me every day in every way. They also believed in the dignity of accomplishment and how important it was for one's sense of self. Dignity was very important because my parents came from China and had to start a whole new life here in the United States. Even if my level of competition wasn't at the level of Venus Williams, I did get the daily sense of discipline, which was ingrained into me in a way that, at sixty, I still possess and that will still be with me every single day of my life.

I won my first regional championship at ten and went on to win many times. There are three sectional competitions throughout the country, and I was frequently within the top five in the East Coast. I competed for fifteen years and was among the top singles skaters in the United States for almost five years. The fact that I didn't place in Nationals kept me hungry. There was a fair amount of politics involved in the judging process. I sometimes felt I didn't get the judging marks I should have, which frustrated me. In skating, as in fashion, judging can be very subjective.

The night before competitions, I used to lie in bed and my feet and the palms of my hands would sweat as I played over everything that could go wrong and everything that I had to remember. I still have recurring nightmares about not being prepared enough, if you can believe that. It has never left me.

I did pairs at the end of my competitive career because I think it's easier for good singles skaters to be good pairs skaters. In the pairs I competed at the U.S. Figure Skating National Junior Championships in 1968 and 1969, finishing sixth and fifth respectively. It was very difficult because my partner, James Stuart, wanted to focus on his singles career. So we broke up the pair, and that's when I really quit skating altogether.

Nothing could ever take the place of skating for me except for fashion. I never had any formal design training. I didn't go to design school but I did graduate from Sarah Lawrence College and attend Columbia University. I had lived, trained, and skated in Paris. I went to the Sorbonne eventually. You can't help but fall in love with fashion in Paris. So when I was twenty during college, I worked as a salesgirl during the summer at Yves Saint Laurent on Madison Avenue. A woman from *Vogue* whom I waited on said, "When you get out of college, call me. I think you could become a fashion editor." I used to read *Vogue*, *Harper's Bazaar*, *Glamour*, and all the fashion magazines because my mother read them, but I didn't even know what a fashion editor did. I told my parents, "Frances Stein, the fashion director at *Vogue*, says she'd like to hire me." My parents didn't believe it.

I wanted to be a designer but my father wouldn't pay for me to go to design school after college. He said, "If you think you're so talented, go get a job." So I called Frances and she remembered me. I went for an interview with the head of personnel and was told I had to first learn to type ninety words a minute. I went to secretarial school and got the job. From an assistant, I worked my way up to become the youngest editor in history at the magazine. At twenty-three I became a full editor and stayed there until I was thirty-eight. Frequently I would ask my father, "Would you help me finance a company?" and he said, "No, if you think you're a designer, go get a job as a designer." Thanks to *Vogue*, I did. I went to Ralph Lauren, where I became a design director.

As I planned my 1989 wedding, I grew frustrated when I couldn't find a wedding dress that was modern and fashion-forward. I sketched my own design and commissioned a dressmaker to make it. Finally, when I was forty, my father said, "I think I'll help you now start your own company, but it can only be bridal." I thought, "Why? I think I can really design anything. Why does it have to be bridal?" But my father was a very astute businessman. He had identified a business opportunity, and at that time I didn't really want to leave Ralph. My appetite for starting my own company was gone because I had seen how hard it was to succeed at both Ralph Lauren and *Vogue*. I had lost my desire for risk. He said, "Well, now that you are really nervous, it's time. I'll help you because now you have a realistic view of what it takes to start a company." Today there are days I'll ask myself, "What did I do this for? I must have been crazy." But the love and the passion spur me on. And since I was seven years old my life has been defined by pushing myself out of my own personal comfort zone. But for athletes as well as designers, any field where you are judged, you have to continually push yourself out of your own comfort zone in order to grow.

My life has always been a series of reinventions, but the real truth is I never got where I wanted to in skating. I wanted to be on the podium at the Olympics and never made it. I wanted to be editor-in-chief of *Vogue* and didn't get the job. My friend Anna Wintour did. A lot of my life's accomplishments happened by default because I didn't achieve what I'd hoped for, so I kept searching. My mother always said, "It's about the journey." It's about learning, and every day I try to be a better designer. I try to learn more about what I'm doing, more about design, fabrics, prints, and about feeling confident enough to express myself fully, and that's totally in parallel with skating. This is my company's twentieth-anniversary year. I still love it. It's the passion that keeps me going. Just like skating did. I was very fortunate last year to be inducted into the U.S. Figure Skating Hall of Fame for my costume designs for Olympic skaters Nancy Kerrigan and Michelle Kwan. That had to be one of the happiest moments of my life. I always joke I didn't make it to the Olympic team but my clothing did. It was such an honor for me after all these years of loving this sport so much.

I don't think anyone should ever underestimate the psychological part about skating. My coaches Sonya and Peter Dunfield, who trained a lot of champions, including Dorothy Hamill, were very, very tough on me. They really believed in the mental element of skating, which is probably as important as the physical. You have to be your own worst critic. The fact that my coaches encouraged the mental part needed for the sport was extremely useful. I've seen many skaters who didn't have any mental focus, only the physical training. They easily blew up under pressure, because there was nothing grounding them. That was a profound lesson for me, because it's what I've had to live through in fashion. I've had so many ups and downs in fashion that I'm often surprised I'm still standing. But that inner belief in yourself, that voice that says, "I have done this before. I have been here before. I can do this," is extremely important no matter what you do.

In skating, if you fall on your first jump, you still have the entire program to get through. You begin to doubt yourself. Suddenly you think, "Am I going to land these jumps and these spins I've done forever or not?" I fell at Nationals in 1968. I could hear the entire stadium go, "Oooh." You have to try to find a way to tune it out because you can't let it affect you. But it is a lot of pressure when thirty or forty thousand people are going "Oooh" together and you're sitting on the ice. It's the same with fashion. I've had a show that I thought represented a great effort, and still a certain reviewer killed it. I mean really killed us. It is very hard to keep my team motivated. They'd not slept. They'd worked fourteen-hour days, and then someone says, "Well, it was really bad." It's not unlike sports where one is subjectively judged! In races, you either win or you don't. Skating, like gymnastics and diving, is subjective. It's the ups and downs of it. You have to be passionate to stay in it. If you don't love it, why put yourself through it? Any time you put yourself out there for criticism or praise, it takes great courage but also enormous passion.

I always tell kids when I'm speaking at design schools, "Listen, this is about passion, and if this isn't for you, if you have any doubts, you must go away and rethink it." The best way to know whether or not it's for you is to work, if you're lucky enough, for a designer you admire and respect. Then you'll see whether you really love it or not. Because once you work in an industry, then you get an idea of what it's really about, and you may discover you don't like it enough. I've had a lot of interns who've said, "Thank you, Vera, but this isn't for me." And I've had a lot that have wanted to go on to design school and really pursue their dreams.

Were it not for what I learned through skating, I could never have reached my dream of becoming a designer. Those principles of discipline, desire, and hard work are one hundred percent responsible for my success. I will quote Anna Wintour, who said, "I attribute Vera's stick-to-itiveness and her desire and passion and who she is to the fact that she was a competitive figure skater." Anna loves sports, specifically tennis, and she will often mention that I was a figure skater.

Very few people in fashion know just how much of a skater I really was or how dedicated I was. It wasn't a passing fancy. It is my past that gets me through the level of pressure under which I have to function day in and day out. I'm also responsible for people's salaries and livelihoods, and still have to be a creative artist. Some people have teams that design for them. They give them artistic direction, come in, and edit. I really do design myself. It's not necessarily the best formula, but it's the only one I know.

As in sports, you have to be able to work hard and train really hard, but then, when you're performing, you have to trust your preparation. You need to be free to create. My friend Olympic figure skating champion Evan Lysacek has taught me how important that is, that trust in yourself. In design, when you create, it has to be in a controlled way, how much you spend, how hard the fabric is to sew, how reproducible it is. You need mental control and mental freedom. That's a hard balance to strike all the time, year after year—or, in my case, show after show. It's challenging, and the only thing that helps as you get older is to know that you have done it before.

I think of fashion as a very highly competitive sport, a continuation of what my life was before. Fashion and figure skating—who would have thought of the connection!

DENZEL WASHINGTON

The importance of building a foundation is something I learned through sports. . . . Your natural ability will take you only so far without a foundation and training. I applied that to almost everything else in my life. I definitely applied it as an actor.

Denzel Washington is a two-time Academy Award–winning actor. He was born in Mount Vernon, New York, and played basketball at Fordham University in the Bronx before transferring to the school's Lincoln Center campus, where he earned a B.A. in drama and journalism. He worked on his master's degree at the American Conservatory Theater in San Francisco.

Natural Ability Will Take You Only So Far

EVEN THOUGH I WAS A little guy when I played running back as a kid, my dream was to be a pro football player like Gale Sayers or Jim Brown. If you look at a picture of me on the Boys' Club football team, you'll see I'm the shortest one. I didn't know I was little. Ignorance is bliss. I knew I could run. I knew I was fast enough. The sad thing about looking at that picture is, half of the people are dead.

My dream was never acting. I had never heard of it and I didn't know anybody who did it. Yet, my father was a minister and my mother owned a beauty shop, so there was always a lot of theater. I did, however, grow up with sports. My parents sent me to the Boys' Club when I was six. I played basketball and football and ran track there. But I didn't go just for the sports. It was like a family, a comfort zone. You belonged and adults told you that you were important. It meant something and you felt good. It was, as they say now, a positive place for kids. I couldn't wait to get back there because that's where the fun was, where you got to make new friends and see who could run faster, who could jump higher, who could climb the rope, who could play pool the best, who could play Ping-Pong the best and be the best in arts and crafts.

Except for one game that my father came to, my parents never saw me play. Nobody's parents came, because they were working. Nobody had time to come to the club. They did as much as they could, spending the ten dollars to get you in. My dad was working two or three jobs and preaching. As a minister, he wasn't that keen on sports. He didn't come from athletics. He came from the farm. He was chopping wood and slopping hogs when he was my age. It was that and the church.

For me it was sports. All the things that I've taught my four children I learned as a youth playing sports—playing fair, playing together, dealing with losing, being on time, washing your uniform, remembering your sneakers, sportsmanship.

I played baseball at Oakland Academy, a prep school in upstate New York, and I was the MVP my senior year when we won the championship. We also played in the football championship my senior year. I was the MVP of the team, the star running back, all of that. That's the only game I remember my father coming to. We lost, 44–12, and I scored two touchdowns. I remember screaming at my teammates at halftime because they were acting like they were afraid. We had played the team in the regular season and they killed us with something like 40–0. We somehow both ended up in the championships. I think we lost before we left the locker room, so I went off.

In general, I don't remember getting down when we lost. I met actor José Ferrer, who had won Tony awards and an Oscar, when I was doing *Othello* in college. He came to see the play and I tried to flatter him. I said, "Oh, I loved you in such and such." He said, "I don't live in the past. That movie is gone." I kind of adopted that attitude from him. It didn't apply to losing that high school football game, though, perhaps because my father had finally come to see me play. And there was an Academy Award that took a while to get over not winning. I wanted it.

P. J. Carlesimo was my freshman basketball coach at Fordham University in the Bronx. I wasn't recruited and didn't have a scholarship. I walked on and never started. I was the garbage guy. They still had freshman ball. Right before I got there, Fordham was a top-ten or top-fifteen team under Coach Digger Phelps. Our freshman team was good. We were nineteen and one. We lost to St. John's, and, boy, did we pay the price. It's not so much the things P.J. said but his work ethic that made an impact on me. How important the fourth quarter is conditioning-wise, though I think we played halves in those days. Our conditioning under P.J. was ridiculous. The last five or ten minutes of practice he'd go nuts if you put your hands on your knees to rest. You weren't allowed to do that. You could not hold your shorts. If you did, everybody had to run. I remember standing over other teams when they were holding their knees. I'd say, "We're going to finish y'all off. You're tired, huh?" And that is a testament to P.J. What I learned from him was never give up. Work harder. Whatever you think your limit is, you can go further. You can push it. You can push it. I took what I learned from him and applied it to my film *Remember the Titans*, where I portrayed a high school football coach. There's a scene when I talk about the fourth quarter and guys falling on the ground.

My freshman year in college I also played football. I thought I was pretty good in high school. When I got to college we had a defensive backs coach who put me on the first unit before we had played any games. But right after that he got a job in the pros and left. The next day I was second string. I never got to start. Little did I know I wasn't going to get to play much either. I figured that I was going to work my way back to the first unit, but I didn't. I didn't quit during the season, but I didn't go back. It was the first time since I was six that I never played. That's when I realized I wasn't going to be a pro football player.

There came a time when John David, my oldest son, who went on to make the NFL, wanted to quit football. I shared that story with him about quitting. And my son Malcolm also wanted to quit because he said football wasn't his sport, which it isn't. His sport is basketball and he plays at Penn. I said, "We don't quit. We're not quitters." I must stress, I did not quit. I didn't return. But I played a full season of football and I played a full season of basketball.

The importance of building a foundation is something I learned through sports. Billy Thomas, who ran the Boys' Club in Mount Vernon, New York, taught me something I'll never forget. I was on a track team and there was a kid in the third grade named Reginald Whitfield who was faster than me. He joined the team at the Boys' Club and the coach knew I was worried. Billy said to me, "What's wrong with you? You're not yourself." It was a relay team and I was the slowest one of the four. I was about to become the fifth, and there's only four on the relay team. I remember Billy talking about how Reginald doesn't know how to run the turns yet. How he doesn't know how to pass the baton. Basically what he was telling me was that your natural ability will take you only so far without a foundation and training. I applied that to almost everything else in my life. I definitely applied it as an actor.

I transferred to Fordham University's Lincoln Center campus, which didn't offer sports but had a real drama program. Once I started acting, in my junior year, I got instant gratification. I had only studied for two years and I had already done two leading roles. I was busy and getting feedback such as, "Hey, you've got it. You can do it." William Morris was going to sign me before I even graduated. I remembered specifically what Billy had told me when I was a kid. I said, "No, I'm going to grad school. I need more work with Shakespeare. I need to study more." I didn't feel ready after only two years. I went to the American Conservatory Theater in San Francisco to work on my master's, or my baton passing, because I knew my natural ability was only going to take me so far.

These are the reasons why I wanted all four of my kids to play sports. I grew up in it and learned lessons from it. I knew it worked for me and that it was a way to interact with them. I live through my kids. My favorite sports memories are through them and not my own experiences. When my youngest kid, Malcolm, won the state Division V high school basketball championship in 2009, I almost ran out on the court with the team and rolled around on the ground. But I thought, "Don't go out there now and do that, Denzel. Don't do that, dude."

Another reason I wanted my children to play sports is because it keeps them busy. It wears them out. I've heard that the most dangerous time for kids is after school between the hours of three and six, because the parents usually are still working. When you're young, you want to fit in somewhere. You're going to fit in with jocks, or you're going to fit in with the geeks, or you're going to fit in with the stars, the handsome people, the Goths, the drug heads. I just felt it was important for my children to stay busy.

I also knew sports would teach them life lessons, like humility. You might have a one-and-ten season where you're just awful. And if I'm coaching, as I was sometimes—not that we had a one-and-ten season—you've got to keep coaching through that and keep teaching and inspiring. Such wonderful lessons can be taught through sports. My son John David was playing a game against Brentwood. It was pouring rain and it was his last game of his senior year in high school. He's running the ball, and it's a sloppy, awful day. He had thirty-something carries and a bunch of yards. He takes the ball all the way down the field. We're losing by five or six points and need a touchdown. He fumbles and the other team got the ball with about four seconds left. I said, "God almighty, don't let this child end his high school career on a fumble." I left my wife, Pauletta, in the stands and went down to the field. I'm on the goal line, thinking how I'm going to build my son back up. He's feeling awful. He's been everything for the team. I'm working on my speech about losing and God having a plan. I planned to say, "You couldn't have fumbled if you didn't play. You had thirty carries and you fumbled because you had the ball all the time." In order to win, all the other team has to do is snap the ball and take a knee. But their quarterback slips and fumbles. Our guy ran around the end and fell on it. Touchdown. We won the game. I told John David, "Go find that quarterback and give him a hug, because think about what kind of a day it is for him." All those lessons I learned from losing and winning.

I still define success in sports by winning, old-fashioned as that might sound. At ACT's acting school they asked each one of us what we wanted to be. I said, "The best actor in the world." Everyone turned around and gave me one of those looks, as if to say, "Who is this guy?" Maybe I was still closer to sports then, so I thought why not shoot for that? When I won my Oscar for *Training Day*, which was my second Oscar but my first for Best Actor in a Leading Role, I said, "Thank you for saying to me tonight that I'm the best actor that I can be."

For a while now, when I've defined success I've asked myself, "Did I do all I can do for this particular job?" It's not just for acting or for sports. The metaphor for life is looking in the mirror and asking yourself, "How do I get better? How do I continue to grow?"

PART 3

The Media Executives

LUCY DANZIGER

The crew team at Andover . . . traveled to races together as a coed team. The funny thing about that is you're sweaty and gross when you come back off the river. Or if it's been raining, you're muddy . . . you have to go straight to dinner. Nobody wants to sit with the crew team because we all look like drowned rats. We were fine with it. It was almost kind of tribal. You lose your vanity and gain this confidence from what I call "function over form" . . . you don't worry that you can't . . . look perfect . . . like the other girls . . . You learn to accept . . . the whole "beauty-comes-from-within" concept.

Lucy Danziger is editor-in-chief of *Self* magazine, reaching 6 million readers. She previously was the editor of *Women's Sports & Fitness*, from 1997 to 2000. She was born and raised in New York City; went to Andover, where she discovered her competitive athletic side; and then to Harvard, before launching a career in journalism.

The Importance of Attitude

I GREW UP IN A very privileged environment, in the sense that I always thought, "Of course girls can be athletes and scholars. That's a given." In 1978 at Andover, a boarding school in Massachusetts, we had whatever the boys had, other than football. It was a very liberal way of thinking and ahead of its time. That put me in a league with the same generation that benefited much later from Title IX, the gender-equity law passed in 1972. The minute I got to boarding school, I loved being outside and made a no-gym edict. I thought, "I've grown up in New York City. I've been in a gym, playing volleyball and basketball." So I decided to do only outdoor sports. So I went out for rowing and even ski-racing!

I tried crew and fell in love with it because it combined everything that I was naturally good at, which was body coordination, as opposed to hand-eye ball sports. Crew is a strength, endurance, and push-yourself kind of sport. You're part of a team and you have to work together, but your individual effort is what you are responsible for, and that's very similar to my work environment. At a magazine, you're part of a team, but every individual is responsible for the work that crosses their desk and for making it excellent. You have to push yourself because nobody else is going to. As part of a team you feel responsible to the other people to do it well, do it quickly, and put in your best effort. It's similar to crew.

As the "stroke," I loved being the leader of the eight-person boat, and had a lot of control over the cadence and intensity. You have to be the kind of leader people want to work with. If you're not, the boat won't set up nice and move steadily through the water, and you will rock and go slower—rowing in a rocky boat is just a miserable experience. It teaches you the importance of collaboration. There's a huge difference in the experience when people all pull together or when they don't. I never forgot that.

I also skied. I've always had this mix of confidence and insecurity, which led me to becoming captain of the ski team at Andover. We practiced on this teeny hill near our school. It was called Boston Hill, but we called it Boston Bump. We had some serious skiers from New Hampshire, Vermont, and Colorado. We'd whistle, yell, use cowbells, and cheer each other on. I was always extremely good at helping motivate other people, even though I was probably one of the worst skiers on the team.

We ski-raced in New Hampshire, which is pretty close to Andover. We'd go up to these icy, frigid-cold, miserable runs. My dad would drive six hours from New York to see me compete. He would stand there on the side of this freezing-cold hill and watch. Usually the first four gates are very, very steep. I would say to myself, "I just want this to be over," and I would fall. And then I realized that if I didn't think that way I could do better. So instead I thought, "I want to do well at this race because he's here watching. I don't want to fall anymore." And lo and behold, I would actually finish the race. I would try to think positively about getting to the lower parts of the course, the less icy or steep areas where I could ski better. I improved because I stopped defeating myself with negative thoughts. I started understanding the importance of attitude. Obviously, there's always going to be somebody better, faster, somebody more fit. But that's not what wins a race. What wins a race is the person with the best outlook. Who can get themselves to do their best on a given day? That became a real lesson for me, and I'm reminded of it in everything I do.

For example, I'm friends with Julie Foudy, former captain of the U.S. women's national soccer team. When I was about to run in the New York City Marathon, she told me, "Your brain only has room for one conscious thought in your head at a time, so you have to make sure it's positive." So I would envision myself crossing the finish line with my hands in the air like winners do and saying, "Yay!" I would also envision myself *running* the whole way so that even when I was in pain and I wanted to walk or slow down, these positive thoughts kept my feet moving!

So now I think that way in business, too. I'm an optimist and try to keep people on track. I say to them, "We can do this." I try to be constructive and positive. Even when I don't like a layout, or something negative is going on around me, I try to stay as positive as I can. That doesn't mean being idiotic or overly naïve about how tough it is to grow in the face of today's economy, or not seeing that I need to enhance the magazine, enrich my product, and engage my reader. I have to do all those things, but I can do it from a positive point of view.

The ski team at Andover was coed and I loved being a captain of a coed team because it has a different dynamic, especially if you're a girl captain. The boys have to listen to you, and that's empowering. If you tell them to clean up the gates and get in the van, they've got to do it. If you tell them we're going to take three practice runs while the coaches are parking the car, they'll do it, too. You don't get intimidated easily because you feel that you've been given the authority to be the leader so you have to be comfortable with that authority.

The crew team at Andover was made up of two squads; we had a female captain for the women's team—our coach referred to us as the women's, not girls', squad—and a boy captain for the boys. But we traveled to races together as a coed team. The funny thing about that is you're sweaty and gross when you come back off the river. Or if it's been raining, you're muddy, and, still, you can't miss serving hours so you have to go straight to dinner. Nobody wants to sit with the crew team because we all look like drowned rats. We were fine with it. It was almost kind of tribal. You lose your vanity and gain this confidence from what I call "function over form." You know you're sweaty and gross but you have to eat before they close the dining room. So you don't worry that you can't go back to your dorm and put on a cute sweater and look perfect at dinner like the other girls. Who you are and how you act are the really important things. You learn to accept, even back in high school, the whole "beauty-comes-from-within" concept and that you don't look perfect all the time because you have grease on your calves and calluses on your hand from being a crew jock.

My crew coach at Andover, Chris Kirkland, used to tell me: "Avoid mediocrity at all costs." Win or fail big, he meant, but don't race for the middle. Go for it. If you go for it and you tip your boat over, that's fine, but go for it, because not trying your hardest is the worst thing possible. I've taken that all-or-nothing philosophy into business by taking risks. Not every risk pays off, but when it does, it feels truly great. For example, we featured Fergie, of the Black Eyed Peas, on the July 2007 cover when she was emerging as a solo artist. No Condé Nast publication had ever put her on the cover before. We tested the cover image and some readers said, "She's a drug addict." Or she had been in the past. She was in recovery by the time we photographed her. But some readers said: that's not *Self*'s image. But that didn't deter me. She was a woman reinventing herself, and readers could relate to the "new" Fergie, I was sure. I also loved her new single. I had met her at a fashion show, and she impressed me as an amazingly nice, intelligent person. When I looked in this woman's eyes, I saw integrity. I also felt that her personal journey toward straight and sober was inspiring, and that women could relate to having more than one chapter in their lives. Fergie spoke openly about it in the interview, and it made me that much more admiring of her success, bravery, health, and well-being, and her commitment to living an upstanding life. We were either going to be called out for the fact that she had been a druggie, or people were going to forgive her, move on, and say, "Look, there's redemption, and everybody makes mistakes." And that's what happened. That issue sold incredibly well. I will always think to myself, "Follow your gut, because you can be wrong, but if you think you're right, the payoff is great."

I wasn't the best in rowing, although I qualified for a Junior Olympics training camp in Colorado Springs when I was seventeen. When I got to Harvard, the crew coach was standing at registration and pulling aside anybody who was about five-foot-ten or taller and built strong. I'm only five-foot-five and pretty small for a heavyweight rower. I walked up to her and said, "I stroked the winning boat in the all–New England championship." She just said, "Uh-huh, can you step aside because I'm trying to find rowers here?" I said, "But I'm trying to tell you that I am a rower." She said, "You're too short." She didn't want me, but there's no way I wouldn't show up for tryouts. When I did, she said, "Okay, you can go in the bow," and that meant learning to row on the other side, as a starboard. But because I was also a sculler, I knew how to do either and I could "feather" with both hands, so I went to the bow and rowed there for a couple of years. I was never as good as these bigger, stronger athletes. And I didn't love the indoor rowing tanks since they're cold, wet, and disgusting. One reason I liked rowing is you're outside on the water, in the fresh air, and there's the beautiful view, sky, and trees. The tanks in the winter were just gross, like a Petri dish of sweat and germs. I decided I was not going to row anymore and told the coach. She was less than heartbroken. I decided to try out for the college newspaper, *The Harvard Crimson*, and follow my heart into journalism.

I wrote my old coach, Chris, whom I adored. At this point he had become interested in the theater and had moved to Colorado Springs to run a theater company. I wrote that I'm giving up crew. It's the hardest decision I've ever made but I'm going to follow my dreams and be a journalist. I've rowed for five or six years, and I've loved it. He wrote back the nicest letter saying, "There are two important days in an athlete's life: the day you decide to commit to your sport, and the day you decide to leave it and move on. Never regret either day." I knew then that I was making the right decision.

It was 1980 and all of my friends who were good rowers from Princeton, Yale, and Harvard were going out for the Olympics and could have made it. Then President Jimmy Carter canceled the U.S. teams going to Moscow because of the Soviet invasion of Afghanistan. We all graduated in 1982 and some of them rowed through '84, trying to make the 1984 Olympic team competing in the Los Angeles games. None of my pals made it. After I quit rowing I ended up coaching house crew at Harvard and teaching beginners how to row, which was fun. I was a pretty good coach. I could take girls who had never rowed before, put them in a boat, and we'd win races against other houses. I realized I could go back to Andover and teach English and coach, or I could go to New York and try to get a job in journalism and leave rowing behind completely. I moved on.

It was the right decision for me. A lot of people who tried and didn't make the L.A. Olympics felt they never had that moment where they decided to put it in a box and walk away. They felt that they had been cheated out of their Olympics. There was a lot of bitterness and sadness; they felt they didn't get out of the sport what they wanted to. I was able to take what I'd learned from rowing and adapt all that good positive thinking and teamwork to become the person I am today, with those lessons intact.

I'm still very active today. I'd wanted to do a triathlon for ten years, but I was a terrible swimmer and scared of open-water swimming. It didn't help that I grew up in the era of *Jaws*. My dad would rent a little cottage on Martha's Vineyard before it was so chic and expensive. They made *Jaws* one summer on Martha's Vineyard, and we went to see it the next summer. It was literally *my* beach where the girl got eaten alive and my town where much of it was filmed. I internalized *Jaws* like nobody's business. I would get in the water and literally hear the music and think I was about to get eaten.

I finally decided to do a triathlon and get over my fear of openwater swimming. I started taking swim lessons, and people would make fun of me. Then I joined a team, which was even more intimidating because not only don't I swim well, but I'm older than these people by twenty years. Some of them literally were born the year I got out of Harvard. There are some Division I swimmers who are Olympic-level swimmers. I said, "I'm just going to keep telling myself I don't suck and I'm going to keep trying." I started to run as well as some of the younger people, and could bike well enough to keep up with some of them because of my experience with skiing and crew. (It's all quads.) The young girls think it's sort of laughable and admirable that somebody who's old enough to be their mom is still trying to compete, and I think not only am I trying to compete, I want to try to finish in the top ten in my age group, at a national level. Doing these triathlon races has been one of the most fun things I do in my outside time.

It's been five years and only in the last two, when I got over my embarrassment and humiliation about being in a team environment, have I gotten fast, and that's because I decided, *I don't care if I'm bad or vulnerable.* The only way to get better is to start swimming more, and be fearless. Plus, being on a team is motivation, and I get inspired by the best athletes around. Five of my Terrier Tri team members went to the world championships at Kona recently.

I say: Play up. Surround yourself with the best people in both work and outside of work, and let them challenge you—and insist on your own best performance to become the best you can be.

Interacting with twenty-six to thirty-six-year-olds on my team has also helped me realize how much I need to stay connected with the young people on my magazine team. It's too easy when you move up a corporate ladder to lose touch with some of the junior people because there are necessary layers of structure in any corporate business. If you have sixty "direct reports," you're not going to get anything done. But I try to spend significant amounts of time with every level assistant and editor at every age at the magazine and say to them, "Make me smarter about the Web. Make me smarter about blogging and Tweeting, help me know all the things I need to know that are going to keep us current and engaged with our young readership." Our readers are in their early thirties or late twenties, and online and on Facebook all the time. I've made a big effort to cut down all the walls and try to create as much fluidity between levels at the magazine as I can and still be effective.

There's a direct relationship between sports and my success. But being creative, curious, focused, and fearless, and trying to be a well-rounded person is always important. I'm not just an athlete, nor am I just a magazine thinker. I feel as if I have this broader view of how to collaborate—on a team—that has served me well, and has been one of the most rewarding parts of my life.

DONNY DEUTSCH

As a quarterback, I usually was the organizer. I would put a disparate group together and try to get them to work down the same path. I had to understand people's motivations, their weak and strong points more than anything. And that's Management 101—knowing how to organize people, how to manage and motivate them, how to get people to work toward a common goal of winning. In advertising, you take fifty, sixty, however many people are working on the pitch, and set a goal of getting everybody to be their best and to come together to work as one. It's very similar in sports.

Donny Deutsch is a television host and the chairman of Deutsch, Inc., a multibillion-dollar advertising agency founded in 1969 as David Deutsch Associates, Inc. In 1989, he took over the company as president and CEO, changed its name, and built it from a small shop into one of the top agencies. He's also a managing partner of Deutsch Open City, an independent film production company, and the former host of the CNBC talk show *The Big Idea with Donny Deutsch*. He was born and raised in New York City.

Management 101

AS I WROTE IN MY book *Often Wrong, Never in Doubt*, in the ninth grade I just wanted to be good in sports and have a lot of friends. I grew up in Bayside, Queens, New York, and everybody was in the streets. We played football in the streets; we played softball on concrete. I was an okay athlete. On a scale of one to ten, I was a six or seven. Not the best, or even one of the better ones. But I always had a good mouth, and it got me an extra point or two. I usually ended up being the organizer of things, more of a leader than anything else. If there were twelve guys, I would say, "We'll divide the teams this way . . ." I was always using my brain. And that helped me in my leadership skills—as did my charisma. It put me in the center of the pack, and it elevated my athletic skills. I never played organized football. I played choose-up games with fourteen guys on the street. We played some tackle. We would buy our own equipment and play other teams in the next neighborhood.

The only organized thing we ever did was Little League, and that was at the Mid-Queens Boys' Club. Most of the sports I played were more social. We were guys choosing up teams, or we'd be in a football league that we organized ourselves. That's how it was growing up in Queens. If I'd have grown up in a suburb I might have been on a basketball team or softball team. But my school, Martin Van Buren High School, had four thousand kids. All the basketball players were six-foot-six and African-American. All of the soccer players were Hispanic. We didn't have a football team. None of my friends played any high school team sports. None of the girls were cheerleaders. It just wasn't part of the social fabric of my high school experience. In a more suburban or rural high school, on Friday nights, basketball games are the social epicenter. In Queens, it wasn't part of the social milieu of things.

I remember in choose-up games I always felt bad for the kid that got picked last. It was a very tough place to be. When I was growing up, guys either played sports or they were nerds. Whereas we just had sports camp growing up, now kids can go to sleep-away camp, theater camp, this camp, and that camp. If you're not an athlete, you can be a super computer whiz.

I was on the younger end of my age group. I was born at the end of November. I was always good in school, but somehow in Little League and camp I was always one of the younger kids. I remember one year in Little League, I didn't get picked the whole year, even though I was a good athlete. That sucked. I think what's very important is putting your kids in a position where they can flourish. I'm not saying you stack the deck for them, but it's interesting to see how today, in school, kids born after September are held back.

My worst moments in sports still stick with me. In Little League I was playing second base. We were up two or three runs. A guy got up in the last inning and the ball went through my legs. It ended up being a home run and cost us the game. Also, I was the last guy cut from my ninth-grade basketball team at Parkway Junior High School in Jamaica, Queens. They cut me for an eighth-grader. That really stung. It was a small, private junior high school, so I have no excuse. I didn't make it. When you're a kid, it hurts. You never want to feel it again. That's the way it is in business and in sports. You don't grow from the wins. You grow from the defeats. Or hopefully you do. I don't believe "Winning is everything. It's the only thing." You want to win. But that doesn't mean that a loss can't turn into an eventual win.

I was very competitive as a kid. I had three friends, and one summer all we did was play two-on-two basketball in this guy's backyard for four hours a day. These games ended with a score of something like 100–98. We'd kill ourselves over these games. The competition was highly acute. It was just four guys, all of whom were very competitive with each other. Still, I think I am a much more fierce competitor in business than in sports. I loved sports. But it was what it was. Business has brought out a much more fierce sense of competition in me.

If I lost an account I would always kick myself. The true failure in losing is when you don't take anything away from it. If you just go through the pain of losing and don't, in any way, advance yourself further for any next game, life moment, or situation, then it's a loss with no caveat or no asterisk whatsoever.

I'd like to think my life has been a great success for the most part, but it's when I'm disappointed or I fail or something doesn't go my way that I think I'm going to somehow use that and get to a bigger place. Take my TV show, *The Big Idea with Donny Deutsch*, which I was doing for four years on CNBC and which ended at the end of 2008, due to a series of events that led up to its end—the economy, and so forth. I'm still smarting about that, figuring it out. Eventually, I'll put the experience in a great place. But until I do, I'm pissed off. I did the best I could. It was a huge success. It was the longest-running talk show they've ever had. It still bothers me that it was canceled. I want to strangle someone. Six months from now, a year from now, two years from now I will be in an even grander place, for lack of a better word. That's the game. It's not always supposed to be easy, and it's not always supposed to go your way—as long as it goes your way eventually. You have to be able to harness the loss and not be bitter about things. But also own them, and use them as tools.

From sports I learned how to get a group of people to work together. As a quarterback, I usually was the organizer. I would put a disparate group together and try to get them to work down the same path. I had to understand people's motivations, their weak and strong points more than anything. And that's Management 101—knowing how to organize people, how to manage people and motivate them, how to get people to work toward a common goal of winning. In advertising, you take fifty, sixty, however many people are working on the pitch, and set a goal of getting everybody to be their best and to come together to work as one. It's very similar in sports.

I would have been a good coach. That's what you are in business, at the end of the day. If you run your business, you're a coach. I'd have been a better coach than an athlete. I know how to motivate and, hopefully, inspire people. I think I'd be a very good play caller, in fact. I'm just a good strategist. That's what running a business is.

Business is no different from sports. Businesses are people, and the most successful businesses find the best talent that works together well. They don't have a star system. I never wanted one prima donna, one creative superstar, in the agency. You want people to work well together. It's so easy for me to see why some sports teams don't make it. The winning teams have the right pieces that come together. It's that simple. You can see it. I never understand how guys putting professional teams together don't understand that. You can't just put a bunch of stats together. It's very clear. And it's no different in a work environment. Over the years, I've hired one or two people who turned out to be a mistake, people who did not foster that team spirit. It was much more about them as individuals. They didn't work out. I've learned from those mistakes.

I've pretty much achieved everything in advertising that I wanted to. That's why I sold the company in 2000. I felt as if I had climbed the mountain with the agency for almost a decade. There was nowhere for me to go. If I didn't feel that way I would still be doing it, because I would have something to prove. I feel that in the ad game I was Michael Jordan. I won. I really felt that way—whether that was true or not—in every way I could measure it: monetarily, outside accolades, quality of product, and the organization I built. Whereas in television I think I've been a moderate success. You could say not a lot of people end up with their own talk show and it was a great show. That's a million to one. But it hasn't been a stunning, continuing unadulterated success. Until I get that, I'll keep punching.

DEBRA LEE

One of the advantages that men had over women is that they learned at an early age to compete and that it's okay to lose and keep going. Girls missed out on that for a long time because we didn't have team sports. I see what my kids have gone through recently and it's a whole different world. . . . The more girls grow up competing and learning how tough it is and that you've just got to get back up and keep going when you lose, the better off we are in the business world because sometimes things don't go the way you planned.

A former attorney, Debra Lee is the chairman and CEO of BET Networks, a unit of Viacom, Inc. Lee graduated from Brown University with a bachelor's degree in political science with an emphasis in Asian politics, and then, simultaneously, earned her Juris Doctor at Harvard Law School and a master's degree in public policy from the John F. Kennedy School of Government.

Learning to Compete

THERE WEREN'T THAT MANY opportunities for girls in sports when I was coming along. We had basketball, but only six-on-six where players had to stop at half court so we didn't have a basketball team at James B. Dudley High School in Greensboro. But we had track and field. I started competing, as it became clear during physical education that I was pretty fast, which I enjoyed. Having the wind going through my hair and being free was fun. I remember the exhilaration of winning. It was a high. You felt as if you were contributing to the success of your overall school. That, and going to other schools to compete, was a lot of fun. I also remember the ugly little blue uniforms we wore.

Dudley was an all-black high school when I went there. Greensboro, North Carolina, was still very segregated at the time. The school had a great sports history and was very proud of it. Curly Neal, who was on the Harlem Globetrotters, went there. I ran the fifty-yard dash and anchored the 400 relay. We practiced hard. I was never great at long-distance running, but I remember being made to run around that track more times than I wanted to. It was grueling near the end. It was all about getting a good night's sleep the night before, being relaxed, going out there and doing your best and hoping it all came together on that day.

I was pretty good for the level of competition. I didn't win all the time. Losing was not fun. I still have problems losing. I think the more of it you do, the better you get at it. You strive to win but you learn that sometimes you do lose. Maybe if I had played more of a team sport it would have been different. That's one of the advantages that men had over women—they learned at an early age to compete, and that it was okay to lose and keep going. Girls missed out on that for a long time because we didn't have team sports. I see what my kids have gone through recently and it's a whole different world.

The coaches I liked best were the ones who encouraged you. Even if you lost, they could find something to say about that loss that would encourage you, as opposed to saying, "You lost, so that's the end of the road." That's true in business, too. You can't just lose and give up. You've got to keep coming back and redefining where you're going and what your goals are. It's an ever-changing environment. You always want to win, but there are things you need to do if you don't win. I remember that when Carly Fiorina was let go from Hewlett-Packard, where she was chairman and CEO, a lot of women in business said, "Well, what's going to happen to her?" Some people thought that she might not be given another opportunity to run a company on par with Hewlett-Packard. The more girls grow up competing and learning how tough it is and that you've just got to get back up and keep going when you lose, the better off we are in the business world, because sometimes things don't go the way you planned. And sometimes you get terminated, or they bring in someone else, and you just have to keep moving. Men are able to do that a little easier than women.

That's why it's heartening for me to see Venus and Serena, the women of the WNBA, and other women out there competing hard on a daily basis and learning how to deal with the agony of defeat as well as the exhilaration of winning. You've got to be able to deal with both.

In the media business, we compete daily. Every day we get something called the Nielsen ratings, which tell us how our shows fared compared to our competitors. We live and die by the numbers because it's what the advertisers use to decide whether or not they're going to buy us. So it's something that we work hard to increase on a daily basis. Early on, when we were the only game in town, ratings weren't as important. We had a lot of advertisers that bought BET just because we were the only black network out there, so they weren't asking about ratings. Now that we're owned by Viacom, ratings are critical to what we do every day, and they're comparing us not just against other black networks but against TBS, TNT, and MTV. Before Viacom bought us, BET was involved in a lot of other businesses, and we were an independent black company. We had attained quite a bit of success and judged ourselves against other black brands whether it was *Ebony*, *Jet*, *Essence*, or *Black Enterprise*. There weren't any other networks like us at the time and we were in a lot of different businesses because the brand worked and there are a lot of services and products that African-Americans need. When Viacom purchased us, almost ten years ago we entered a new realm of competition with general market networks. We always competed against them in a way, but when we became part of Viacom, all of a sudden we had sister networks such as MTV, VH1, Comedy Central, and Nickelodeon, to which we were compared.

It's very competitive in business and we want to win. When we do our awards show, the BET Awards, or our Hip Hop Awards, or Celebration of Gospel, we want it to beat every other show on television that night. The BET Awards '09 show drew 10.7 million viewers, which ended up being the most-watched award show on cable that year. Michael Jackson died on a Thursday afternoon and the show was Sunday. We only had a couple of days to revamp the whole show. The team put forth the effort and worked around the clock to make it happen. Even with the tragedy, it was a high point in terms of seeing it all come together and the teamwork involved. When we received the numbers, it was a real high for us. There were a number of executives still in Los Angeles, where the show took place, and we went out and celebrated. It's like winning a game or a track meet. Our awards show is our version of the Super Bowl. It takes a lot of preparation, and people work on it for six months. It's live, and you want it to be great.

Sports also teach you about motivating other folks. A good coach is great at motivating athletes and getting them ready for a big game. Sometimes part of what I do as CEO is to make sure executives and employees are prepared and ready. It involves everything from budget presentations to annual meetings to our new brand strategy or our "upfront" presentation, where we're presenting our new programming to the advertisers. It's all about being prepared and performing when it's time. When it comes to management style, I don't like to put all men or all women in the same category. Depending on how you were raised, you approach it differently. Most of us were raised to be good girls and wanting to be liked. That doesn't necessarily jibe with running a business and having to terminate people or make decisions that are unpopular with people. Sometimes women have to learn that.

Through sports you learn a lot about discipline, preparation, competing, and giving that extra energy needed to be able to win. I try to teach my kids that that's what studying in school is all about. You've got to learn how to prepare and study. But you always have to do that little bit of extra in order to be successful. I learned that early on, and athletics was a big part of that. Once you get out of school and you don't have those exams and deadlines, it's a little easier, but even in the work environment, you still have those moments that feel like exams. You can't always just do what the job calls for. You usually have to do a little bit more and show that you're open to new possibilities and that you are always prepared. Before Viacom bought

BET, I used to say that giving speeches to analysts was like taking an exam, because you had to know everything there is to know about the company. You had to be able to answer questions and be prepared. To be successful in the business world, you find something you love and work hard at it. Just as in sports.

I love track and field to this day and go to the Olympics every four years. It's always my favorite event because it brings back the excitement of living it in high school. The discipline of practicing, being prepared, and getting ready to tackle a goal, which was the track meet itself, has served me well in business.

SOLEDAD O'BRIEN

One of the reasons I wanted my kids to play sports is I just love the idea of thinking of your body as something positive as opposed to thinking, "I'm fat. I'm unhealthy." I want my girls to feel like they're strong. To think, "I can do a backflip. I can stand on my hands. I can jump a fence with my pony. I can run faster than somebody." To think of your body in those terms for girls is a really empowering thing, because girls have so many body issues.

Soledad O'Brien is an anchor and special correspondent for CNN. She joined the network in 2003 from NBC News, where she had anchored the network's *Weekend Today* since July 1999. She began her career as an associate producer and news writer at the then-NBC affiliate WBZ-TV in Boston. The Harvard graduate grew up in St. James, on New York's Long Island.

Endurance

M Y HUSBAND WAS A TERRIFIC athlete in college and high school. He played lacrosse, hockey, and soccer and was a ranked junior tennis player—a naturally athletic guy. I wasn't. I was good at some things. I ran track. But there's something in being able to use your body in an accomplished way that comes from playing sports. And if you're great—and sometimes I was great—then so be it. But if you're not great, then it's also fun to be part of a team that's accomplishing things.

At Nesaquake Middle School on Long Island I ran the quarter mile, the 400-meter hurdles, and the 4-x-400. I ran track with Coach Len Carolon. He was one of those people who made everybody feel that they were contributing to the team—even the worst runner, people who would never get to be in the first heat or even the second heat. I look at him now and say wow, what a great manager in business he'd be because he made everybody feel very valued and valuable. Even people who really, on the face of it, weren't contributing became the biggest cheerleaders. They stayed for the entire meet and cheered for their friends. We were definitely a very tight team.

I remember once we had this young woman who was a naturally great athlete but wouldn't do the work. Coach Carolon said whoever comes in last is going to have to run an extra mile. This woman just wouldn't do the work, so she came in last. She had to run the extra mile, and all of us ran it with her. We said, "We're part of your team." None of us were anywhere as good as she was. But in order for us to all win, she had to realize that she had to deal with her mental half. Being great physically was just part of the battle.

In sports, what you put in is what you get out. I know so many people who are naturally gifted athletically but don't work at it. They can be beaten by the people who have a lot more drive. I tell that to my kids all the time—that you may be taller, you may be stronger, but really at the end of the day it comes down to how hard you are willing to work. I really want them to understand the value of teamwork, the value of hard work, and the value of putting something in to get something out.

As a kid I always played sports. In high school I mostly ran track, and did a lot of horseback riding, too. At Harvard we had a club running team. I played rugby and tried out for the lacrosse team. Right after that I tore my knee up. I was a freshman. It was sad to not be able to do the sports that I really enjoyed, but I never felt that, long term, I was going to be some kind of professional athlete.

I always thought I was competitive until I met my husband. On our first date we played croquet with this little lawn-croquet set. He's trying to figure out how to beat me, and I'm holding a glass of wine. I thought, "We're on a date. You're going to try to kill me?" He loves to win, whereas I want to play a great game for me. I want to be better. Whether it's in running or jumping. In life it's the same thing. I'm always competing with myself, trying to top myself. When I started to report, I used to screen everything I did. I'd come in during my free time and try to improve by watching every little nuance and try to make it better. It really paid off. Five years later I got better, and people would say, "Oh my God, how did it happen?" Well, I really sweated every detail, which is as it is with sports. I'm a fairly athletic person, but not *the most*, and so I have to work hard at it.

A lot of sports is just sticking it out and doing the training. Not giving up when it gets hard. It's not giving up when you're tired or your legs hurt the next day. For me, journalism was always like that. You don't necessarily have to be the best, and you may not be the smartest. You may not be the prettiest, but you can work harder. The beautiful thing about television news is that hard work actually counts. It counts more than all those other things. It's great to be smart, but you can learn stuff. It's great to be talented, but you can learn. It's great to be cute, but you can clean up fine. Sports are kind of like that. I know so many people like that girl I ran track with, a natural athlete who didn't want to put the work in. At the end of the day, some of us did better than she did.

A lot of my job is endurance—covering the tsunami in Southeast Asia, covering Hurricane Katrina, covering the conflict between Israel and Hezbollah. It's hot. Your backpack is heavy. It's not a sit-down kind of job, unless you're anchoring. I like to land somewhere, figure out the story, sleep on the floor of an RV. You better be in pretty good shape. Covering Katrina was certainly an endurance race. We were there for weeks at a time. You camp out and just keep running and running.

One of the things I've always liked about having played sports my whole life is sports are really helpful for getting very comfortable with your body. I had four kids and gained fifty pounds with each pregnancy. I had three pregnancies, with one set of twins. One of the reasons I wanted my kids to play sports is I just love the idea of thinking of your body as something positive as opposed to thinking, "I'm fat. I'm unhealthy." I want my girls to feel like they're strong. To think, "I can do a backflip. I can stand on my hands. I can jump a fence with my pony. I can run faster than somebody." To think of your body in those terms for girls is a really empowering thing, because girls have so many body issues. For me, as a lifelong athlete who wasn't top-notch, who wasn't ranked outside of Long Island at any point, I just always felt like my body was on my side. I'm strong. I can lift things. I can haul things. I can carry things. I could carry my backpack through New Orleans while covering Katrina. I can hang in there when it's ninety-five degrees because I'm strong. And for girls that's really important.

I talk to my girls about it. Little girls are all about body. Even at eight, my daughter will say, "Is this fat? Is that fat?" I'm sure she's hearing all sorts of things at school. It's happening much younger than it ever happened when I was growing up. I say, "That's not fat. That's a muscle, and that muscle is why you are able to jump over that fence. This is the muscle that runs up to your butt and the one that makes you strong. So, you know what? This is a great muscle. You need that one." I really feel very comfortable in my body, and I think sports got me there.

I never had any of the eating-disorder type issues a number of my friends had because I believed my body had a totally other purpose. I was running track. I was playing rugby. Having a good strong foundation is why every time I had a kid, I kind of popped back into shape. Before long I was within ten pounds of what was normal for me. A lot of that is having a core strength and muscle tone that has come from playing sports since I was seven or eight years old.

There's a big connection between doing well in school and in athletics, and some of that is you don't get in trouble. I look at my daughter who does gymnastics. She's really into it. She goes to gymnastics. She comes home. She eats. She does her homework, and she's tired. There's no time to get in trouble. I was a much more focused student because I didn't go hang out with a bunch of kids. I went and played sports. If you're playing sports, you're not smoking. If you're playing sports, you're not hanging out smoking pot. If you're playing sports, you're not getting into trouble after school. You're exhausted. You roll home, scarf down dinner, do your homework, and go to bed. You have to be a very focused person, and that's what I really got out of sports. I was very focused and knew how to get stuff done.

My husband and I talked about it all the time before we were parents: "When we have kids we're going to make sure that they are immediately into sports." We spent a lot of time trying to figure out what sports my daughter Sofia would be in because she's a shyer and quieter kid. With Cecilia, we figured gymnastics. She was good at it right away. She was a kid that came out of the womb with very developed calves. She's a tough, strong child. Sofia didn't take too well to sports immediately, but we knew that that was going to be very important and we wanted her to have a great grounding in that. Now she's on the swim and tennis teams and loves it. She could win every game or lose every game. I do not care. I love that she has a thing that she likes, that she feels good about, and that she's working on. If she won every game but was a jerk at the end, then I would be sorely disappointed, as if I had failed as a parent.

Everyone says that it's the process, the road, not the end result. That's really true in sports. My daughters are seven and eight. After their horse show the other day we witnessed one mom light into her daughter. It was very strange. You have these big giant horses and all the girls are in bows with their hair done. They're all gussied up. My daughters were so uncomfortable watching this mother just rip into her child about how she should have done this and how she should have done that, and this was well after the fact. I mean, she'd done her course.

The message I always try to give them is, if you win and you have terrible sportsmanship, then that's not winning. That is the last thing you want. Winning at all costs is not winning. My son, who's five, plays soccer. They're so little, and they literally run in the wrong direction. They're truly cute kids. They were out there playing and he said, "Mom, I scored a goal!" And I said, "Yeah, but you also had great sportsmanship." The other day he played in the rain. He said, "Mommy, I had good sportsman, didn't I? I had good sportsman." I love that at age five he understands that it's great to win, but winning and being a horrible winner is not victory. That's a really important lesson.

Not everybody is going to be beautiful. God, we all wish. But sports can enhance your life by making you a better person. It teaches you how to self-critique. It teaches you how to treat people. It teaches you how to push yourself to get better. It teaches you how to lose and stick a smile on your face and say, "Next time I win because I'm going to work hard to get there." For us mere mortals who are not going to go out there and win Wimbledon, that's the amazing real changing power of sports. It's really remarkable. There aren't a lot of things in life that have the transformative power of sports.

ROBIN ROBERTS

The greatest thing I learned from sports is that you always get another chance to prove yourself. . . . I can remember playing tennis. I'd lose a match, I'd go back out the next day. . . . I think this idea helped me when I graduated from college in 1983 and sent out my tapes. I was trying to get hired as a sports reporter. Most people, especially women, would give up. I wasn't really the smartest or the best. I was just persistent, and that was because I felt, "Well, I'm going to get another opportunity. The game's not over."

Robin Roberts is a co-anchor at *Good Morning America*. From 1990 to 2005 she worked at ESPN. She also hosted ABC Sports' *Wide World of Sports*. She was born in Pass Christian, Mississippi, and graduated cum laude from Southeastern Louisiana University with a Bachelor of Arts degree in communications. She ended her college-sports career as the school's third all-time leading scorer in basketball.

Discipline

I WAS ALWAYS FASCINATED with everything to do with sports. Bowling was my first sport. My dad was in the military, and on base, when I was six or seven years old, they didn't offer much else. I became a Mississippi State bowling champ in a matter of a few years because I became obsessed with it. Then I started playing basketball, but tennis was my passion. I *really* wanted to be a professional tennis player. Every time I took up a sport, I thought, "Okay, I want to go pro."

Because my dad was in the Air Force, sports were a great way to meet new friends. I was rather tall for my age at an early age, so I was always a big hit when I moved to town. They'd say, "You're on our basketball team." And there was also just the intangible joy of it. I liked to see how fast I could run, how high I could jump and how far I could throw a ball. You can't describe it. I'm the best doggone average athlete you'll meet. Yes, I went to college on a scholarship, and had a thousand-plus points and rebounds in basketball, and won some state mixed doubles championships in tennis, but I just liked how sports made me feel. I competed with myself and didn't really feel like I had to prove anything or say I was number one. I loved sweating, the strength that I felt. I loved the mental aspect of it. I'm coachable. I was horrible in pickup basketball games. I needed a coach to say, "You go down on the low block. You do this. You do that." And then I was incredible. But left on my own to freelance, not so much. Maybe it's the military background from my father. I appreciated the structure.

Louisiana State University recruited me in basketball and I had pretty much committed. The spring of my senior year in high school, I went to LSU to practice. I was on campus and said, "No, this is not for me. It was too big." Driving back to Mississippi with my high school basketball coach, Ann Logue, in her little green Corvair Monza that barely got us to Baton Rouge, I saw the sign for Southeastern Louisiana University and asked her if we could stop. It was the perfect little college campus in a small town, Hammond. The basketball coach, Linda Puckett, had already given all her scholarships out, but she said to Coach Logue, "Technically, it's going to be a tennis scholarship, but she's going to play basketball. And she can play tennis, too, if she's got some energy at the end of the year and still wants to play." I didn't play tennis. She knew I'd be whipped. Plus, I wanted to do well in school, and there was no way at that point I could do both because basketball season was such a long season and tennis was in the spring.

My freshman year in college I remember doing a drill during basketball practice. We had to stay down in a crouched defensive position and slide our feet all the way around the court. I was in the middle of the pack. It was painful to stay down all the way around the court, but Coach Puckett told me to stay down and so I did. We're all huffing and puffing. She gets right up in my face and says, "Hon, hon, you're going places in life because you listen. You're disciplined. You were the only one who stayed down." That meant so much that she acknowledged me like that. It was a simple thing of just following the rules.

I had so many coaches who were instrumental in my development. The first one, Coach Steve Burns, was my physical education teacher at Jeff Davis Elementary School in Biloxi, Mississippi. He was our track coach, and he was stern. We had a proper way of doing things. At the time I thought he was so mean, but he's someone who's still in my life to this day. I see him at Christmas almost every year back home. He really made me feel like I was a champion. There was one track meet a year and we'd go against the other schools. I was the fastest at my elementary school, but we would get to this track meet and I would get smoked. These girls were running without shoes, and I had my new Keds or whatever. I think the highest I got was fourth place. Still, he never made me feel like I let the team down. But he also taught me about how important sports were, not just that they were fun. He knew that what I got out of sports was going to be something I would keep for a lifetime, and that it would shape me. Boy, was he right.

Being disciplined in sports has helped me. I have to get up at three forty-five in the morning to do *Good Morning America*. The focus that it takes is quite similar to what I experienced as an athlete. The show has a team aspect. It's not just the people that you see that I work with on camera but people behind the scenes as well.

Sports have helped me handle pressure. I remember one game against Louisiana State University. They had a point guard that was so cocky. She just thought she was all that and a bag of chips. It was a really close game and they were ahead by a few points. We needed the ball back. I purposely fouled her so she would have to shoot the free throws, hopefully miss, and we would get the ball. She went to the free throw line and was a wreck. Here she had been so confident and so cocky until the game was really on the line and her team needed her. I thought, "You are the biggest fake. What a façade. You're not so cool, honey." Sure enough, she missed the free throws. We got the ball and ended up winning the game. I don't know why that has stayed with me. I know about pressure: I've got to get the story right. I've got to get it fast. It's so competitive.

I remember when I was covering the University of Georgia.

Willie Anderson was the star basketball player. Two guys from the other two stations in town had gone in the locker room and gotten their interview. It was a time when they wouldn't let women in the locker room, so they were keeping me outside. I realized that if I didn't get that interview I wasn't going to have a job. How could I keep a job if the news director is watching that night and sees a sound bite from Willie on the other two stations and not ours? All of this was going through my head. As polite and southern as I am, I said to the sports information director, "You either get Willie Anderson out here right now, or I'm going in there." And sure enough, thirty seconds later, Willie Anderson, in a little-bitty towel, is in the hallway talking to me. I get my sound bite and go running to the satellite truck to make the feed in time to make the eleven-o'clock news that night. I felt my job was on the line—that's pressure. Those kinds of moments kick in, and a sports background has made the difference.

My sister Sally-Ann has had an exceptional career in broadcasting. She's a morning anchor in New Orleans. I remember one time she was about to go into contract negotiations. I was on the road and talking to her on a pay phone. (It was before cell phones.) I was giving her advice, like, this is what you do. You go in and this is what you ask for. You are great blah, blah, blah. Someone overheard the conversation and said, "Boy, you're a great big sister." I said, "Well, actually I was talking to my big sister. I'm the little sister." I relayed that story to Sally-Ann and she said, "It's because you played sports. You have this attitude about yourself." That's why she made sure that her children, especially her daughters, were exposed to sports.

The greatest thing I learned from sports is that you always get another chance to prove yourself. There's always another game. I can remember playing tennis. I'd lose a match, I'd go back out the next day. The same was true for basketball. You'd lose this horrible game and then you'd get to go back out and play again. I always felt that it gave me a chance to prove myself again to myself. I think this idea helped me when I graduated from college in 1983 and sent out my tapes. I was trying to get hired as a sports reporter. Most people, especially women, would give up. I wasn't really the smartest or the best. I was just persistent, and that was because I felt, "Well, I'm going to get another opportunity. The game's not over." Having that spirit helped me land my first job in Hattiesburg, Mississippi. Because I felt if I could get the first one, things would be okay. It was just so hard to get that first one. I remember classmates of mine who were at the top of the class. I would see them and ask what happened. They said, "I sent out a couple of tapes and a couple of résumés and they said no." They didn't take rejection well; but I didn't take it as rejection. I looked at it like this: I have to have a better game plan. I didn't win this round, so I've got to figure out how to improve my tape. But I never looked at it as: I'm not good enough. That was the difference.

Some of my coaches thought I was too gracious in defeat. They wanted me to be a little angrier, a little more upset. I mean, I *was* upset, but I was my father's child. He was never too high and never too low. I wasn't boisterous. If we won, I wasn't jumping up and down with my finger in a number one, launched into the air, nor was I boo-hoo-hooing if we lost. I was competing with myself. I always wanted to do well, and I always wanted to do better than I had done before. I always wanted my team to do well.

What really stuck with me my senior year in college was that we had a losing record, my only one. For that last organized team that I was a part of to have a losing record was hard. I'm not going to lie. That was a tough one to take. It was a team thing. Had I been playing tennis and had a losing record I would have hated it, but I would have gotten over it a little bit quicker. I was MVP. How can I be MVP and we have a losing record? I've pretty much moved on, but it wasn't until the summer of 2007. I got cancer and said, "All right, I'll let that go."

Cancer is an opponent. I've faced big, bad opponents. I'm not trivializing it or trying to minimize what cancer is. It's extremely serious. I was embarrassed, because I thought, "Oh my goodness, I'm an athlete and my body let me down for the first time. What's going on here?" My doctors quickly told me that it didn't let me down. In fact it was going to help me beat it, which is true. I approached it as this big, nasty opponent and developed a game plan. My doctors were coaches, and they had a strategy. I said, "I'm very coachable." They clearly laid out the plan: "Okay, you're going to have to have surgery. You're going to have to have this amount of chemo. You're going to have to have this many months of radiation and this is going to be the end result. Victory." I said, "I can do that." It put it in terms relatable and beatable for me.

Sports have truly shaped me. There's no two ways about it. I believe I would have successes in any area of business that I chose. I chose broadcast journalism, but if I had gone into sanitation I would have been the best sanitation person that you'd ever seen. I really feel that sports gave me an incredible advantage. I had the tools. I had what it takes to work with people, to solve problems.

JEFF ZUCKER

On the tennis court then, and even today, I always balanced taking risks with playing safe. I'd like to think I always played smart on the court, and I'd like to think that I do the same thing at NBC Universal, which is: balance. Balancing the right amount of risks with the right amount of safety.

Jeff Zucker is president and CEO of NBC Universal. He has spent his entire career at NBC Universal, joining the company's Olympics unit in 1986, straight out of Harvard. In his more than twenty-four years with the company, he has had a diversified career as an award-winning producer and business leader. He was born in Homestead, Florida, and grew up in Miami.

Don't Make the Same Mistake Twice

I STARTED GOING TO MIAMI Dolphins home games when I was seven years old with my family. And that was in 1972. For anyone who knows anything about professional football, that was the year of the perfect season. They won the Super Bowl the first year I went, and they won the Super Bowl the second year. I was used to having my team win, and so why wouldn't I expect the same thing on the tennis court?

I started playing tennis when I was six years old, and thereafter I played almost every day of my life up until I was eighteen, including competitive junior tennis in Florida. I wasn't a big kid, so contact sports weren't really something for me, although I loved and played touch football. Because my parents played tennis recreationally, I gravitated toward tennis.

When I was younger I had a pretty bad temper on the court. I had a pretty substantial collection of Jack Kramer wood racquets that weren't in one piece. I eventually learned to outgrow that, and by the time I was playing 12-and-under, 14-and-under, I realized that a temper wasn't helping my game. It was only holding me back.

Early on, I had a lot of success and for many years was state ranked. When I didn't quite grow the same way that some of my peers did, I wasn't quite as successful. The same players that I was beating in the 10-and-under and 12-and-under, by the time we got to the 14- and 16-and-under, had developed a strong serve-and-volley game because they had grown. I was still playing from the baseline. I would think, "What's going on here? I used to beat you guys." That was difficult to come to grips with. There's always going to be obstacles, whether you're on the tennis court or you're in the boardroom. You have to figure out ways to overcome them. Nothing is clean. Nothing is easy.

Despite my size limitations—saying I'm five-foot-six now would be generous—my competitive spirit drove me. I was captain of my high school team and played number one on the team in the tenth, eleventh, and twelfth grades. When I was captain of my high school team I was always supportive, which is what I hopefully still am every day in business. Being supportive of your teammates is really important.

When I was younger I had dreams of Centre Court at Wimbledon, as every little young tennis player in Florida would have. By the time I was in the 16-and-under, the 17's, I knew that I wasn't quite at the caliber of the top-tier players because my game did not keep pace with the young boys that I used to beat. I thought about playing college tennis. I played on my freshman team at Harvard, but eventually gave that up because I pursued other activities, including the school newspaper, the *Harvard Crimson*. And, frankly, after that freshman year in college, I don't think I picked up a tennis racquet very much for the next decade. I may not have played at all. I was kind of burnt out. I had played almost every day from the age of six to the age of eighteen, and it did run its course.

Sports have always been the vehicle for me. I was sports editor of my high school newspaper and then became the sports editor of the *Harvard Crimson* and then president of the *Harvard Crimson*. I came to NBC through NBC Sports and the Olympics. When I went to the

Today show after NBC Sports, I went there as a producer covering a segment called "Sportsman of the Week." And then I went on to what I've done at NBC Universal. Sports have always been an entrée for me.

I love all sports. I'm a huge football fan—I'm still a huge Miami Dolphins fan. I'm a big New York Yankees fan. I still play tennis. I play golf. Sports are a central part of my life, and I think I bring that drive to win into the corporate offices. There's always the desire to be the best you can be, whether you're on a tennis court or in a corporate office, and you never give up.

I hate to lose, and that's part of my personality in business as well. I'm always trying to find a way to win, even when the odds are against us. I never mind being the underdog. If people don't expect you to win and then you surprise them, that's okay. But you can't always win and you can't always be expected to win. There's probably some people who think I am too competitive, and sometimes that probably is true. I hope that it's more plus than negative, and when it gets in the way I hope I recognize that.

On the tennis court then, and even today, I always balanced taking risks with playing safe. I'd like to think I always played smart on the court, and I'd like to think that I do the same thing at NBC Universal, which is: balance. Balancing the right amount of risks with the right amount of safety.

The key in business is doing a good job and growing your business. You can't be afraid to make a mistake. Fear is the worst thing you can have. You can't be motivated or live in fear of failing. You have to know it's okay to make a mistake. Just don't make the same mistake twice. I think all of those principles apply to both the tennis court and the business office. When I played tennis competitively, my goal was just always to do the best I could do. I didn't have anything beyond that. With NBC Universal it is to do better than we did yesterday. To do better than we did last week. To do better than we did last year. To keep improving on ourselves. The fact is, we're going through a tremendous transformational time in media where digital is changing everything we do. Nothing is the way it was and everything will be different going forward. Navigating that world is incredibly exciting and terrifying at the same time.

One of the lessons in life is that you can't always win, whether you're on the tennis court, in business, or in your personal life. The joy of victory is exhilarating, but you can't win all the time, and that's okay, too. And it's as important that you handle that as well as you do winning. In the end you learn that it's much more important how you deal with losing than winning. There's nothing more important in life than being a graceful loser.

I got colon cancer twice in my thirties, but I still play tennis. I'm a weekend player because I don't have a lot of time during the week because of my job and four kids. Every time I step on the court, I still want to win. I don't really like to go out and just hit. If I'm going to go out, I want to play. Even when I was younger, I always liked to play matches. I probably only have one speed. It's funny to me, now that my kids are playing, to see how lessons are taught: they warm up for practice. We never had this whole concept of "mini tennis," where people warm up from the two service lines.

After I got sick with colon cancer the first time, when I was about thirty-two years old, I couldn't play tennis. I just had surgery and was going through chemotherapy, so I took up golf as a way to be outdoors and do something. I love golf because I haven't played it all that long. When I play tennis I invariably remember how good I was when I was young and realize I'm never going to be that good again. I'm not that good in golf but enjoy it because I know I can only get better. My tennis game peaked probably when I was fourteen. I'm forty-four. I'm hoping my golf game will peak when I'm about fifty.

PART 4

The Business Executives (Part II)

PHILIP KNIGHT

In a lot of ways there's more lessons to be learned from the defeats than there are from the victories. [Losses] motivated me to work harder and to compete in school, to really understand the value of competitive response and what was needed. . . . [The] equipment business is very, very competitive, so lessons in how to prepare and fight hard are applicable to a business.

Philip H. Knight is the chairman of the board of directors of NIKE, Inc., a company that began as a partnership between Knight and his former track coach at the University of Oregon, the legendary Bill Bowerman, in 1964. Knight, who earned his M.B.A. at Stanford, was born in Portland, Oregon.

Competitive Response

I WAS INTERESTED IN SPORTS from the time my dad took me to my first baseball game when I was six or seven years old. We watched the Portland Beavers, the Triple A team, play. I was consumed by sports. I read the sports section cover-to-cover and subscribed to sports magazines. I was a pretty good youth baseball player and played shortstop. But when I went to high school they didn't have a freshman baseball team. They only had a sophomore-and-under. I was the last guy cut from the team as a freshman. My mother said, "I'm not going to have you moping around the house. You're either going to get a paper route or go out for track." A lot of times they would have you run before and after baseball practice and I could win those races a lot of times, so I thought I would go out and try it. That's how I went out for track and I was better at it than baseball. Within two weeks I was the best distance runner on the freshman team. By my senior year I was probably the second-best half-miler in the state, and I was MVP for my team.

Think of how my life would have been different had I not been cut from the sophomore-and-under baseball team. I didn't think so at the time, but obviously it was the luckiest thing that ever happened to me.

By the time of my senior year at Cleveland High School in Portland, University of Oregon track coach Bill Bowerman was recognized as a national-caliber coach. It would be another fifteen years or so before he was named the head coach of the 1972 U.S. Track and Field Olympics team. But his record at Oregon was so strong, the only place I ever really thought about going to college to run track was Oregon, and that was to run for him. That's where it started. I guess you could say I started Blue Ribbon Sports, Inc., which became NIKE, to stay close to Bowerman. There's an element of truth in that.

I ran four years for him. The first year was really tough, because he was very, very demanding. He almost believed in hazing the freshmen. He always used to say, "The most important thing for a teacher is to get the student's attention," and he would come up with some bizarre way to get your attention. He was very psychological, getting in your brain, pushing you to compete hard and get you to do things that you really didn't think you could do. He was a master at that. For example, Bowerman always said, "Okay, if you got the flu, if you get sick, just come by and tell me and you'll get excused from practice." I remember I was sitting there one day my sophomore year, coming down with something and feeling terrible. I waited for him for about fifteen minutes and he didn't come, so I left. As I was walking out of the track complex here he comes. He says, "Where are you going?" and I said, "Well, I waited for you for fifteen minutes and then I got the flu. I was going back to go to bed." He said, "Get your ass out there on that field." I remember thinking, "Darn it, that old son of a bitch." But I had one of my best workouts ever. I had to sit down with myself when the year was over and say, "I'm either going to do it his way or I'm going to quit." But I never came close to quitting. You ultimately learned to get along with him or you didn't compete for him.

I worked hard in practice. I went to college, like so many kids, thinking track was a three-month-a-year sport, but at the University of Oregon it was a twelve-month-a-year sport. So he had to get that through to me, and to everybody else. When I came there out of high school, I was working hard, by the old standards. But there were the new standards, and I learned that. He became certainly the most important teacher in my life, other than my parents. He had a huge impact on me—not just because of my interest in developing running shoes but in ways beyond that as well.

He never considered himself a track coach. He always said, "I'm a professor of competitive response." It was more than just about running, although that was where you proved whether you could win or lose. It was about competing well in life. He was very encouraging on the academic side and every other way.

What he taught me about life is that how hard you work and prepare is critical, and that sometimes you can prepare hard and still get beat. Four hundred yards around the track was just sort of life in microcosm.

One thing I appreciated most about him was his caring. It was quite clear that when you broke all the barriers that he put up for you how much he cared about the people who ran for him, and about his students. He had a wonderful house that he built himself out on the McKenzie River. He would have the athletes out to his house for dinner, and there was a lot of off-track time spent with him.

The other thing I appreciated is what a phenomenal innovator he was. He was always playing around with shoes and uniforms and how to make things lighter, looking to improve the weight, either of a shoe or even just a pair of shorts. He was constantly concerned about that. That kind of carried over when you thought about how much it meant to him and how hard he was trying on your behalf. Obviously, his experimenting with the shoes planted the seed for what I would do later in life.

He was never a cheerleader coach. He was always very reserved. When one of his runners would run a great race and break the finish line, Bowerman was nowhere to be seen. A lot of times the coach would be right there with the athlete. Instead, he let the athlete bask in the glory. But sometime within an hour after a really good race, he'd come up to you and he'd put that big paw—he was about six-two and he had big hands—on your neck, look down at you, and say, "Nice race." That was the ultimate. Jim Grelle, who was my nemesis and also went to Oregon and made the Olympic team, once said, "You know, everybody else, they're running for a girlfriend or for their parents. We all run for Bowerman."

There were some races at Hayward Field that were big to me at the time. I remember we went one two three against the University of Washington. They were expected to beat us, and I'll never forget the roar that went up when I went into second place behind Grelle. Washington was one two, and Oregon was three four five going into the last lap. Going down the backstretch, Grelle went by and then I went by and then another Oregon guy went by. The roars just got louder with each step. I can still hear them.

My best time in the mile was 4:10. When I started out I was hopeful I could make the Olympic team, but my talent just didn't take me that far. I probably had some more years of running in me. Runners don't really make their peak until probably late twenties. But I quit long short of that, so there was some thought that maybe if I had kept going I might have improved a lot. But there wasn't any money in it, and I had to get about getting into a career and selling shoes. I made the right decision.

Bowerman continued to tinker with shoes after I left Oregon. I went into the Army for a year, and then I went to Stanford Business School. In the entrepreneurship class they said write about something you know. I wrote a paper on whether Japanese track shoes could do to German track shoes what the Japanese cameras had done to German cameras. And in the course of that I made contact with the Japanese company. When I got out of college I went over there and visited. I came back with samples and showed them to Bowerman. I thought he was the best coach, and he was certainly the most innovative in terms of equipment and shoes. So getting his blessing that these were good shoes would be an important step, I thought. I got more blessing than I'd counted on. He said, "Hey, let your old coach in on this." I said, "Great," and we shook hands.

We learned lessons as we went along. Bowerman had instilled a lot of values in me personally, and obviously that showed in what became the culture of the company that became NIKE. He was hugely impactful on the value of and attitude toward innovation. Running the company, or measuring units of sales or profit, wasn't of great interest to him. He kind of let me do all that.

The lessons from running track helped me running a small business. First of all, this equipment business is very, very competitive, so lessons in how to prepare and fight hard are applicable to a business. There have been plenty of bumps. We got kicked out of two banks in Oregon. There were only two banks in Oregon at the time. We had some tough moments early on. I really loved the business and knew that if it fell, I was just going to start it all over again.

We fought hard, and I give a lot of the credit to the early group at NIKE. In the early days we would blow right by our sales forecast and we'd have to adjust our goals on the fly. The people that I was working with really did have an ambition to be number one in the industry. We never let up.

Initially, the goal of being number one was so far out there that we really didn't think of that. We were just trying to get a toehold, make a living, and be one of the good competitors in the business. But the flip side of that is that we always thought we had good products and we knew what would make better products. So in some ways that number-one thing was hovering off in the distance because it wasn't good enough for us to just make a good running shoe. We wanted to make *the* best running shoe.

We had become number one in the United States, and Reebok was gaining on us after creating an aerobics shoe for women in the early '80s. I can remember the day that Reebok went by us. That was a killer. I went out and ate lunch by myself, closed the doors, and turned the lights off. It was a very tough day. We vowed we were going to beat them. We were going to fight like mad, and we did. That's all part of who we became. It's all part of the NIKE culture.

I've always felt the sting of losing more than the joy of winning. In my senior year there was only one guy, Grelle, who beat me, and I didn't take those losses very well. I just couldn't get by him, and those losses became pretty heavy. Those bus rides home were always difficult. You prepared all week, and, to some extent, all year. So it was just a tough period, but it teaches good lessons, too. In a lot of ways there's more lessons to be learned from the defeats than there are from the victories. It motivated me to work harder and to compete in school, to really understand the value of competitive response and what was needed.

You get an attitude toward competition from any of the athletic fields you can't get anyplace else. Those lessons are irreplaceable.

SCOTT MCNEALY

Being an entrepreneur, a CEO, and the head of a fast-growth global company, my job required way more physical stamina than most people realized. There was traveling, dragging luggage, doing late-night meetings, running from meeting to meeting, staying sharp, and staying focused. And my sports background was useful here. I found that being in good physical condition was absolutely critical in maintaining an even keel and maintaining focus in meetings—not falling asleep and putting my head in the salad bowl at an important business dinner—dealing with jet lag, and trying to have a life also.

Scott McNealy is the co-founder and former chairman of Sun Microsystems, which merged with Oracle in January 2010. With three other young entrepreneurs he founded Sun in 1982, and from 1984 to 2006 he served as Sun's CEO and chairman. He graduated from Harvard in 1976 with a B.A. in economics and received an M.B.A. from Stanford in 1980. He's an avid hockey player, a single-digit-handicap golfer, a husband, and the father of four boys. He was born in Columbus, Indiana.

The Scoreboard

GROWING UP, MY SUMMERS WERE perfect. I'd get up and play eighteen holes of golf in the morning. Then I'd do a two-mile swim practice by noon. I'd have sailing until two o'clock on the lake. From two o'clock to four o'clock was tennis practice, and then my mom would pick me up and give me my baseball uniform and a couple sandwiches. I'd change into my baseball uniform and play Little League baseball before going home to have another meal and a bowl of ice cream and eventually passing out. There was never a better day than that for me. I just loved it.

I was never great at any one sport, but I was good at lots of them. I always loved competing. If I go for a bike ride or if I go skiing, I always wonder who won at the end. I've always liked score-keeping in sports.

I went to eight schools by eighth grade and lived in Columbus, Indiana; Rockford, Illinois; Kansas City, Missouri; Racine, Wisconsin; and Birmingham, Michigan. I'm basically a product of the Midwest. Golf was probably the first sport I played. My dad was a golf nut. Vice chairman of American Motors, he'd play golf Saturdays and Sundays and take me to play with him. To be with my dad, I used to pull his pull-cart. I remember having to jump up to grab the handle, which will give you an idea of how tall I was at the time. There were a couple of elevated tees on the golf course in Wisconsin that were very downhill, and about fifty yards down below the tee was a creek. Dad would tee a ball up on these two tees and I would swing his hugely oversized club. All I had to do was hit it about four feet and it would dribble off the front of the tee and roll down into the creek. He'd go into histrionics about how I just lost his golf ball. I'd giggle and laugh. What really got me excited about golf was spending time with Dad.

As I got older, I got to play golf with Lee Iacocca, as well as with the chairman of Ford and the chairman of General Motors. As a young teenager I was hanging around these folks, and probably one of the best life lessons I learned was that though they had a high level of intensity and competitiveness, they could shank a ball, chunk a ball, and hit one OB just as easily as anybody else—they're all human. So when I started Sun Microsystems, I wasn't intimidated to call up anybody at any level at any organization and start a conversation. I didn't feel like I needed to start by calling somebody in the mailroom and look for an introduction to the CEO. It was just as easy to call the CEO directly and say, "I'd like to meet with you." Of course, you certainly have to execute when you get there, or the word gets around that this is not worth doing.

I settled into two sports, hockey and golf. I just loved hockey. I went to Harvard and tried out for two days with the freshman junior varsity team. I remember thinking, "Holy mackerel, these guys are good." At the end of the second day of practice I was sore and tired. I'm thinking I'm probably not at the right caliber here. The coach said take two laps around the rink and then take it into the locker room. I thought, "I'll bust butt on this two-lap race and make a decision after practice." Well, I got lapped—in a two-lap race!—and that's when I decided I'd play house hockey.

About two years into Harvard, I was sitting with the junior varsity hockey coach and we're talking in the stands and watching practice. He said, "I'm leaving in a couple of weeks for the spring golf trip." And I said, "What? You have a golf team here at Harvard?" He looks at me like I've been hanging out in the library too long. I asked if I could try out. He said you can try out after we get back from the spring trip. I tried out, and in my senior year I was captain of the golf team at Harvard.

The thing about both sports is, you can actually be quite competitive as you get older. I stopped playing hockey two years ago when I broke my leg crashing into the boards at the age of fifty-three. I haven't played any competitive hockey since, although I think I might go out and try again. One of the things I loved about golf is, it created an interesting bond with some pretty interesting business people that I've gotten to know and have learned a ton from; people like Ron Sugar, who runs Northrop Grumman; Jack Welch, who ran General Electric; and Riley Bechtel of Bechtel Corporation. These are all people I admire enormously. I've learned a ton from them.

Being an entrepreneur, a CEO, and the head of a fast-growth global company, my job required way more physical stamina than most people realized. There was traveling, dragging luggage, doing late-night meetings, running from meeting to meeting, staying sharp, and staying focused. And my sports background was useful here. I found that being in good physical condition was absolutely critical in maintaining an even keel and maintaining focus in meetings—not falling asleep and putting my head in the salad bowl at an important business dinner—dealing with jet lag, and trying to have a life also. I also found that when I got on the hockey rink, survival was my number one area of focus, not what was going on at the staff meeting earlier that morning. It was a nice release and a nice break.

One of the greatest lessons I learned from playing sports that helped me run Sun is: practice makes perfect. I always tried to outwork my competitors. One of the reasons I stepped down from CEO is that I wanted to spend a little more time with my family. I've got four little startups I'm working on and I wanted to make sure I gave them enough time, energy, and focus. I take raising my children very, very seriously, and I wanted to make sure I spend the time to impart to them important life lessons—the importance of integrity, and the focus on hard work. I think these are especially important for kids who grow up in a fairly well-to-do environment. I want my boys to know there's no sense of entitlement, and that they're going to take personal responsibility.

Instead of growing up thinking everything should be handed to me, I always grew up thinking that if I were born with a platinum spoon in my mouth, then I had to do a little extra to prove to the world that I didn't get where I got because of the family I was born into, but through hard work. I want to make sure my kids know and understand that. There's a lot of people who are going to say, "Aw, they just had every advantage in the world." Well, they do. But they better totally outperform through hard work because of all of the advantages. Sports has taught me that.

Golf is all about mental agility. It's quite a physical sport—if you've ever tried to play golf with a sore elbow or something you'll understand how an injury can massively throw you off. But it really is about mental toughness; and, unfortunately, it's one of those sports where you can blame no one but yourself. And in that way it is much more like being CEO than any sport I've played, because you're not even playing a real opponent. You're playing the whole field and the whole golf course. It is all up to you. You can't blame anybody, because you fundamentally have control over that little white ball.

I love having my boys play golf because I can't tell you how many times they'll say, "This nine iron just doesn't work" or "That was such bad luck." I'll sit down and explain to them, "I've seen you get a lot of good shots with that nine iron. Here, give me that nine iron and watch this." I'll hit the ball really well with it and say, "I don't think it's the club." I have another conversation with them when they have a bad hole and start getting grumpy. I'll say, "You don't practice hard enough to be grumpy about that. Now, if you spent eight hours a day working on that shot and you hit it bad, then maybe you'd have a little right to be grumpy about it. But I don't see you practicing hard enough." And the next day I'll see them out there working on it. It's being able to give them those life lessons.

Integrity is also a quality I picked up through sports. You call penalties on yourself in golf. It's self-policing that way. If your ball moves while you're in the woods, you come out of the woods and say, "My ball moved. I took a two-stroke penalty." If I went out and came in with a score and told my dad what I shot, it didn't feel right to come in and say, "Hey, Dad, I shot eighty-three" when I really shot eighty-seven. "Who are you cheating," I'd ask myself, "and can you sleep well at night?"

I remember one time we had a stupid, frivolous lawsuit against us at Sun. During the discovery process we had to produce all the documents around the time period that the event was going on. About two years later the lawsuit was still going on. I was doing spring cleaning in my office on a Saturday morning and I looked under the cupboards where I never went and there were some e-mails that weren't going to help our case and would maybe cost the company millions of dollars if we turned them over. I remember holding the bundle of documents with a big rubber band around them over the garbage can thinking, "Should I just throw them out? Nobody will ever know. These lawyers with the ridiculous greenmail lawsuit will never get a chance to abuse these documents in a court case, and it's the right thing to do for my shareholders." But then I thought, "It's not the right thing to do." I walked them down the hall and put them in the in-box of our general counsel. I said, "I found these and they should probably be submitted for discovery in the lawsuit." It turned out it did cost us many millions of dollars in the settlement because there were documents written by sales reps in an emotional moment that wouldn't have looked good in front of a jury. But I slept better and felt better about running the organization by doing that. It's just like not coming in and saying you shot eighty-three when really you shot eighty-seven.

I didn't like losing in sports. The two toughest losses for me were in swimming, when I was a teenager. There was always this big strong kid who was about twice my size and looked like Arnold Schwarzenegger. He swam the same event that I swam, the breast stroke. He beat me for four years. I kept working at it and working at it. Finally, in the finals of my last year of swimming, in the qualifying I swam faster than him, so I had the pole position. In the finals it was just him and me. Nobody else was close in the pool. I swam as hard and as perfect a race as I could—and he touched me out. That was a little tough to deal with, but I gave it my best and think I scared him, which was actually pretty cool. I'd much rather lose to somebody who was really good than beat somebody who's really bad. And I would rather lose to a great team than beat a team that didn't provide any competition. So I always tried to "play up" in tennis and golf. It was always more fun to beat a guy I wasn't supposed to beat than win over somebody who just clearly wasn't at the same level. When we started Sun, we decided to go after IBM, Hewlett-Packard, and DEC. We figured if we're going to go after somebody, let's go after the biggest and the best. We also went after Microsoft. We didn't choose a little guy to beat. That's no fun.

Running a business is a team sport. Every person has their position to play, and everyone has to work together in order for the team to win. The scoreboard is the public value of the company. But it is very different from sports. Sports are games. Business is not a game. If someone does badly in professional sports, they might lose their job. If a boss blows a "three-foot putt" or "double faults," literally thousands could lose their jobs, billions of dollars of investors' money could be at risk, and the boss is likely to lose his or her job, too. Worse yet, if you cheat in sports, it seems to be okay as long as you don't get caught—or maybe you'll get two minutes in the penalty box, or have to forfeit a match. But in business, if you cheat, you have a real chance of going to jail. Very few sports figures have gone to jail for breaking the rules on the field of play.

I thought I became a way better CEO later in life, when I had kids and got involved in coaching. I've never been head coach because I just never had the time. But as an assistant coach, it was quite fascinating to see the behavior that I saw in my kids' youth hockey teams. I would think, "That's sort of like so-and-so at my staff meeting." I started to explain to my staff that it's never good when the activities or actions I see you taking remind me of my kids' youth hockey teams. But we don't ever really grow up. We are humans. We have normal, natural, inescapable human traits and tendencies. I don't care what culture you come from, they're all mostly the same.

Every leader uses their life experience in business. I use what I learned in the ice hockey rink, on the golf course, and in raising and coaching my kids' sports teams. I probably would have come to the same realizations anyway, because they are essentially my core values. However, sports were always part of my life and helped me stay both fit and competitive, as well as see the striking similarities to the boardroom.

SUSAN MERSEREAU

There's an etiquette associated with each sport. Don't choose tennis and expect it to operate like a football game. That notion of "Whatever sport you choose, play within its rules, and play it well" helped me a lot later in business, because my natural tendency would be to change the corporation to fit what I needed.

Susan Mersereau served as senior vice president of information technology and chief information officer at Weyerhaeuser from 2003 until her retirement in 2008. In addition, she held various information-systems management positions. She was born and raised in Portland, Oregon.

Play Your Game

M Y FAMILY WAS VERY ATHLETIC; it was just part of our DNA. I have two brothers, and all three of us were involved in sports for as long as I can remember. I started skiing at three and playing tennis at four. I was on a junior golf team at six or seven. I was on the swimming team for a while. I did the trampoline. My mother and father just assumed we would all be involved in sports. It was never discussed. It just was.

They thought it was important we get into team sports to learn how to be part of a team. But they were also focused on using individual sports as a way to develop us, in the hope that we would maintain the interest for the rest of our lives. Sometimes athletes involved in only team sports stop playing once they graduate from school, when it becomes harder to organize teams. And there was clearly a focus that we would be doing these things for the rest of our lives, not just doing a childhood thing. I can remember my mother saying how important it was that we learn things that we could do later in life and that were mobile, because they were also very much into exposing us to a lot of travel and didn't want us to spend time and energy with things that we couldn't do if we moved.

I played tennis at Scripps College and today still play singles, mixed doubles, and doubles with the United States Tennis Association. Both my mother, Barbara Munro, and father, Roland Mersereau, were excellent tennis players and downhill skiers. My mother was on the Scripps tennis team, too, and later was considered a top senior woman in golf. I still have her trophies. They coached us—particularly my mother, who coached me in tennis, golf, and skiing. It's normally the father who coaches. But our mother was the one that got us out there and really taught us everything in terms of the values side of sports.

That whole issue of working hard and focusing was instilled in us at a really young age. My mother would take us out with a big basket of tennis balls from the time we could hold a racquet. When we wanted a snack or to rest in the shade, she would continue to throw balls at us. She would always say, "It's simply a matter of how many balls you hit. Let's hit ten more." She would sort of negotiate with us early on to stay with it and hit ten or fifteen more balls before we could have a snack. She would do it with schoolwork, too. It's focus. Do your chores and then you can have a snack but don't take the easy way out early. It's how many miles you put in. The difference between you and the next person is how many tennis balls you hit in a lifetime.

What motivated me was the consistency of improvement. It was sort of that joy of getting better through practice, improving and feeling like every time, every year, I was better at something, or I could then do something that I hadn't done the year before. I saw that through practice I got better, and felt better at it. It was the discipline and focus of staying with something. Practice was part of our daily life. I can't remember a time when I didn't want to go out and hit tennis balls, or spend time on weekends skiing or playing golf. I wouldn't say it was a joyful experience, but joy wasn't how we were raised. It was more about getting better at something.

I listen to people on the tennis court today saying how much they're just out there to have fun. That concept was foreign to my family. We were taught to go out there to win and don't try to dumb down your game just to make the person you're playing feel better. There was no confusion about the purpose. There was a lot of focus on how we did it, with etiquette and graciousness, but it wasn't about getting on the court and saying, "Well, I'm just out here to have fun."

There were a lot of women when I was growing up who were always afraid of beating the boys because then they wouldn't be popular. I remember thinking that was the stupidest thing I'd ever heard. If you're playing tennis, you're out there to win. No one ever said you can't do exactly what your brothers do. In fact, I was taught to beat my brothers, and we still to this day are very competitive with one another. I'm eighteen months older than my next brother and close to five years older than my youngest.

The idea of playing to win carried over into the business world. In a business negotiation or deal, I never walked into it saying, "Well, I'm just here to negotiate the best I can. If it doesn't work out that's fine." It was more about what is it I want and how am I going to get there, and focusing on that, as opposed to some ambivalence about winning.

Growing up, we had a very, very strict way of handling defeat. I remember my brother once didn't do well in a set and threw his racquet. My mother just came unglued. She pulled him off the court and basically said he would never play again if he did that again. And one of the things that helped me later on in my business career was not seeing failure or losing as a bad thing so much as something you can learn from. Was there something you could do next time that would be different? How could you apply what you learned in this game to the next? Make each loss a learning experience. Losing never felt good emotionally, but how we handled failure was almost more important than the failure itself.

The other piece of that was, if you're never failing, you're not pushing yourself hard enough. You're not taking risks. You're taking the safe way out. I remember holding back in some of the tournaments, not hitting shots as hard as I could, not trying for the lines because I was focused on the outcome and thus not playing the best I could. When that would happen I sometimes would lose. In business it's the same thing, if you're not taking calculated risks, then you're probably not playing your full game. In a business sense, you're not operating from a full capacity. You're holding back. You're being too cautious. You're too worried about failure.

Losing and failure give you information. It's feedback. If you start to get down on yourself, take it personally, or start to think that you're a failure, associating the event with who you are, that's when you run into trouble. I think in business there aren't enough failures. The most successful people have gone through a lot of areas and problems where they have had major issues. And it's the overcoming of them; it's how they handle them; it's what they do next; it's the person who goes into bankruptcy, comes out, and starts a new company and is wildly successful that is inspiring.

So much of sports is mental. One thing that my mother particularly taught me was mental toughness. Don't let the other person get you down. Don't let them suck you into their game. Find out where their weaknesses are early on and then adjust. Don't just play your game and if it's not working simply keep doing it. That's kind of the definition of insanity.

All through grade school and into high school my mother would coach us on the side. She taught us to stay calm under pressure and how important it was to hold our own. That has helped me so much, in both business and in continuing to play sports today.

Two anecdotes are sort of related to this. I was at Weyerhaeuser for twenty-eight years. I became a vice president in 1988 and the company's first female senior vice president in 2003. As a female in a predominantly all-male work environment, there were so many times along the way when I would say something in a meeting and the man across from me would look at another man as if the man had said what I just said. And they would talk to each other about it. I kept thinking, "Wait a minute. What's going on here?" Or the pressure would be for me to go along with the program, and somewhere along the way I had to learn to stay with what I believed and be okay with that and not worry about what people thought about me or if I was going to be rejected. They used to call it the ability to belly up to the bar and hold your own. I think a lot of that came from my experience of holding my own in tennis, regardless of what was going on with the opponent or the people watching us in tournaments. You've got to stay in your own voice and not try to accommodate or become what the rest want you to become. But I found so many people, women in particular, who worked for me who would tell me they couldn't be who they really were, or that they lost their own voice, or they had to become like the people around them to survive. That was foreign to me because I believed if you couldn't be who you were, what could you offer the corporation?

Another thing that I remember really well is the lesson that it's not about failure, it's about how you handle it that makes a difference in the long run. Because you're going to fail, and you're going to run into challenging situations. There was a time in my career when someone from outside the company was brought in to "shake up" the area I was managing. I was in Montana, fishing at the time, when I got the call that this was going on. Although I was assured a comparable role and a long-term future, I disagreed with the company's decision. There were a number of women in particular who said, "Oh, you should fight this. You should cry foul. This isn't fair." After some reflection, I chose to see this event not as a personal failure, but as a natural shift that often occurs in large organizations. The lesson for me was that this event was not about fairness or what was right or wrong, but about how I chose to deal with it. In embracing the change, I moved on to what turned out to be an extremely fulfilling career with the company.

People looked more at how I handled it than the event itself. And in the long run I ended up getting promoted. Whereas if I'd ranted and railed against the system and tried to make some big fuss about it—you know, a lot of people would have said, "Well, I'm going to get an attorney"—it would not have served me well. Again, it was more about how you handle yourself in a challenging situation, because no one can take your sense of who you are from you. If they can, then you're on the wrong track. A lot of my thinking has come from earlier sports lessons: sometimes things aren't fair. People make the wrong call, or the umpire doesn't do something, but it's how you handle it. I was always taught to not let my emotions get the better of me because that could then derail my game and my opponents could exploit that. That was a really important lesson for me: I had the responsibility to manage my own emotions. No one else did.

This whole issue of emotional intelligence that's recently been talked about is so valid in the business world. I see people's anger, and their ways of dealing with things, to be so destructive to the people around them. I recall colleagues saying to me, "I can't even tell him something because he's going to explode." So they wouldn't tell the person what was on their mind and then it festered. If I worked with people who were affecting other people because they were emotionally up and down, I would have to take them out of their role, because they would soon impact the whole organization.

My mother also talked about having a plan. Before someone hits the ball to you, have a plan about where you are going to hit the ball, and then if it doesn't work have another plan. But don't just sit there like a bump on a log and allow someone to serve to you. And not just in tennis, in life itself. Her whole thing was, yes, things happen to you. Life happens to you. But have a plan. What are you going to do about it?

I had a plan toward self-sufficiency. I did not have a plan toward a position. I actually evolved from one point to the other in my business career based on what I was interested in at the time and doing very well at that. That was my goal. But my overriding plan was to be self-sufficient financially, mentally, emotionally. I wanted to have a career that allowed me to stand on my own and not be dependent on anyone. I never had a role longer than four or five years. Every four or five years something started to shift and I would be on to something else. But I didn't have a goal of, say, becoming senior vice president. I thought of my career more in terms of me being a change agent, so wherever they plopped me I would go in and try to improve something. As long as I was able to get into a situation where I could make major changes, I was very happy. I'm not a maintenance person, so when things are working well and running, I would go on to the next thing. I need a challenge, mostly because I need to keep learning, and as long as I'm learning I'm fine.

One of the things that came from both my mother and father is that when you choose a sport, play by the rules. There's an etiquette associated with each sport. Don't choose tennis and expect it to operate like a football game. That notion of "Whatever sport you choose, play within its rules, and play it well" helped me a lot later in business, because my natural tendency would be to change the corporation to fit what I needed, as opposed to playing by rules that didn't make any sense to me. Being a change agent, my inclination in certain situations might be to say, "Well, this is stupid. Let's not do it this way." But I kept remembering what I learned as an athlete—that an organization has its own rules, and that I should learn them well and play by them. And if I do I'll end up coming out well, as opposed to constantly fighting, complaining, resisting, spending a lot of energy on what I would change or what doesn't work.

In this regard, and in so many others, sports are a wonderful metaphor for how you handle life.

ROGER MINCHEFF

The second I see high-level sports on a résumé, I know there's most likely a confidence and an attitude that comes with those experiences. There's also the teamwork element. If I know they're an athlete, then I already know certain things about them. But the other thing I consider is: Did they play team or individual sports, and how does that fit the positions I happen to be looking to fill?

Roger Mincheff is senior vice president of branded entertainment at Fox Filmed Entertainment, launching a new division of News Corporation that will define how brands and Hollywood interact. He joined Fox after serving as president and CEO of Spacedog Media, a full-service digital marketing agency he founded in 1998, and Spacedog Entertainment, a film and television company, which followed in 2003. He was born in New York City and spent most of his childhood there, with a four-year stint in Ft. Lauderdale and Plantation, Florida.

Game Day

BASEBALL AND FOOTBALL WERE ALWAYS the two sports that drove me, but you'd be hard-pressed to name a sport that I haven't actually played competitively—or tried to! If it's an organized sport, at some time in my life I've probably played it. I'm forty and have played some form of baseball—softball these days—nonstop every single year of my cognizant life. My earliest memories are of being in my room and my dad teaching me how to swing a baseball bat. I've been a skier my whole life—at points even competitively. There are sports where you compete against yourself and a clock. There are sports where you compete against someone. I cannot help it. I am drawn to any scenario where there's a winner and a loser. Do you want to thumb wrestle?

My dad grew up in Argentina, where soccer is not a sport, it's a religion. My father prayed at the altar of soccer. But I remember vividly in the fifth grade that I had to make a choice between soccer and football, which in New York were played in the same season. It was a little bit of a no-brainer for me—but not the way one might guess. I chose *American* football because with my father, I think his son playing football was a form of acceptance, of assimilation, because the game is so uniquely American that it's become symbolic. My dad's first language was Spanish. My mom's Brazilian, and her first language was Portuguese. We never spoke anything but English in the house. So I think football and baseball both definitely fit in with my family's goals of first and foremost being American.

My parents divorced when I was nine. I lived with my mom. At the time of the divorce, my mom didn't know how supportive my father was going to be. He ended up being very supportive. But without that assurance, she thought, "Well, at least Roger will have sports," my assumed scholarship the key to our future because I was one of those who was on every all-star baseball and football team. I was recruited by coaches. As a teenager the Yankees invited me to their spring training facilities in Ft. Lauderdale. Mom looked at sports as almost a ticket, a guarantee, because while I was a good student and excelled in other areas, she figured sports could propel my career. For my father it was assimilation. For my mother it was assimilation *plus*. My mom went to every baseball and football practice because that was her guarantee that everything would be okay.

Due to the divorce I spent about four years in Florida with my mother, going to public schools. Because of my parents' desire to improve their lives, we kept moving to better neighborhoods, with better schools. I went to nine schools before I graduated. Based on my experience, I don't know how someone without sports could have dealt with that. Football players are asked to go early and start practicing before the school year starts. So for me having so much transition in my life, no matter where I went, I had teammates right off the bat. And then when you excel, there's a respect and a credibility you get in sports that translates off the field in a very tangible way. To be able to leverage that was huge.

I played football and baseball the best I could at Emory University in Atlanta. Unfortunately, I went to a school that didn't commit to sports the way I committed to sports. I thought the baseball program was decent for Division III . The problem at Emory was that—unlike at my high school, where the entire school campus was in the shape of a "U," with the football and baseball field in the middle—the baseball team literally had to get on a bus and drive to a distant baseball field. We didn't have a lot of fan support; more people attended intramural than varsity sports! Looking back, it took something like that to actually stop my sports career in schools. I'm convinced I would have made a Division I team—though would I have been a starter? Probably not. I might have been that senior who maybe got to play the last couple of games but whom coaches don't ever want to cut. I hate to draw the analogy, but I'd like to think I'm kind of like Rudy, who dreamed of playing football at Notre Dame, was too small to earn a scholarship, but walked on and finally got in a game the final play of his senior season—and that's self-deprecating. I'm not necessarily that good, but I believe a great work ethic and always executing what the coach wanted of me would have won the day.

Sports and family are most influential in who and what I am—that is, in terms of how I process the protocols that I use on a day-to-day basis. My parents never officially coached me, but they're probably my biggest coaches in terms of attitude and addressing the problems and the challenges that life throws at you. I've had several defining events in my life that have helped my self-esteem and confidence but sports gives you a confidence that just continues to translate and grow throughout your life. How do you face winning, losing, adversity, bullies, weaklings, mismatches, friendships? How do you deal with those situations? What else in life teaches you these lessons?

The first thing sports teaches you is about your own thresholds and your own capabilities. Until you've run, until you've made yourself vomit and then start running again, until you push yourself past where you think you can go, until you do something and achieve something that you didn't think was possible, I don't know that you can understand what an athlete has learned about his or her limits. So when people say to me, "You can't do that," it makes me want to do that. When people say that's impossible, it makes me want to do it in spite of it. I think the biggest differentiator is competitive fire, that competitive spirit, that analyzing a situation and trying to find the win in it. All of that is about understanding your own limits and how broad they really are.

The second thing sports teaches you is teamwork. I smile thinking about some of those exercises that people do at executive and/or motivational camps. To a competitive athlete, if you know what it's like to rely on someone else to pick up your slack, what it's like to have someone else's back—then standing on a box and falling backward and having people catch you is a metaphor for something you have been doing your whole life. Any athlete who's played in a team sport understands how important teammates are—to capitalize on someone's strengths and yet minimize their weaknesses and use those relationships to find victory.

I think the concept of teamwork has absolutely been massive in terms of the lessons it's taught me. If you look at today's workplace, for example, retention and recruitment are huge issues and problems for companies. There are a whole lot of fancy ways to say what I'm about to say, but here's the thing: create a team that people want to play for, and you will see how much easier it is to recruit and how much easier it is to keep people. At Spacedog people asked me how I kept my retention rates so much higher than the rest of the industry. It was simple. I created a team people wanted to play for, because I believe that the emotional dynamic is so much more powerful than a lot of other factors that affect people's decision-making.

There's a discipline to sports—different types of sports and personality traits—that absolutely affects me when I'm looking at potential candidates. The second I see high-level sports on a résumé, I know there's most likely a confidence and an attitude that comes with those experiences. There's also the teamwork element. If I know they're an athlete, then I already know certain things about them. But the other thing I consider is: did they play team or individual sports, and how does that fit the positions I happen to be looking to fill? There is a very egocentric (not egotistical) attitude you *have* to have to excel at an individual sport that is incredibly relevant for certain types of roles. And there are other positions that are all about being a cog in the machine that a *different* type of athlete in a team sport makes so much sense for. One of my female senior executives ran track and still holds records at the University of Pennsylvania. One of my other female senior executives played tennis at Division I level. I mix it up though—there are also musicians, fashionistas, and comedians! Sports did not drive my career to the extent that I looked for a career in sports, but there is no doubt in my mind that almost everything I've learned in sports is translated into work, because work is sports. The same passion that I brought to baseball and football I bring to work. Scoreboards change. What's my scoreboard now? I can't look up at the board and see 14–7. I approach it as I would a competition: I'm going to win or not. I want to be on a team that maximizes strengths, minimizes weaknesses. I've got to like my teammates for it to work. I still speak in sports metaphors, in terms of what I'm trying to do at work, and I still look at the deals and accomplishments as a scoreboard.

There's this concept that many people talk about: the game face. I am a little bit different in that I'd like to think I'm one of the nicer people you'll meet. Hopefully people think I'm sweet and outgoing. I almost never raise my voice. I rarely ever get mad. But the thing about game day is, when you get on that field, it is hard-core. It is balls-to-the-wall. It's everything. There will be one winner, and there will be one loser, and the question is: What are you going to do to make sure you're on the right side of that equation?

The game itself was never a problem for me, in terms of motivation, because the second I'm in the game I don't need any more motivation. Spacedog once pitched Ernest & Julio Gallo. We thought they'd make a fantastic client. I walked into the meeting with my partner, sick as a dog. It had been so hard to get the meeting, I had no choice but to go. I was down and my energy was low. As we walked, I said to my business partner, Dustin Callif, "You may have to step up today, D. I'm definitely feeling out of it." I think Stephanie Gallo is a spectacular woman now that I know her a little bit, but I didn't know her at all then. On that day, less than five minutes into the meeting, Stephanie starts interrupting with questions. She was probing, aggressive, and definitely challenging. It was a very intense meeting—an hour and a half of talking and maybe a little yelling—but it was great, and we got the business.

We walked out and Dustin said, "Uh, what happened to you feeling out of it?" I said to him, "Dustin, when someone punches you in the face, I don't care how you feel. You're in a fight." The implication was that once in a fight, natural instincts and adrenaline take over.

There's a really interesting question that a lot of athletes ask themselves, and that is: "Do I compete because I want to win, or do I win because I'm so afraid of failure?" There's a balance there. "Am I trying to win or am I refusing to lose?"—which a lot of athletes ask, and the truth is, most athletes, myself included, don't know. I can't answer the question, but come on—how incredible is the feeling of winning?

For example, recently I was playing softball, and my wife, Yvette, was in the stands, but close enough that I could hear her. It's the last inning, two outs, bases loaded, and we're down by two or three. Cliché, I know—but true, and why we play the game. I get up to bat and I hear my wife's friend say, "He must be so nervous." Yvette says, "Oh no, he lives for this." I would be remiss in not telling that I hit a game-winning grand-slam home run.

We've all had those bad endings: "I lost it for the team"—is miserable. Why do we put ourselves there? Why risk the heartbreak? Why take time away from our kids, our job, our family, your spouse? Why sacrifice all of that to put ourselves in these potentially anxiety-ridden situations? It's what we do. Yes, there is that moment where we're nervous, but it's those nerves that a real athlete loves and lives for. I'll tell you why we do it: they are defining situations and they validate us. We want to validate that we're here. We want to validate that we're good. We want proof: records, trophy plaques, scoreboards, etc. And I believe that's where a little of the competition, the winning and the losing, comes from.

When I lived alone, every sports trophy I had was displayed in one room, a trophy room, in my house in Los Angeles. I think the earliest one I had was literally from fifth or sixth grade, a tiny MVP trophy. When my wife and I moved into a house together in New York, Yvette said, "There's no way those are going into the house." So she got a huge box labeled: "Fragile—Trophies."

Most of my trophies are for victories in baseball and football. They represent memories of all the friends I played with, the stories we told, the memories I have. If I were a tennis player and all my trophies were individual, I don't know that I would have been that brazen about them. But because they were so team-sport-oriented, and I'm so proud and happy about the teams that I've played on, I created a trophy room.

Both of my kids have already taken golf lessons, tennis lessons, softball lessons, et cetera. So many issues that are important for kids are all tied into self-esteem issues, and I don't know that anything builds self-esteem like sports does. However, I'm a pretty easygoing guy. If not sports, then what? Acting? Art? Music? I literally don't know. I'm open-minded; if it's not sports, then someone needs to convince me that acting can instill that sense of self-confidence. If acting or music will give a child that sense of pushing himself or herself, and instill discipline and goal orientation, as well as a feeling of achievement, fantastic. I'm one hundred percent supportive of it. Personally, I just don't know anything that does it like sports does.

MELISSA PAYNER

I'm the same in my job as I was as an athlete. I'm able to compartmentalize. I stay focused so that I'm not terribly affected by external issues. I stay the course, remain calm and collected at all times, which allows me to be much more rational about what the next steps are.

Melissa Payner is the president and CEO of Bluefly, Inc. She previously served as CEO of Spiegel Catalog. Prior to that she held senior executive positions with Pastille (a division of Neiman Marcus), Henri Bendel, and Chicos FAS, where she served as president. She graduated from Arizona State University with a degree in fashion merchandising. She was born in Elyria, Ohio.

Consistent Improvement

MY FAMILY WAS COMPETITIVE BUT not necessarily in organized sports. For example, I remember major fights over *Jeopardy!* that literally almost got physical when someone didn't put their answer in the form of a question. I was always quietly competitive and always loved sports. I started taking competitive roller skating lessons when I was five or six years old, probably because it was something I could do year round since it was indoors. I had no fear. I was completely confident if it involved spinning or something in the air. And I had no fear of being judged, either. It made no impact. I could be practicing or in a situation where I was being judged, it made no difference to me, which is odd.

Roller skating required me to be at the rink five days a week. I was the only one whose parents never came. They dropped me off at the front door and I did my own thing. Eventually my mother thought it was silly for a five- or six-year-old to be spending that much time skating and stopped taking me. I couldn't get a ride there anymore, so I quit. I ran track, and by the sixth grade was the fastest runner in the school. When I got to junior high school, I joined the school track team but was pretty small for my age. I took twice the number of strides to reach the finish line because all of the other girls had long legs, a real advantage. I thought, "That's ridiculous. That will never work, because I can't run any faster." I decided to become the best female pole-vaulter but was told that girls don't pole-vault. I tried everything to get them to let me do it but they wouldn't consider it. When I was about eleven, someone told me about tryouts for the gymnastics team at the Y. "That sounds interesting," I thought. I was small and it seemed reasonable to me that I could do something like that. I stayed in gymnastics, which was really the sport for me, through college.

One of the things that attracted me to everything that I got involved in was being part of a team in a sport in which you have to count on yourself. Everything I was interested in was individual, whether it was the pole vaulting, roller skating, track, or gymnastics. And this idea of individual competition stayed with me after college. I skied, played tennis, and learned English riding. I even got involved in competitive mechanical bull riding. You can't blame someone else in these sports. It's about how *you* perform. I like being part of a team, but when it came to personal performance I preferred not having to rely on anyone else. I'm the middle of five kids, with an older brother and sister and a younger brother and sister. Being the middle child made me very independent and maybe a little radical. I didn't like a lot of attention. My sisters, being the first and last born, wanted the attention. I preferred being left alone, which might explain why I selected the sports I did.

My parents never supported me during gymnastics, so I walked to the gym, which was a few miles away from home. They thought the sport was too dangerous and that's why they refused to give me a ride. They figured I would eventually quit. At eleven years old, I walked back and forth every day for a year except for the time there was a snowstorm. After a year, they agreed to give me lessons because they knew I was serious. I started private lessons and practiced up to seven hours a day. Even when I was competing, there was very little involvement from my parents. I think it was because I didn't appear to require it. I was more focused on what I was doing and accomplishing.

At home I used to stand on a four-foot-high brick wall in the backyard and do backflips. I knew it was risky, but every time I stuck the landing—and of course didn't crack my head open—I had this enormous sense of accomplishment, especially the times when I knew my mother was looking out the window uncomfortably. I loved that wall. Some of my fondest memories are of that brick wall.

Although my mother wasn't supporting my gymnastics, she set a very good example in terms of working hard to achieve your goals. She was one of the few mothers in the neighborhood who had a professional career. After giving birth to five kids, she went back to college and got her master's and then her Ph.D. She became the superintendent of the Lorain County Board of MR/DD. The work she did was highly regarded. Ultimately, my mother was invited to the White House for what she had accomplished, so it was a pretty big deal. She was a great role model.

When I was around thirteen, I was hit with something life altering. My coach insisted on ballet training for everyone who was doing gymnastics, and it was in that class that she noticed I had an issue with my muscle development. After a visit to the doctor, it was determined that I had scoliosis and would require back surgery to prevent future problems. I was, needless to say, devastated. I was told that not only would I be unable to do gymnastics but most sports would be off limits. I walked out of the doctor's office with my father and said, "That's not going to happen. I'm not going to get the surgery. I'm going to continue to do gymnastics and work to figure out how to overcome this." I didn't have the surgery and worked to compensate by strengthening the right muscles. I started spending more time in ballet and in balancing gymnastics. The most important thing I realized from that was that my mental focus was going to have to be as critical as any physical training. The determination to overcome this disability made me more motivated than ever.

Gymnastics requires you to internalize your emotions, so I became very focused, disciplined, confident, and controlled about everything that I did. During competition, if somebody yelled something while I was on the four-inch-wide balance beam, I wouldn't hear it. I never heard anything. Something else that maybe changed about me was that winning or losing was not the issue, it was about improving on my previous performance. Consistent improvement in my performance—became my focus.

My determination paid off, because as a college freshman I made the varsity gymnastics team at Ohio State University. The one time I lost focus, it was a disaster. I had the flu and was trying not to let it affect my floor-exercise routine. The coaches were tough, and they didn't care if you had the flu. Right before a tumbling pass, I briefly lost my concentration. I remember thinking I wasn't going to stick the landing, and that's the worst thing you can ever do. You cannot think outside of what you're about to do. I lost consciousness midair and hit the ground. When I came to, the lower half of my arm was kind of twisted behind me with my hand resting on my shoulder. My elbow was dislocated so severely I was told my arm would be permanently paralyzed from the elbow down. At the hospital, I was told that for me gymnastics was over. I was eighteen and thought, "That's the most ridiculous thing I've ever heard." That was not an option. It was almost as if it went in one ear and out the other. I transferred schools, went through rigorous therapy, did tons of hard work, and was able to make the varsity team at Arizona State University. As soon as I achieved that goal, I quit the team. I had achieved what I set out to achieve. I overcame this disability.

Eventually I accepted that I would have to have the back surgery; and that, together with my injury, meant that I wasn't going to be an Olympic gymnast. Still, I felt that I had become the best I could be at that sport. It wasn't about being better than anyone else. Overcoming the challenges in gymnastics reinforced what my father always said, that life is problem-solving, and if you stay calm and think it through, your next move will come to you. That's how I've lived my entire life.

The mental discipline I learned in gymnastics certainly helped prepare me for a career that has focused on turnaround companies and startups. Like gymnastics, turning around a company is a task that requires daring, determination, and consistent improvement— successes in moving this type of company forward is that much more fulfilling. Sort of like doing the backflips off of my brick wall in the backyard. If you land it, it's really something that you've figured out, and you've moved forward. If you don't land it, you've got to fig- ure out how to get yourself back up and moving again. You have to stay positively motivated. In business, even in tough times, I always say there can be positive stress and negative stress. Positive stress is remaining motivated and excited, even in the most challenging situ- ations. Negative stress is simply deflating. I had coaches who were tyrants. My first boss out of college was a screamer, and I learned how to get along with her, but I knew as I progressed in business that that was not going to be my MO. I believe you get much more out of people when you make them feel that they're making a positive con- tribution and are a positive partner. To be in a startup type business, you have to want to feel the results of your efforts every single day, so if you blow it, tomorrow you're going to fix it. And that's okay, too, because we only learn from the mistakes we make.

I'm the same in my job as I was as an athlete. I'm able to compart- mentalize. I stay focused so that I'm not terribly affected by external issues. I stay the course, remain calm and collected at all times, which allows me to be much more rational about what the next steps are. I don't ever believe that giving up is an option. It never crosses my mind. I believe that in business, if we're truly as good as we can be, and we learn something every single day, our results will generally be positive. If I didn't come in first in a meet, I felt I would do better next time, and it's the same thing in my career. People got promoted around me, and I would hear that I looked too young to get a promotion. I didn't go home and think, "Oh, I can't believe they're getting promoted." I thought, "These are the things that I need to do to get better at what I do." Part of life is problem-solving. I'm very self-critical. I was that way in athletics and I'm that way in business. If somebody says something, I'm not defensive, because I've probably already thought of it myself.

It's interesting when I look back at how I handled situations in sports. When I was about twelve I had a bad experience with a coach. He had very strict rules, one of which was that if you invented your own gymnastics move, you would be the only one who could perform it in competition. I worked very hard to develop a unique move on the uneven bars, and, without any conversation with me about it, the coach proceeded to pass that move on to another girl on the team who was older and more experienced. At the end of practice I walked into his office and reminded him about his rule. Because I was challenging him he became furious and threw a pencil at me. I remained calm and walked out of his office. But on the way out I slammed the door and the glass shattered. I never turned around. I kept walking down the stairs and out of the building. There was a snowstorm, and I got into my dad's car very quietly. I said to my father, "I just quit," and for a split second he was relieved. He didn't know anything happened. I was completely calm. As we drove home I said, "So, I'll be looking for another coach." I remember seeing his face, which said, "Ugh," in the rearview mirror. But that was how I was: very focused and unflappable regarding situations around me.

It's the same in business. When I came to Bluefly, I said to the board that I wanted to prove a certain merchandising strategy I was developing. Part of my marketing strategy was television advertising, and they thought that was impossible, that that was not the way to get people to shop online. Because we were a "pure play"—meaning, an online-only business—the belief was that all of the marketing should be online. I explained how, if they supported me, I would prove my approach to them. My belief was that people who shop, shop every-where, so you won't only find them online. It became the beginning of a whole world of opportunity for Bluefly, leading to a groundbreak-ing and very successful relationship with the reality-television show *Project Runway*. So I did prove that to them.

My philosophy was, and remains, that as long as I'm learning something new every day and can contribute in a positive way to a team, then I'm in the right place. I believe you have to love what you do in order to be the very best. I had a gymnastics coach, Denise Gula, who stressed this. What I learned from her was, it wasn't about winning or losing. It was about believing in yourself, and that in order to achieve, you had to love what you do.

IRENE ROSENFELD

I am inherently a competitive person. If anything, sports just gave me a place in which I could play that out most productively. The experience of honing my competitive skills really gave me a leg up as I came into the business world, because women of my generation didn't necessarily have the experience of being competitive and playing to win. It certainly didn't hurt that I could hold my own with colleagues on the tennis court. So, in addition to whatever I could do from a business perspective, playing tennis and golf were really important in terms of establishing my credibility.

Irene Rosenfeld is the chairman and CEO of Kraft Foods. A twenty-nine-year veteran of the food and beverage industry, she held a variety of leadership positions at Kraft Foods, and previously was chairman and CEO of Frito-Lay. She holds a Ph.D. in marketing and statistics, a Master of Science in business administration, and a Bachelor of Arts in psychology, all from Cornell University. She was born in Brooklyn, New York, and grew up in Westbury, New York.

Creating a Vision to Win

GROWING UP, I PLAYED JUST about every sport—tennis, softball, hockey, volleyball, badminton, basketball—and I swam. Although I played a variety of sports, I started off as a bit of a disaster, athletically. I was typically the last kid picked for the kickball team. I played dodgeball and I missed everybody. In elementary school they put me in a program called Gym X for the people who were not quite competent enough. I was so embarrassed, and hated it so much. And then I had occasion to go to summer camp at Tyler Hill Camp, in Tyler Hill, Pennsylvania, when I was about eleven years old, and I decided it was time to get my act together.

Psychology plays a big role when it comes to success at sports, and I think for me the ability to start with a clean slate, to think I could do it, was all that I needed. It was really when I left elementary school that I kind of blossomed, from an ugly duckling into a swan. Tyler Hill Camp was a fabulous place for me to be able to spread my wings, to be in a different environment, one where I hadn't been labeled, and miraculously I blossomed into one of their star athletes. I was an undefeated pitcher on the softball team. For many years I played inter-camp tennis. Amazingly enough, if you go on the Tyler Hill Camp Hall of Fame website you will see me there. They're very proud that one of their alumni became a CEO.

I attribute my early experiences playing junior varsity and varsity sports under the leadership of Joan Case and her staff as key to my development as a competitor and as a leader. Joan coached me in a couple of sports at Tresper Clarke Junior High/High School in Westbury, New York, but I was involved in a lot of activities in school that she was involved in as well, so I had lots of interaction with her. She has been a lifelong friend and mentor to me. In fact, next to my parents, she's the single most important influence in my life. At that time my mother was a homemaker. For me, Joan was one of the few role models I had of a self-sufficient working woman. She was not married. She did not have children of her own. I think her students were her family. She genuinely took pride in our accomplishments and really pushed us to do our best. A lot of what I did was because I wanted her to be proud.

She coached me in volleyball, and she was also the hockey and softball coach. I played softball in junior high, but by the time I got to high school, the only varsity sport that I played that she coached was volleyball. However, we had this thing called Leader's Club, which was for the top girl athletes in the school, and she was the head of that program. That's really the context in which I got to know her. The members of the club assisted the PE teachers in class, and in the process learned a great deal about presence and leadership. It was Joan who encouraged me to run for president of the Student Council, which I won. I was the first girl and first athlete to do so.

Joan was inducted in the New York State Public High School Athletic Association Hall of Fame in August 2007. I went to Lake George for her induction, because that's how important she is to me and how proud I was to see her honored in that way. I wrote a letter on her behalf to nominate her and wrote about the ways in which she influenced not only me but also thousands of other athletes whom she mentored over the years.

I was the first person in my high school to win an award for playing on twelve varsity sports teams. I also won a female athlete-scholar award. I graduated high school in 1971, and Title IX was passed in 1972. Women's sports were not at the forefront of anything at that point in time, but they were instrumental in my choice of college. I selected Cornell, first of all because it was one of the few Ivy League schools at that time that had been coed throughout its existence, unlike Yale, Princeton, or Harvard. I thought that was a terrific thing. So they had a much better male-female ratio. And, though they didn't recruit for women's sports, they had a fabulous women's sports program, with great facilities for women, which really impressed me. A lot of the schools didn't even have a women's locker room.

I was not a major college athlete. I played freshman basketball but broke my leg the first season. But the real complication was that sports competed with my studies, and I was on a work-study program to put myself through school. I had a job, so I quit basketball after the first season. The rest of the time I played intramural sports. People who knew me at Cornell joked that when I changed my dorm room my freshman year, I had to move more sports equipment than books—my skis, my baseball bat, my tennis racquet. They'd laugh and ask, "Do you have any books?" Basketball continues to be my favorite sport. One of my first jobs was at General Foods. We had a women's pickup basketball team. I was always able to find like-minded women that were interested in playing, so I continued to play. My birthday present when I was forty years old was a basketball hoop. I made a donation to Cornell about three or four years ago in honor of my parents, an endowment for the women's head basketball coach. There's actually an Irene Blecker Rosenfeld Head Basketball Coach Office at Cornell.

I've always been willing to practice and train, but I have been exceptionally competitive from the beginning. When I was in

Brownie Patrol, I always wanted to collect the most money, sell the most Girl Scout cookies. I wanted to always make sure I could win in Candy Land. I have a cartoon that somebody gave to me when I first had my kids that showed a mother in a suit who had just come home from work. She has her briefcase off to the side. She's busy playing with her little baby with blocks and says, "Look, Mommy can make a bigger tower than you can."

I am inherently a competitive person. If anything, sports just gave me a place in which I could play that out most productively. The experience of honing my competitive skills really gave me a leg up as I came into the business world, because women of my generation didn't necessarily have the experience of being competitive and playing to win. It certainly didn't hurt that I could hold my own with colleagues on the tennis court. So, in addition to whatever I could do from a business perspective, playing tennis and golf was really important in terms of establishing my credibility.

There are a lot of similarities between sports and what I do now. The same kinds of visualization routines that I would have followed preparing for a tennis match or a basketball game and the notion of practicing to be my best—I now use at work. As I get ready to deliver a big speech, for example, I visualize it, think about what I want to get done, think about what I'd like the outcome to be. A lot of the sort of self-taught, motivational exercises that I did when I was playing sports are exactly the kinds of things that I use here. And many of the skills that I acquired watching great coaches are skills that I bring to my role as a leader in a big organization, such as the ability to figure out who plays what position and how to complement one player with another to bring out the best in a person, as opposed to focusing on what they're *not* so good at. (Most of my sports tended to be team sports; more so than individual sports.)

I found, for example, some of the business books that I value most were written by coaches. When Don Shula, Phil Jackson, or Pat Riley talk about what they have done to create a winning team, it's really powerful. I've invited a lot of coaches, guys like Ohio State football coach Jim Tressel and Bill Parcells, to speak at meetings of mine, because that whole notion of creating a vision to win, mobilizing the team to go get the job done and figuring out what you need to do to help them play together to accomplish that task, is exactly the game of business.

There's a lot of psychology involved in sports, and I think that same psychology—understanding people's motivation, understanding what inspires them and how to bring out the best in them—is invaluable when it comes to making any team work. Business and sports require the same kinds of skills.

There's also the notion of keeping score. One thing that is most important in getting a business to execute well and to win is to be able to have clear metrics against which to evaluate output. A critical part of being an athlete is keeping score. And I think in business, people who keep score, and keep trying to better their scores, perform better. There's a fabulous book by a guy name Charles Coonradt called *The Game of Work*. I've given it to many people. And the concept is, whatever job you do, if you figure out how to keep score, you can do it better. Coonradt was a grocery clerk and he stocked shelves at night. There's nothing more boring than that. He was driving himself to distraction, until one day he decided to count how many cans of tuna he put on the shelf and then the next night he said, "Well last night I put forty-two cans on. Tonight I'm going to put fifty-two on." And in that way he kept himself motivated, and he was able to get better and better at what his job was at that time.

In business, guys and gals in sales are in the best position because they have a clear scorecard each and every day as to how they're doing. But I think the closer that we as leaders of the organization can come to providing the rest of the company with those kinds of scorecards, the better able we are to motivate them to perform better.

I hate to lose. The best way to handle losing is to make sure you learn something from it so that you have higher odds of winning next time. I analyze things after the fact—what could I have done better, and what can I learn from it? I would say I drive my kids to distraction in that regard. My daughters were both debaters. They'd go to these debating tournaments, and after a competition they just wanted to know "Did I win the tournament or not?" Instead, I would read their judges' assessments and say, "Hey, did you read this? Maybe you ought to stand up straighter. Maybe you ought to look around the room more." They had no interest in that kind of thinking, but for me that's a critical piece of continuing to get better at what you do.

My dad used to joke with me. I'd be off playing basketball all the time and my dad would say, "Irene, you can't be a basketball player for the rest of your life. What are you really going to do?"

I'd like to think I could have become chairman and CEO of Kraft Foods even if I hadn't been an athlete, but I truly believe I am a more focused, more competitive, more successful leader as a result of my experience in sports.

PART 5

The Former Pros

BILL BRADLEY

Through basketball I learned that preparation and discipline are important, that defeat has a richness of experience all its own, and that it's better to win than lose. I learned that it's important to cede part of your own individual potential to the group and in the process have the group be able to achieve more.

Senator William W. Bradley is a managing director of Allen & Company LLC, a merchant bank headquartered in New York City. He served in the U.S. Senate from 1979 to 1997, representing the state of New Jersey, and in 2000 was a candidate for the Democratic nomination for president of the United States. Prior to serving in the Senate, he was an Olympic gold medalist in 1964 and a professional basketball player with the New York Knicks from 1967 to 1977, during which time they won two NBA championships. In 1982 he was elected to the Naismith Memorial Basketball Hall of Fame.

When You Win Don't Crow,
When You Lose Don't Cry

I GREW UP IN CRYSTAL City, Missouri. I was the only child of
parents who married late in life. My father was forty-three when
I was born and my mother was thirty-five. My father, who was disabled, never played sports with me. He lived with a painful, calcified
arthritis of the lower spine. I never saw my father drive a car or tie his
shoes. I had to tie his shoes every day if my mother didn't. But I grew
up with the story that he once was an athlete—a good baseball player.

I started playing basketball in the fourth grade. My parents didn't
really encourage me to play. I used basketball in order to separate
from them and have my own identity. It had a positive-feedback loop:
you practice, you get better, and you achieve. You practice more, and
you get even better, and you achieve more.

I had good coaches. At Princeton Butch van Breda Kolff was perfect for me. He let me freelance on offense and taught defense. He
preached court balance and how it was achieved by moving without
the ball. He appreciated the nuances of the game. And then in the
1964 Olympics I played for Hank Iba, who used set plays on offense
and strict rules on defense. It was a fairly rigid system. I thought Red

Holzman, who coached me when I played for the New York Knicks, was a great coach in terms of how he handled the team. He had only a few simple rules such as "help out on defense" or "hit the open man," and he also treated each of us as adults. But the only person I ever called "Coach" was my high school coach, Arvel Popp. I guess because he got me when I was young, Coach Popp had a big influence on how I handled success. Among the things he said was, "When you win, don't crow. When you lose, don't cry." That even temperament was drilled into me early.

When I was a freshman in high school, Coach Popp, who coached both football and basketball, felt that I should have played football in the fall. Instead I practiced basketball alone during the football season. Then we got to the basketball season, and after four games he moved me to varsity as a freshman, which was unheard of because usually only juniors or seniors played on the varsity.

We came to a practice over the Christmas holidays during my freshman year. A guy who graduated from the high school three years earlier and was at that point an all-American tight end for the University of Missouri came too. The coach said, "Bradley, come over here to the mat. Put on the gloves. You're going to box Danny." The tight end weighed probably two hundred and fifteen pounds and was six-foot-four. I was six-three and weighed one hundred and sixty-five pounds. I didn't tell the coach I'd had boxing lessons when I was a kid. The tight end pummeled me, but he didn't destroy me. I think I proved something to the coach because I didn't back down.

A key moment for me was when I was fourteen years old and went to a basketball camp run by Easy Ed Macauley, a forward for the St. Louis Hawks who had returned to his hometown in a trade that sent Bill Russell to the Boston Celtics. I was challenged most profoundly when Easy Ed said, "Remember, if you're not practicing, somebody somewhere is practicing. If you two meet, given roughly equal ability, he will win." I never wanted to lose because I didn't practice. Whether it was in the United States Senate, along the campaign trail, or any number of other projects over the years, I was determined that no one would outwork me. Basketball had lit that fire, and it burned in many directions. I would practice three hours a day from June until April, and then I would do five hours on each weekend day. I often practiced alone.

There weren't a lot of players in Crystal City who loved the game as much as I did. In the off-season maybe one other player and I would shoot baskets. He would leave, and I would continue to shoot. I did all kinds of things. I piled chairs up so that they were eight feet tall and shot over them. I wore glasses that blocked the area below my waist so I couldn't see the ball when I dribbled around chairs practicing crossovers, reversed pivots, changes of pace. I had my routines, like hitting twenty-five shots in a row from five spots. If I sank twenty-four and missed, I'd go back to zero. That routine left me eating many cold dinners when I eventually got home from practice.

In the fall, before basketball season began, I did cross country. I ran along streets in town, through fields, over railroad tracks, down to the banks of the Mississippi and back. In order to improve my vertical leap, I wore weights in my shoes and jumped to touch the rim for four sets of fifteen jumps each, with alternating hands.

And then the season began, and I would practice with the team five days a week. On the weekends a lot of the older alumni—*older*, meaning in their twenties—would come back and play in the gym. I'd play with and against them. And then in the summertime I remember driving forty-five minutes to St. Louis on occasion to play pickup games. There were summer games in the Washington University Field House that occasionally attracted professional and college players. I would play in those games. I tried to play against better talent as often as I could.

I loved playing basketball and I was always good at it. I was taller and better coordinated than other kids, but then I developed because of hard work, too. My natural attributes weren't as good as some people's. But I had better eyes and better hands and in some sense better feet, so I made up for my physical shortcomings such as leaping skills.

My most unpleasant memory was my entire rookie year in the NBA. I was drafted by the Knicks in 1965 but didn't begin playing for them until 1967. I was a Rhodes Scholar at Oxford and at the same time played in Italy, where I won a European Champions' Cup. When I returned to the United States, I was supposed to be the "white hope"—the savior of the Knicks. When I took a shot in warm-ups, the standing-room-only crowd at Madison Square Garden shouted and screamed and applauded wildly. Yet, within fifteen games I realized that guard was the wrong position for me. I wasn't quick enough to play with the pro guards. It was then that the crowd turned on me. They spat on me, threw coins at me, accosted me in the street, and called me all kinds of names. That year was a nightmare. I had been used to having people praise me, and then suddenly I was being cursed. Cab drivers told me I was an overpaid bum because I wasn't effective playing in the backcourt. Nothing like that experience has ever come close to happening in business or politics. There were a few town meetings in which there was a ruckus, but it wasn't quite as personal. People were angry at government, or angry at some law or at me because I voted a certain way. Still, they didn't personalize it quite as much.

After my rookie season in the NBA, I retreated into my work ethic, and said, "Well, this is what has happened. You haven't done well. You need to get better." And so I practiced harder and harder in the off-season. Still, it was difficult for me to move, to play defense against the other guards. Then, in my second year my Knicks teammate Cazzie Russell broke his ankle and I was moved to small forward, where I was quicker than most of the other forwards and where I saw a role I could play. We had five guys that year that played forty-two minutes a game for forty games after Cazzie's injury. We gelled as a unit. I had found my place.

The title is clearly the mountaintop of the sport and once you've experienced it, it's a lifelong memory. I think that I had a very full experience in sports. It allowed me to see things, go places, meet people, attain recognition, feel a sense of accomplishment within myself, a sense of great joy in doing something I loved and being paid well for it. I not only have no complaints, I have a great deal of gratitude for having had the experience that I had.

In 1998 I wrote a book called *Values of the Game* in which I talked about ten values, things like responsibility, discipline, imagination, courage, selflessness—those are values I learned through basketball, but they spun out to the rest of my life.

Through basketball I learned that preparation and discipline are important, that defeat has a richness of experience all its own, and that it's better to win than it is to lose. I learned that it's more important to cede part of your own individual potential to the group and in the process allow the group to achieve more. I felt the joy of doing something I loved. I felt my body do whatever I wanted it to do. I came to understand the public, the crowd, the audience, and what it wanted and what it didn't care about. I came to respect people from totally different backgrounds from mine and to find in them things worthy of learning.

Ten years in the NBA was enough. The team began to change and I got a step slower. My interest in public issues was growing as my interest in the team situation at the time was decreasing, so it was a natural evolution. I'd been planning for the end from the beginning, so I was ready to move on.

Winning an election is a tremendous honor but it doesn't compare in exhilaration to winning an NBA title. When you win a Senate seat you have six years to work sixteen hours a day to prove that the people weren't wrong. But when you win the world championship it's over. Clear-cut. Black and white. You're the champion. You're the best in the world and people recognize that. You have chills going up and down your spine. Your face aches from smiling and you have that incredible feeling of accomplishment that lasts about three days and then you have to start all over to try and do it again.

In politics, there never is as clear-cut a moment of victory. Occasionally, the passage of a particular law gives you a great sense of achievement, but it's not as dramatic as a world championship. There were two laws that stick out, however. One was the Tax Reform Act of 1986. We reformed the entire income-tax code. The top tax rate for individuals dropped from fifty percent to twenty-eight percent, and what amounted to billions of dollars annually in loopholes were eliminated. That was a big thing for me. The other was the passage of the largest exchange program in history between Russia and the former Republics of the Soviet Union and the United States. That program has brought over twenty thousand high school kids from Russia and other Soviet Republics to live with American families for a year.

Life's a continuum. Now that I'm in merchant banking, the values I learned when I was young and those I learned in the game are still relevant. They'll apply for a lifetime in whatever I do. Basketball, politics, and merchant banking are all very competitive environments. Perspective is important. Being able to listen, being analytical, having the judgment to determine who's telling you the truth and who isn't, having a set of standards that you live by—all those things are important as is the curiosity to learn something new.

DYLAN CASEY

As an athlete, I couldn't control what my teammates or the people against whom I was competing were doing, but I could control what I was doing, how hard I worked, and how disciplined I was about aspects of my training. . . . That's something that has translated into my work here at Google. As a company, part of our culture is not to fixate on what our competitors are doing but rather to stay fixated on what we want to do for our users. That's a positive attribute and a healthy way of thinking.

Dylan Casey is a product manager at Google. He was a cyclist for the U.S. Postal Service Pro Cycling Team from 1998 to 2003, rode on the U.S. Olympic team in Sydney in 2000, won a gold medal at the 1999 Pan Am Games, and became just the third U.S. cyclist in history to win national championships in both road and track. He was born in Berkeley, California, and graduated from the University of California, Santa Barbara.

One Deliverable at a Time

I GREW UP IN OAKLAND until I was thirteen. My BMX bike was my source of freedom. I rode it all over the place. I remember reading the magazines, going to the bike shop, and hanging out with the guys there. But for whatever reason, I never took riding to the next step. When I was fourteen or fifteen, my parents took me to a barbeque in Los Gatos, California, and there was a big bike race that mesmerized me. I'm always asked, "Why didn't you get into cycling then?" I think I was distracted with other things. Although I liked sports, I hadn't done a lot of them in high school, and definitely not any endurance sports. I liked to play baseball and football, but wasn't necessarily very good at them. I tried to play football in high school as a freshman but got injured during the first week of tryouts. I didn't make the team and was really discouraged by that.

I went to UC Santa Barbara and decided I needed a bike to get to class. That's when I got my first real road bike. Some guys saw me on it and said, "Hey, you should come out riding with us." I was a real newbie. I fell in love with the area. Santa Barbara is so majestic and beautiful, with the mountains and the ocean. This group of cyclists encouraged me to keep going. There were always group rides to do. Everybody was always sprinting for a stop sign or something like that, and I liked that competitive part of it, especially since I was all of a sudden better than everybody else. It struck a chord with me. I got a real high off of it. I was encouraged to enter some local races.

How I got into cycling is a little different, compared to my peers. Lance Armstrong, George Hincapié, and most of the Europeans who made it to the highest level of the sport started when they're ten. I'd already made a commitment to finish school, so I didn't have the opportunity to pursue cycling as a professional career until I graduated from college. After graduation I moved to Philadelphia to work at a consulting firm, with the ambition of going to business school. Six months into the program I realized that all I really, really wanted to do was race my bike, so I quit and moved to northern California.

My first year I had some early successes, as well as some setbacks. Fortunately my successes outweighed my setbacks, and every year I improved and got smarter about training. I wasn't an instant standout like Lance was when he came into the sport, but I was good enough to capture the attention from some directors and coaches, who said, "Maybe this kid's got something that could be developed into future successes."

I learned how to deal with the failures and stay focused on the successes. The way that I perceived myself was essentially defined by how well I was doing on the bike. Every time I won a race, I got all these positive accolades, interviews in the press, and everybody wanted to be my best friend. It's an aphrodisiac almost. It's like a drug, and I was motivated by the fact that when I worked hard I could see the results. There was a real cause and effect between working hard and being successful, and I liked that feedback loop.

There is a significant physical component to cycling successfully. However, I knew cyclists who were far more physically talented than I was, yet they were mentally or psychologically weaker. I always liked that, too. Cycling is a very strategic sport. It requires a lot of analysis and on-the-site decision-making during the actual race, yet at the same time it also requires a huge amount of work, dedication, and physical talent. In order to be successful with the sport, especially at the highest level, you have to have every element in place, because the competition is so high.

In 1998 I started working with Chris Carmichael, who was Lance's coach at the time, and was the national team director at USA Cycling, the governing body for cycling in America, from 1989 to 1997. He was also the cycling coach for the U.S. Olympic team in 1992 and 1996. Chris had a lot of positive input. He was always very good at keeping me focused not just on the big picture but also the objective right in front of me. And he'd sometimes help remove all the pressure I would put on myself by saying, "Don't worry about the rest. Just focus on this one deliverable right here."

Johan Bruyneel, who was the director of U.S. Postal Service Pro Cycling Team when I was there, taught all of us on the team how important it was to be prepared. That's been something that's really stuck with me. He honestly believed that we would win races simply because we were better prepared. We had done more work. He removed the element that some people believe you're not capable of something because of who you are. The U.S. had fewer riders who raced at the highest European level, and the races in Europe are much harder than races here because the depth of the field is much greater. When Johan took over the team, Lance hadn't won the Tour yet and the U.S. Postal Team wasn't fully proven, but he knew we had the talent and ability to be one of the best teams in the world. He didn't want us to accept less of ourselves just because our critics said we weren't up to the task. He instilled in us the idea that it didn't matter who we were. If we worked hard enough we could get it done; we could win. That was a very empowering lesson.

As an athlete, I couldn't control what my teammates or the people against whom I was competing were doing, but I could control what I was doing, how hard I worked, and how disciplined I was about aspects of my training. That's something that has translated into my work here at Google. As a company, part of our culture is not to fixate on what our competitors are doing but rather to stay fixated on what we want to do for our users. That's a positive attribute and a healthy way of thinking.

When I retired from cycling in 2003 to come to Google a lot of my peers thought I was a little bit crazy. I was thirty-two, which is younger than most guys are when they retire, and I still had a lot of opportunities to race in front of me. When I retired I was the reigning national champion, but it just seemed like it was the right moment, and the right opportunity. I always had an affinity for technology, and Google was a great opportunity. But I was still ambivalent because when I came to Google I had no idea how I was going to get that same rush that I got from racing and winning.

I remember being in a closed-door meeting in a conference room with a bunch of our executives during my first couple of months at the company. I was still trying to find my way, trying to figure out how to get up in the morning and come to this office. How was I going to survive here? At the meeting, one of the executives stood up and pounded his fists on the table and said, "We're going to win. I don't care what it takes, but we're going to win, and we're going to beat that competitor." He went off on this fifteen-minute tirade about it. When he said, "We're going to win" and "We're going to work really hard to do it," I realized, "Oh, I know this game. I know how this works. This is the same thing that I was doing before. It's just a different set of deliverables and it's measured slightly differently." Before that I was very uncomfortable. Most of my peers here at Google were rock stars in their own right, so that was intimidating at first. I didn't have the same education that my peers did. I didn't have the same business experience. I wasn't a Ph.D. I hadn't already started my own company. But after that meeting I was extremely comfortable.

Google as a company, and the people that work here, have such high expectations. Everybody expects everyone to perform at the highest level. My peers really celebrated my background as a successful athlete. I had interesting anecdotes to tell, and I'd had the opportunity to travel around the world. Being a part of U.S. Postal and being Lance's teammate was always intriguing to everybody. I remember one of my first reviews with my manager at the time. He said, "Dylan, I want you to realize that some of your peers and the people who you work with are very intimidated by you." I was really shocked to hear that, because I was always a little bit intimidated by them. I felt I didn't measure up oftentimes. When he told me that, I asked why, and he said, "Well, I think people are intimidated by your confidence." I think that's maybe a nice way of saying that I was arrogant. I think some of that came from the fact that when I was on the U.S. Postal Service team, the expectation for you to deliver was so high that you just kind of operated in that realm at all times.

I started off in Google's marketing department and have worked my way over to the product side over the last couple of years. I'm responsible for a set of products and I'm part of a team made up of engineers and user-interface designers. We have a marketing team. My role is to help get everybody to work in symphonic fashion toward reaching the objective of the product, which may be more users, or whatever the metric that we use as determining success. It's prioritization. It's product management. It's influencing others, keeping everybody focused, knowing what people are good at, putting them in the position to do it, and understanding how people are incentivized—and relying on people to be responsible and deliver what they're responsible for. It's almost like being a coach or a director; it's very team-oriented.

The skills that I developed and use to be successful as an athlete have transferred over to Google. I thrive in high-pressure situations. That's when I'm at my best. When I raced, I coined a phrase: "The sweet taste of victory is afforded to those who can eat bitterness." I thrive in those moments where you've got to really work hard and suffer. That ability has served me well here at Google, because launching products or working with people in high-stress situations requires so much clarity and focus. Sometimes I feel like there's not enough pressure. I recall being way more stressed out as an athlete than I have been here at Google. That's not to say that there haven't been moments that I've been stressed out. Maybe it's just a different kind of pressure. I don't have somebody coming up to me, saying, "You better do this or you're out."

I'm very good at methodically preparing for a deadline and being held accountable for my work, and that's a skill that has served me well at Google. I was always a game-day performer. I used to joke that there were guys who were really good in training during the week but then on Saturday and Sunday, when the race was on, you would never see them. They were kind of "professional trainers," and for me it was always the opposite. I could always rise to the occasion. In fact, I remember some coaches would get a little bit tense because in the days leading up to the event I wouldn't look so good, wouldn't look so comfortable on the bike, or I wouldn't turn in the best times. And then on race day, inevitably, I would always figure out a way to win or to do my job for my teammate. I definitely am at my best when there's a deadline looming. One of the things that I've done to try to make myself better is to set intermediary deadlines so that I can maintain that pressure.

An attribute that made me successful as a cyclist that has bled over into Google is prioritization. When you're an athlete you have to prioritize everything you do. I would always make my training the number-one most important thing of the day, because I figured anything else that I didn't get done that day I could always push off to the next day. But if I didn't do my training, I couldn't make it up the next day. That's something that I try to do here at Google, too. I sit down in the morning and look at all the things I have to do. I start with the most important or the hardest things first. I turn off my phone. I turn off my computer, or whatever it might be, so I can limit the number of distractions.

One other nice thing about Google is, it's such a metric-driven company that it's easy to measure success—not always, but some elements are easy to measure. I tend to focus on those. The rush from winning in business will never be the same as winning in cycling. However, there are similarities. Part of my reward for working here, besides compensation, is the personal satisfaction that comes from launching a good product, or having a project that I work on turn out really well. There are moments and occasions where I've done something and said, "That was a win." Winning as an athlete—and I experienced this emotion here at Google, too—is often more of a relief. I was often more relieved after I won than elated, which I'm sure psychologists would say is not the healthiest response. But I always had a fear of losing, and a fear of not meeting my objectives, and I was driven by that.

When I was racing, I was aware that the lessons I was learning would help me later and would become defining elements of who I was as a person, something I didn't discover until I retired from professional cycling. I was nineteen or twenty years old, and the lessons that I learned as I was maturing, becoming a man, continue to have a big impact on me.

EARVIN "MAGIC"
JOHNSON

*I don't know if anything else produces that type of rush
that winning in sports does. Winning in business is a high
but you just don't get the rush. . . . But, touching and saving
communities and putting people to work is a high I never
got from sports.*

Earvin "Magic" Johnson is a National Basketball
Association legend, chairman and CEO of Magic Johnson
Enterprises, and founder and chairman of the Magic John-
son Foundation. He won five NBA championships with the
Los Angeles Lakers and a gold medal at the 1992 Olympics.
He was inducted into the Naismith Memorial Basketball
Hall of Fame in 2002. He was born in Lansing, Michigan,
and attended Michigan State University.

Making Assists

ALTHOUGH I PRACTICED and played basketball constantly while growing up in Lansing, Michigan, I never dreamed that someday I would play in the NBA. My goal was to be a rich businessman, like Joel Ferguson or Gregory Eaton. When I saw Joel and Greg making a difference in Lansing, owning businesses that I had never dreamed an African-American could own—who knew we could own buildings and car dealerships?—I said, "Wow, wait a minute. Nobody told me we could do this. I want to be like them. I've got to meet them. I've got to go talk to them." I'm bold. I went up to them, and they said, "Hey, we've been watching all your games." I was shocked when they said that to me. You never know who's in the stands. You just care about your family being there. I said, "I want to talk to you guys, because one day I want to be a businessman." They said, "Okay, we're going to give you your first start by giving you a job."

I was sixteen and started cleaning one of their office buildings. It had about seven floors on it, and I cleaned the offices from Friday after five o'clock until Sunday night. I would go in, get to my favorite office, sit in a big leather chair, put my feet up on the desk pretending I was the CEO, running the whole company. I would push the phone button as if I had an assistant out front and say, "Cathy, can you bring me some coffee and doughnuts?" That's really where my thirst for business knowledge came from. I would ask Joel and Greg a lot of questions. Our friendship took off, and they became my mentors. They're so proud now. It's really a joy for me to see how happy they are with my success. But I couldn't have done it without basketball.

I thought about turning pro after my freshman season at Michigan State University. We came within a game of the Final Four in 1978. Kansas City had the second overall pick in the NBA draft and couldn't offer me the money I wanted. So I decided to stay in college. I knew could benefit from another season at Michigan State, too. After we won the national championship the following year, there was no holding me back. When I declared myself eligible for the draft as a sophomore, there were a lot of doubters. Even in my home state they were taking shots at me and saying I should stay in college one more year because I wasn't ready. I couldn't shoot. There were a lot of skeptics who thought I was going to be just an average pro. That made me go to the gym and really get on my horse and start working to prove people wrong.

It was the same in business. People said, "Oh, you were great on the basketball court, but I don't know if you can be great as a businessman." Again, I had to go back to work. I thrive on challenges and proving people wrong. So, they fueled my fire. Don't put a challenge in front of me, because I'm going to go for it. While a lot of people buckle under that, I thrive in those situations. When everybody thought I was going to die after I announced I was HIV-positive in 1991, I said, "That's another challenge in my life." And I stepped up to it.

The Los Angeles Lakers drafted me with the first pick in 1979. After I made a little money, I knew what I wanted to do with my life after basketball. I started making investments. The first thing I did was buy an AM radio station out of Denver, Colorado, and then move the towers to make it an FM station, because that's where you made more money. We sold off the land where the towers had been, then sold the station and made some nice money. I met entrepreneur J. Bruce Llewellyn and John Mack, who led the Urban League of Los Angeles for more than thirty-five years, both of whom encouraged me to think about making my business a catalyst for positive change in the community. In 1987 I formed Magic Johnson Enterprises, the umbrella company for all of my business ventures, which provides high-quality entertainment products and services to ethnically diverse urban communities, and four years later I launched the Magic Johnson Foundation, which focuses on the educational, health, and social needs of those communities.

When I first came into the NBA I sought mentors and people who could help me. Lakers owner Dr. Jerry Buss became the first one, and then Lon Rosen, who was the director of promotions and later became my agent. I met Joe Smith, who had courtside seats and was running Capitol Records at that time, and Peter Guber, the former head of Columbia Pictures who'd become CEO of Sony Pictures and who sat a couple of seats away from the Lakers bench. I later turned that relationship into a business deal with the Magic Johnson Theatres, the first of which opened in 1995.

These people saw I wasn't your typical athlete and thought, "This guy is serious. Let's sit down and talk. Let's map it out. Let me see what he's about." At one point everybody pointed me to Michael Ovitz and said, "If you want to be in business, he's the man." Michael founded Creative Artists Agency. The way he treated me in that first meeting let me know that it didn't matter if I was Magic Johnson or not. He wanted me to be serious and start reading *Forbes*, the *Wall Street Journal*, and the *New York Times* and *Los Angeles Times* business sections. The first thing he said was, "If you want to be a businessman, you've got to read the sports page second." Then he said, "Why should I represent you? Because most athletes are not serious. They're serious about their sports but nothing after that." I said, "Well, I'm different." When he called me back a couple of weeks later, he said, "I've done my homework on you. You say you want to be a businessman and you're serious about it. So come on, let's get started."

Michael did my first major deal, a Pepsi distributorship with Earl Graves, the founder of *Black Enterprise* magazine, in 1990. And he talked to me about how to dress, how to talk, how to position myself. It was great to have that type of mentorship. I needed somebody like him. He said it's going to be a tough road, and he was right. I had to deal with people saying, "We'd love to have a meeting with you," but they weren't serious about doing business with me. Executives would hand me a basketball and ask for an autograph, but they didn't want to hear my pitch for investing in neighborhoods populated by blacks. After I showed them the Pepsi concept and that we were going to be successful, we started doing a lot better as far as having more productive meetings. People said, "Let's watch this guy." But it still took a while for them to really take me seriously, and it wasn't until the Starbucks deal in 1998 that people really took notice. That turned all the heads. When my deals and I were profiled in the business section of publications, that's when I knew I'd made it.

With a proven track record, the way I'm treated now in the business world, versus the way I was treated ten years ago, is night and day. People can quote my successes better than I can now. When I go to a meeting, I can tell they've done their homework. They already know that they want to do business with me, whereas before I was selling, selling, selling. Now it's, "This is what I think we can do together." Now I'm in a position where I can say no. I can pick and choose who I want to do business with. Before I had to take what was given to me.

I have the same discipline in business that I had on the basketball court, and that same winning spirit and winning attitude as well. Even as a kid, I always wanted to be good in basketball, so I practiced and played constantly. No matter what, I always had a basketball in my hand. Even if I was running an errand for my mother, I'd dribble on the way to the store, switching from my right hand to my left, block by block. Sometimes I'd wake up before the sun came up. As soon as it did, I'd dribble on the street and run around the parked cars, pretending they were players on an opposing team. Sometimes neighbors used to open their windows and yell at me for waking them up. I started playing in school around the third or fourth grade, and won championships from the fourth to the eighth grades. I finally lost in the ninth. My senior year at Everett High School we won the state championship. We won the national championship at Michigan State and the NBA championship my rookie season with the Lakers.

In college, Coach Jud Heathcote preached repetition. For Lakers coach Pat Riley, it was about preparation, preparation, preparation. He drove that home, and now in business I'm so prepared. I do my homework and research and then it's about execution, which is something else I took from Pat. You just bring it over to the boardroom. Those things that I learned from him have helped me to be a successful CEO.

I'm a guy who will prepare all the way until I go into a meeting. I don't sleep well the night before because I'm dreaming about my pitch and making sure I've got it right. It's just like a game and I'm a point guard again. The night before a big game I would dream about the offensive plays that the other teams would run and what they were going to call when they needed a basket. It's the same thing going into a meeting—who am I talking to? what's their mission statement? what's the core value of their company?—because when we go in, our whole mission is to tell that company how we can add value to their company. I'm replaying all those things in my mind so that I can be ready and prepared when I go into the meeting.

Not every deal has been a winner, but I learn from failure. I ask why did we fail and then make sure it doesn't happen again. But we have to understand that a lot of things are out of our control. It's not like basketball, where you can control the outcome. In business, you can control some of it, but a deal can be set and then for some reason it will fall apart at the eleventh hour—and not for anything that you've done. The company may just say, "Hey, we can't do it right now" or "We decided to go in a different direction" or "We've changed our business strategy."

In the beginning the deals that went sour kept me up at night. Then I started understanding that this is how it's going to be. But it took me some years to get used to that. I had to say, "You've got to take off your super-competitive hat and understand it wasn't you. You did everything you were supposed to do." There have been one or two businesses where I failed. When we opened our T.G.I. Friday's restaurant in Atlanta, we were not ready for the onslaught of people, so our customer service was bad. People got frustrated and went to other places. Eventually, we closed the restaurant. We failed the people of that community, because our customer service was not up to par, so what we do now is make sure that never happens again.

I think back to Game 2 of the NBA Finals against the Boston Celtics in 1984, when I let the clock run out. We lost the game, and the series. I was thinking too much. I should have gone with my gut and taken the shot as I was going to do. Instead, I said, "Oh, no, maybe I should pass it to Kareem." Because of that indecision, the clock ran out. I was hoping and wishing I could be in that same situation again, and God blessed me with the chance to have that play again in '87. But this time I said, "Oh, no, I'm taking this. I'm coming across the middle with this hook." Everybody saw what happened. I was able to deliver. I didn't think about it. I just went with my instinct, as I do now. I go with my business gut when considering something like: Is this the right partner? Is this the right deal? If I'm comfortable with it and I don't have to keep thinking about it, then I know it's good. If I have to keep thinking about it, then something's wrong.

When I formed Magic Johnson Enterprises, I had no idea it would be as big as it is today, with partnerships with Best Buy, Aetna, and others. There's no way I could think this big. My mind wasn't there. When you think of us starting off with three Starbucks, and now we have over 100. And the Canyon-Johnson Urban Fund, the country's largest private real estate fund focused on the revitalization of underserved communities, has a billion dollars in cash. And we've got my equity fund, Yucaipa Johnson Corporate Growth Fund, which has $420 million dollars in cash; and in late 2009 we teamed with TCW Leveraged Finance Group, to form the TCW CapitalAsset Fund, which focuses on providing debt financing to middle market companies whose access to capital has been constrained by the frozen credit markets. We employ over thirty thousand people across the country through different joint ventures and businesses such as SodexoMAGIC, our food-services company, and 24 Hour Fitness Magic Johnson sports centers. I'm proud to be the first player to have a licensing agreement with the NBA. We do many different things. I started off with one little radio station, and now it's turned into all of this.

I established my brand in sports initially, which opened up doors for me to start establishing my brand in business. I still had to excel, but reputation played a part in it, too. A lot of athletes want to get into business and become entrepreneurs, but they have a bad reputation. People don't want to partner with them because they're going to be bad for their brand. That's why a lot of them don't get commercials. They don't understand that you have to have a good reputation.

Athletes and entertainers often come to me for business advice. I met with Shaquille O'Neal before he got started. I met with Derek Jeter, Alex Rodriguez, Jay-Z, Steve Harvey, and Grant Hill. They want to know how I got started. How can they do it? What to look out for? They have the money, but they don't know how to start a business.

Who would have ever thought that I would have the number one brand on the basketball court and then the number one brand in urban America? But the experience of winning is different. I don't know if anything else produces that type of rush that winning in sports does. Winning in business is a high but you just don't get the rush. You're competing in a different way. But, touching and saving communities and putting people to work is a high I never got from sports. Seeing abandoned buildings knocked down and turned into something beautiful is a high I get from being a businessman. We're sending young people to college who thought they would never get a chance to go, and they go on to become successful teachers and entrepreneurs. They come back and say thank you. Basketball could never bring that to me. I always say there will always be great basket-ball players, but I don't think too many people will be able to touch a community like we've been able to.

We were touring Mt. Sinai Hospital in New York and a young Hispanic lady came up to me and said, "Oh, my God. It's you!" She runs over and hugs and squeezes me. She said, "You can't believe it but because of your community empowerment center I was able to improve my computer skills and just got a raise and a better job. I've been looking for you to say thank you." We built eighteen community empowerment centers through our foundation. We're making a difference. So that's what I love now. I'm getting a different type of high.

I'm still passing and making assists, just in a different arena.

BILLIE JEAN KING

Sports are a microcosm of society and already [as a twelve-year-old] I was seeing that things weren't right. As I got deeper in tennis, I found out that the Southern California Tennis Association didn't give girls any money, but they gave boys prize money. I didn't like that.

Billie Jean King is a champion of change. She won twelve Grand Slam singles titles, sixteen Grand Slam women's doubles titles, and eleven Grand Slam mixed doubles titles. She founded the Women's Tennis Association in 1973 and the Women's Sports Foundation in 1974, and co-founded World TeamTennis in 1974. She was inducted into the International Tennis Hall of Fame in 1987. She was born and raised in Long Beach, California, and attended California State University, Los Angeles.

What Am I Doing Today?

I WAS ENGROSSED IN TEAM sports the first ten years of my life. Then, when I was in the fifth grade, my friend Susan Williams introduced me to tennis. We went to the Virginia Country Club in Long Beach, and I wore white shorts my mother sewed for me because you had to wear all white. I thought it was fun but didn't think I'd ever get to play because I couldn't afford to go to a club. Susan lived in the rich section of Long Beach. My softball coach then told me about free tennis instruction on Tuesdays at Houghton Park. I went home and said to my parents, Bill and Betty Moffitt, "I really want to play tennis. Can I have some money for a racquet?" My dad said, "If you really want to play, find a way to earn it." I thought, "Here we go again." I wanted a baseball bat when I was younger and he wouldn't do it. He cut a two-by-four and I had a paddle. He said, "If you show me you like to practice and like to hit the ball and it's fun for you, then I'll get you a real bat." And he did.

I went to the neighbors and begged. I tried to figure out what they might need done around the house or garden. I had a Mason jar in the cupboard and when I got eight dollars and twenty-nine cents in it, I couldn't wait any longer. My parents took me to Brown's Sporting Goods, where I told a salesperson I wanted a tennis racquet, and asked what eight dollars and twenty-nine cents would buy. I chose one with maroon strings and slept with it. I read everything in the library on tennis, which was only three books—*Tennis with Hart*, which I probably read fifteen times and which was written by Doris Hart, who won thirty-five Grand Slam titles despite having a permanently impaired right leg; *Use Your Head in Tennis*, by Bob Harman; and a book on the U.S. Nationals, which is now known as the U.S. Open. There was literally one chapter about women in that book. It was very interesting. I had already started to notice inequities in society. I couldn't articulate it but I was more aware.

I loved the history of tennis and tried to learn the names of all of the Wimbledon champions. I went to Houghton Park with my new racquet and met Coach Clyde Walker, who was sixtyish. I adored him from the first moment. I loved the instruction. As I was leaving I told Clyde, "I want to be the number-one tennis player in the world." When I was growing up, if you won Wimbledon, you were number one in the world. He said, "That's great," thinking, "Yeah, great, sure." It was a done deal. I was so excited. I remember that day so clearly.

My mother came to pick me up and I bounced up and down on the car seat, saying, "Mom, this is it! I've found what I'm going to do with my life." She said, "Well, that's fine. You've got piano and you've got your homework." I said, "No, Mom. I'm going to be number one in the world. This is what I'm going to do with my life." I got home and told Dad and my brother, Randy. I was over the top that day. She was trying to keep me grounded, thinking this will last two weeks. After a month I was still crazed. I couldn't get enough.

Clyde was tennis director for the City of Long Beach and would go to a different park every day. I started showing up at all of them. Silverado was Monday. Tuesday was Houghton. Somerset was Wednesday. Ramona Park was Thursday. Rec Park was Friday.

Thanks to my mother and dad, they found a way. They were working three jobs so my brother and I could have our dreams. By the time he was ten my brother wanted to be a Major League baseball player. My parents rolled their eyes at both of us and thought, "What is going on here?" They used to check in with us every so often and ask if we were doing this for them. We'd say no. They only wanted us to do it if we loved it and it made us happy. My brother played thirteen years in the majors.

I loved hitting the ball, running, and jumping. I wanted tennis to be a team sport because I came from team sports. But at least we had doubles. I don't know if I was good in tennis immediately but I was a good athlete. I was quick and had good hand-eye coordination. I'd stand at the net and want to hit the ball before it bounced. Clyde would say, "Would you please get back on the baseline?" I'd respond, "But I like it up here. It's more fun. It's quicker."

I practiced for a year, and when I was twelve I played in a novice tournament where you had to bounce the ball, hit a groundstroke, and not serve overhand. Then I started to play Long Beach tournaments against adults. That was exciting. I didn't care about junior tennis that much because I always envisioned Wimbledon in my head. Clyde coached me until I was seventeen years old. He didn't go with me to tournaments because he was always at the park. Then Clyde got cancer and a few of us helped teach classes. He taught us so well and he really believed in us teaching. He said, "If you can teach it, you know it."

After high school all of these college coaches wanted me to play for them, but we couldn't afford it. Back then, there were no full athletic scholarships for women. This was pre–Title IX. My dad said, "We'll get a loan if you want to go to one of these schools." I said, "Absolutely not." My dad knew Scotty Deeds, the coach at Cal State Los Angeles, and he said I could practice with the boys' team if I wanted. I already had my vision for the sport. I went to college more for my parents. They wanted us to go to school. Randy, who went to Long Beach State, and I both quit after three years. I hardly went to class, to be honest. I was terrible. I already knew what I wanted to do.

When I was twelve, I had an epiphany that I wanted to change not only our sport but society. I was at the Los Angeles Tennis Club and the sun was setting. It was a beautiful night. I was sitting by myself in the grandstand, looking out at the sky. I loved that time of the evening. I got into this almost trance. I went to this place in my soul. It was like a calling. I'm a big believer in faith. I think God puts you in a certain place at a certain time for a reason, yet I don't believe in predestination. I believe in free will. Sports are a microcosm of society, and already I was seeing that things weren't right. As I got deeper into tennis, I found out the Southern California Tennis Association didn't give girls any money, but they covered the boys' expenses. I didn't like that. Even being white, I felt discounted as a girl, so I can't imagine what my sisters of color or disabled people must have felt like. Even when I was young I used to think about that.

When we started the women's professional tour, I said to the other players, "Do not play for the applause. Do not do it for the money. We'll make more than the generation before us, but believe me, we're not going to make the big bucks. The big bucks are going to come as the years go by." And they looked at me and said, "Yep, let's do it." We talked about women, society, and the rest of the world. We wanted every little girl born in this world, if she's good enough, to be able to play professional tennis. We wanted it to spill over into life. We wanted to raise the bar for all women.

Not only do sports provide opportunities for people to make changes but they teach invaluable lessons such as to keep going, whether you win or lose. It teaches you to fight your best and still go out to dinner with somebody you've either had a disagreement with or with whom you don't agree, whether they beat you or you beat them. You find a common ground and realize that relationships are everything. The culture of most businesses was developed by men, and sports better enables you to understand that culture. In business, women are still talked down to. Ilana Kloss, the CEO and commissioner of World TeamTennis, and I go to business meetings and we're talked down to most of the time. We just suck it up, come out of those meetings, and exhale. That's the way it is. But we also knew what it was to be on the outside looking in, back when you couldn't even get in.

Tennis makes you aware of things, because as an athlete you have to notice space, the sun, the wind, and the score. They've proven that athletes do better in math because we're learning how to count when we're younger. You start to look at things differently, like spatial relations. Geometry was not fun for me until I started relating it to my tennis. All these things add up over time, and they help you in everyday business. They help you notice body language, which is really important in sports. You've got to understand your own body language and somebody else's body language. If you aren't observant, you usually don't do as well.

Sports also teach you about the other person. You learn about your teammates and their lives. You look at these movies like *Remember the Titans*, where Denzel Washington made a white kid and a black kid become roommates. They were going crazy and didn't like it. But they started to learn about each other, see their commonalities and tolerate their differences. Hopefully, eventually you want to celebrate differences. But you've got to get to the tolerating first. Another way you learn about people is through the crowd of spectators. A crowd can get really mean and go against you. But you have to persevere. Alternatively, people can get behind you and give you adulation, but you must understand that that's gratification and not love. The athletes and entertainers who get that mixed up are the ones who are usually miserable after they retire.

You learn to face your fears through sports. I'm always scared and always pushing myself to do things that frighten me. I almost failed reading because I couldn't get up in front of a class and give an oral book report in the fifth grade. My teacher called home and asked, "Does Billie Jean read?" My dad said, "She reads every night. I have to tell her to turn off her light." The teacher said, "That's interesting. They have to give two oral reports a year and she won't do it. I figured she doesn't read." I told him I wasn't going to do it and he said, "Yes you are." I was scared to death.

Another time, I was playing in a 13-and-under tournament and was in the finals against Carole Caldwell Graebner at Lincoln Park in Santa Monica. Near the end of the match I realized I was going to have to say thank you because you have to stand up after a tournament when you win and say thank you to the lines people and the people who run the tournament. I got really scared and as I played, I thought, "I can't do this." Then I thought, "Well, do you want to win?" I'm having this talk with myself as if it's about another person. I did win and had to get up to speak. I'll never forget that.

But usually I don't remember my victories. I've said in the past that victory is fleeting, losing is forever. I hated losing. I'm getting slightly better now, but not much. If I'm around another tennis player and we start talking about when we were playing, which I try not to do very often unless they bring it up, I get this feeling inside. I think, "It's still there." People tell me I won more than I know. The only reason I know the titles I've won is because when I do speeches, I'm introduced and they'll give a little of my bio. I don't live for yesterday. I live for today and tomorrow.

My dad gave me a great lesson when I was fifteen. He wouldn't let me read my press clippings because the first time I ever made the front page of the *Long Beach Press Telegram* sports section, I had lost love and love. I was just devastated. I said, "I've won all these different matches and they put this one on the front page, finally." My dad said, "I don't want you to read your press anymore. It's about yesterday." That hit me to the core. I thought, "Boy, is he right. I lost yesterday. I didn't lose today. What am I doing today?"

My accomplishments off the court, such as receiving the

Presidential Medal of Freedom from President Obama last August, mean more to me than my victories in tennis because I'm connecting with today's generation. As a performer it's fleeting, but something like the Medal of Freedom doesn't feel fleeting. And I'm not finished yet.

BOBBY RAHAL

I don't hire people and then start to micromanage them, because if I'm going to micromanage them, then there's no point in my hiring them in the first place. You presumably hire these people because you believe they have the capability to do the job very, very well. At that point you have to let them do that, and it's the same thing in racing. I couldn't be the driver and the mechanic at the same time. I had to be one or the other, and then I had to entrust.

Bobby Rahal is a former Indy Car champion, co-owner of Rahal Letterman Racing with David Letterman, and chairman of Bobby Rahal Automotive Group, which encompasses sixteen car dealerships in western and central Pennsylvania. He retired from competitive driving in 1998, ranking first in career starts, second in career earnings, third in laps led, fourth in wins, and fifth in pole positions in CART/IndyCar history. In 2004 he was inducted into the International Motorsports Hall of Fame. He was born in Medina, Ohio, grew up in Glen Ellyn, Illinois, and graduated from Denison University.

Innate Drive

MY INTRODUCTION TO RACING came from my father, Michael Rahal, who raced as a hobby. In between playing baseball in the summer, I'd go to the races with him. He raced one or two times a month from April through September, and I tagged along with him from an early age. I enjoyed every second of it. Like any kid, it's pretty easy to become enthralled with the sights, sounds, and smells.

As I got older, my responsibilities to help him race and work on the car became greater. I did everything from cleaning the car to making sure nuts and bolts were tight. Growing up, there was never an expectation that I would become a professional race car driver, or even drive as an amateur, because your basis for racing then was to have a successful job and be able to financially afford it. I started racing when I was in college, and that was only because my father gave me the chance to do it by giving me his old racecar, a Lotus. They didn't even have driver schools like they have today. Back then, if you got a car, you went to the "driver school" and as long as you didn't do anything ridiculous you got your "license." Off I went. I won a national championship and an amateur championship when I was in college.

In my early college years I took a lot of courses and by my senior year had a pretty easy schedule, which allowed me time to race and not miss too much school. I skipped my college graduation in order to compete in my first professional race, which was in Canada. To this day I feel a little bit bad about missing graduation, not for my sake but for my parents. They had invested all that money and wanted to see me with the cap and gown. I saw my graduation as being a celebration of the past and thought my first professional race was a celebration of what was the future.

From the day I got into a race car, I was never interested in just sort of being there. I was interested in winning. To me there was no other reason to do it, which is why I retired when I did in 1998. I came to the point where I didn't feel as if I was able to commit the personal resources necessary to win. Yes, I could have continued to race and stayed in the sport, but that was the antithesis of why I was there in the first place. Either you do something to be the best at it, or you find something else. Even when I ski, I try to improve every time I go out. In a race car, you do one lap and then you enter the next lap. Your thought process is: "How can I do this one better?" It's not: "Well, I think I'll do that same one again." I had a lot of that innate drive to be better the next time, and that was driven to a large degree by my family.

In our household, my father was very much a taskmaster. He didn't have much patience for you doing something unless it was contributing either to your own well-being or to that of the household. There was always the idea that if you're going to do something, you do it right. That was drilled into you at an early age. You always wanted to be the best. No matter what I tried, I always wanted to be the best.

There was some degree of natural ability. If my father gave me talent, my mother, Barbara, gave me the intelligence to handle the talent. She's a pretty cool customer. There are few people in racing that have immense amounts of natural talent. But it's interesting, most of them don't have the mental discipline in order to take advantage of it. They excel up to a certain point and then they can't deal with the mental demands of it. I was a little bit of a late bloomer in the sense that I think I had a lot of natural talent in the race car right from the start, but then I was able to hone it mentally with my discipline so that as time went on I got more successful—and more successful in the more-demanding categories than I was in less-demanding categories.

Aspiring to be a professional race car driver, you have far more lows than you have highs. That's just the reality, because your success is dependent beyond your own efforts. There's a piece of machinery that you're in, and people that work on that piece of machinery. So there's a multitude of people contributing in one way or another to your success, or lack thereof. At one point very early in my career I retired because I'd had a bad year. I thought, "I'm not sure I want to put up with all this. I don't want to waste my life. I don't want to waste my time." And it was very immature of me. Luckily, I was asked back and convinced to give it a second chance.

I think at the time my father was probably a little pleased I retired. He said, "Okay, you got it out of your system." But my mechanic at the time and the fellow that I had driven for said, "You're making a big mistake if you do this. You need to go back, don't give up so easily." They were right. Even after that, there were some good days and some bad days. The one thing I wanted to make sure of was that I would be honest with myself and that I wouldn't deceive myself and say, "Next year will be the year. Next year will be the year." I felt that after I retired the first time and I went back and started succeeding some more, in the end I was convinced that I had to put more effort into it.

I've always said to young drivers, dedication and perseverance can probably claim as much for your success as your innate talents or anything else because of the difficulties and challenges you face as a driver and the fact that your success is not just dependent upon your own efforts. There are times you have to have a very thick skin and you have to have a very strong degree of commitment and dedication to it.

I never had the desire to be a team owner until very late in my career. The only reason I set forth on that voyage was because I was getting into my late thirties and wanted to have control over the final stages of my career. The best way I could do that was to own the team. Also, at the same time I put forth so much effort over the years as a driver in bringing sponsors in, I thought I might as well work for myself if I'm going to continue doing this.

All the traits that you have to have to be successful in sports— doing things right the first time, committing yourself, being dedicated to what your goals are, perseverance, a work ethic—these are the traits that you have to have to be successful in business. Those are the things that I was able to bring to bear from my experience in motor racing to business.

Bobby Rahal Automotive Group, which began with one outlet in 1989, came about because thanks to our past successes in motor sports we were able to make the necessary connections to get opportunities in the business. Right after I won the Indianapolis 500 in 1986 I met the top Honda people. We'd occasionally get together, and I expressed an interest in becoming a Honda dealer at some point. At that time, Honda dealerships were like gold. When we opened, I don't think we imagined ever having more than one store. Now we have sixteen.

Car dealerships are run the same way a racing team is, where we bring in the best people we can find. We watch them grow. We allow them to exercise their skills. One of the things I'm most proud of is that we have people start out in the wash bay and they end up running one of the dealerships years later. There's a tremendous amount of satisfaction in seeing the team grow, and that's one of our hallmarks. That's also the reason why we are able to attract so many good people. We have a track record that says we actually walk the walk when we talk about how the sky is the limit for you as an individual based on the commitment that you're willing to make for the company.

I have to say, our dealerships are doing quite well, even in this economy. I can explain why in several ways, but in the end I think it comes down to having people who aren't quitters, having people who rise to the challenge, whatever that might be, and people who are dedicated to us. Everybody looks good when times are good. When times are bad, *then* you see who your A players are. In the midst of probably the most difficult time we've seen in the automobile business, let alone other things, our dealerships are selling. I lay that squarely at the feet of our people and the leadership. As I tell our team members, "Everybody has to be a team leader. There's nobody that's any better than anybody else. You cannot think that you can just perform at fifty percent of your skill level and succeed or rely on somebody else."

If I've been good at one thing in my business life, it's that I've been able to attract great people who can do a super-fabulous job, and I give them the mandate to do it. I don't hire people and then start to micromanage them, because if I'm going to micromanage them, then there's no point in my hiring them in the first place. You presumably hire these people because you believe they have the capability to do the job very, very well. At that point you have to let them do that, and it's the same thing in racing. I couldn't be the driver and the mechanic at the same time. I had to be one or the other, and then I had to entrust. Many times in a racing car you're entrusting your life to the people that work on the car. Not many other sports or in many businesses do you have that kind of potential for devastating results if someone doesn't do their job. Ernest Hemingway said there are only three sports—mountain climbing, bullfighting, and auto racing—and the rest are games. There is an ultimate cost to any of those three.

One of the biggest lessons I learned through racing was the value of good people, the value of teamwork, and how you could use that to its best effect for your own career. A racing car driver's success is based on a lot of people. It's not like a golfer, where it's just him against the course in the end. For me there were multiples of people that had intimate connection with what I was doing, and by their own performance on their job they could positively or negatively affect my career. I came to understand the value of good people and that you had to bring them in. You had to lead them, but more than anything you had to attract the best people, and if you did that, then you would be successful. Because nobody in and of themselves does it all. I don't care who it is. Especially as you look at a corporation, there are thousands of people involved.

The Indianapolis 500 in 1986 was the most important win for my career, but I can name ten other races that were difficult to win. In some respects, the sense of satisfaction that I got from those races was greater, or there were races I won where I had an emotional attachment to the event because my father had raced there. I derived a great deal of satisfaction, other than monetary, from winning. To me it's the achievement of the goal. My father used to say the only way you make money is by excelling at what you do. For me, it was going out and doing the job extremely well on that given day, and doing it better than anybody else. It's nice to see your bank account go up, but for me it's the inner satisfaction of having beaten the competition.

In business we preach the same thing. If you commit yourself to excellence, then your personal goals, whatever they might be, will be achieved. That's not to say everybody hits their goals all the time. There are good days and bad days. We teach our team members in all of our dealerships that it is the commitment, it's the satisfaction of having been the best you can that day and doing the right thing that make the difference. The car business is based upon a relationship that you have with the customer. There are a lot of people selling the same kind of car, so why should a consumer go to you versus anybody else? It's all about providing a level of service that is world class and that is unmatched by your competition. I'm proud that our franchises have won thirty customer-satisfaction awards, including the BMW Center of Excellence Award, which is given to less than ten percent of the BMW dealerships nationwide.

From a strategic standpoint, I am very involved in the Bobby Rahal Automotive Group and feel that as the majority shareholder I have a responsibility to the business and to myself to stay involved. Our early dealership opportunities came as a result of my racing success, but our subsequent opportunities have come as a result of our successes with the dealerships, which is very important to me. Ultimately, it is my name on the building, and it is vital that I stay vigilant in making sure that our business continues to meet the high standards we have set.

BRUCE SMITH

I've often told people that in football I'd rather have my worst enemy playing next to me, making sacrifices and committing himself to that common goal, than my best friend if he's cutting corners and not doing what he's supposed to be doing.

Bruce Smith is a former National Football League player. He was the first selection in the 1985 NFL draft and spent fifteen seasons with the Buffalo Bills and four with the Washington Redskins. He started in four consecutive Super Bowls with the Bills, holds the NFL's all-time sack record, and was inducted in the Pro Football Hall of Fame in 2009. He is president of Bruce Smith Enterprise LLC, a commercial real estate development company. He was born in Norfolk, Virginia, and starred at Virginia Tech.

Attention to Detail

I STARTED PLAYING SPORTS BECAUSE it was the thing to do when I was growing up. I didn't realize then that it was also a way to stay out of trouble. It was being a part of a group where everyone was striving for the same goals of being a great player or winning a championship, whether it was Little League or high school. I was always very fond of basketball and was quite good at it in high school. It wasn't until the tenth grade that I gave in to peer pressure and started playing organized football.

Because my first love was basketball, I had no desire to play football. But it was somewhat lonely since all of my friends that I had grown up with were playing football. I was the only one on the school bus going home. The football coaches at my high school, Booker T. Washington, were in collusion to get me on the field. They thought I would excel because of the agility and speed I showed on the court. They told me, "Come out. You'll be good at it." I agreed to give it a try.

I was accustomed to hard work, but the first day of practice was a nightmare. The high school was in the inner city, and we saw the coaches scouring the field for broken glass and bottles left from guys drinking the night before. It was ninety-five degrees and the humidity was high. The sun was beating down on us and we were practicing on this half-dirt, half-grass field. After that first day or two, I said, "The heck with this. I'm not cut out for this." And I quit. My coach, Cal Davidson, called my house and talked to my father. Afterwards, my father asked me, "Son, why weren't you at practice today? Are you sick? Is something wrong?" I answered, "No, sir, football is just too hard. It's too hot and it's too painful." My father gave me a look that I'll never forget, and in his baritone voice he said, "Son, whatever you do in life, don't ever quit." My father's words resonated with me and at that moment I decided to commit myself to every endeavor.

I didn't know much about football. To show you how my knowledge of football was not up to par, in the eleventh grade I was playing offensive tackle and I went out for a pass. It was a learning process, as is everything in life, which I later experienced when I became a commercial real estate developer. Whether it's football, basketball, or business, it's a process and it requires some patience. You could see the progression, and my confidence become stronger in football.

I played center on the basketball team. Even though there were a couple of guys that were a few inches taller, I used my height, size, and the way I was built to maximize my ability at rebounding and doing the dirty work on the inside. Once I developed the foundation and the fundamentals, it might have appeared as though it was natural, but it took a lot of work for me to excel. We went to state just about every year in basketball. In football we were decent. We'd win six or seven games a year. Even in the midst of adversity we'd just continue to work hard and persevere. Being accustomed to winning in one sport and not another didn't get me down, though. You have to take it in stride. You're not going to win at everything. The fact that you're competing and giving it your all is what matters, and if occasionally you come up short, that gives the smart ones, the ones who really care about the team and care about their performance, the motivation to go back, to try and get better. That's what I was trying to do.

My senior year I received scholarship offers in both basketball and football from all across the nation. But at six-foot-three, 260 pounds, it seemed like football was my destiny. When Virginia Tech recruited me, the Hokies weren't the football powerhouse that they are now. But Coach Bill Dooley left a lasting impression on me when he said, "If you come to Tech, you will receive an excellent education, and if you can play, they will find you." He was right. In 1985 the Buffalo Bills selected me as the number-one pick in the NFL draft.

In the pros I applied the work ethic I watched my parents display. It was encouraging seeing my father, George, and mother, Annie, going to work and doing jobs that they didn't necessarily like. But their work ethic of not missing any days, and their commitment, even under those circumstances, had an effect on me. They were the perfect examples after which to model myself when I had an opportunity to play a sport I had a passion for.

Marv Levy, who was hired as the Bills coach midway through my second year and was my coach for twelve seasons, reinforced my work ethic. For me that meant conditioning myself. I didn't go to training camp to get in shape. I was already in shape, so I was a step ahead of everyone else. It was that paying attention to detail, doing that little bit extra that no one else was willing to do, and performing the ordinary tasks in an extraordinary manner that I strived to do. For example, we would play a game on a Sunday. The first thing Monday morning, I would go in around eight o'clock, before any of my teammates arrived, and study the film of the game that we played. I would study film of the next opponent and write down notes on how I would defeat that offensive tackle and guard. We had our meeting at eleven or one o'clock. I was already ahead of the game. The coach would study the film of our last opponent with the group and critique us all, but to hear him and his perspective was very helpful. I would take the constructive criticism and digest that. But I had already done that myself.

I don't think there's any such thing as being overprepared. I needed that time to prepare myself, and that's what made me satisfied. That's why I'm in the position that I'm in today; I committed myself to the job at hand and had a passion for it. I would love to have won a Super Bowl, but that doesn't define me as a person or as a Hall of Famer. When you add "Hall of Famer," that speaks for itself about your integrity, your passion for the game, your commitment, and the legacy that you left behind. Being inducted represents a career of excellence.

Along with preparation and hard work, some of the most important things that I've learned from the game are character, professionalism, and paying attention to detail. Marv had a tremendous impact on my life. He's seen me mature from a second-year player to the man I am today. He was the consummate professional. He wasn't one that cursed. He rarely raised his voice, and he treated us like men. He would tell you after you made a big play, "Please, by all means, show some excitement, but don't do it to the extent where it will hurt your team." His favorite line was, "Act like you've been there before." When running back Thurman Thomas scored, he would hand the ball to the official. When I sacked the quarterback, I immediately started helping that opposing quarterback up instead of standing over top of him, dancing. We might think that those little things are fun and exciting, but there's better ways to go about and represent not only yourself but your teammates without degrading the opponent.

That carries over to business, from the standpoint of being a professional and carrying yourself in a professional manner. The first thing people that I've done business with will tell you is that I'm a man of my word. If I say we're going to do a deal, even before we've signed the contract, the deal is pretty much done. Naturally, I do my due diligence prior to making the statement. When I told my strength and conditioning coach or Marv, "I'll be there at eight o'clock in the morning for my workout" or "After practice is over, if you need to find me to talk about some things, you'll find me upstairs, studying film by myself," they could always rely on that.

I became involved in real estate in 1995, a couple of years after meeting Dan Hoffler, who has been in the business over thirty years and is chairman of the board at Armada Hoffler, a real estate development and construction company in Virginia Beach. I started investing with him, and as I did so, I started learning more and more about real estate. When I retired, following the 2003 season, they took me under their wings, and it's been a learning process ever since. I've been in the business with my own company, Bruce Smith Enterprise LLC, for about four years.

As a former professional athlete, in some cases it was hard to earn people's respect in the business world. But when I decided to become a developer, I put my mind to learning about this business, educating myself and building a strong and formidable team that's well qualified to deal with a municipality, city, or university that's putting out requests for proposals or requests for qualifications. They can see that we have an experienced team and the capability to deliver a project to fruition in a timely fashion. Just like it was a process in playing football, it's a process in learning this business as well. You have to be taught. You have to be eager and willing to learn. It helps having partners who have the experience and integrity that my guys have here.

Just like in sports, we have a team in real estate. There's no substitute for having strong partners that have the experience, the knowledge, and the wherewithal of putting a deal together. The idea of being part of a team where everyone has the same common goal is special. I've often told people that in football I'd rather have my worst enemy playing next to me, making sacrifices and committing himself to that common goal, than my best friend if he's cutting corners and not doing what he's supposed to be doing.

One thing about my business now is the total opposite of playing football. In football we have a sense of immediate gratification. You prepare; you practice; you play a game within seven days. In real estate, you can work on a project for a year or two and it still might not yet have come to fruition. This is a long process that's filled with many different variables and moving pieces that all have to come together before you see a finished product. But when that project comes together it's certainly worthwhile, and you have a sense of accomplishment. I've told my partners a number of times that I'm just not used to the slow pace of this particular field, but it's something you get used to after a while.

I partnered with Armada Hoffler on the Mandarin Oriental and the Swedish embassy in Washington, D.C.; and on Smith's Landing, a thirteen-acre mixed-use property with apartment buildings and a Hilton Garden Inn within walking distance of Virginia Tech. It was formerly the Sheraton Red Lion Inn and the place where I stayed during my recruiting visit. I'm most proud of Smith's Landing because it's at my alma mater. I had already left an athletic legacy at the college, and now I've had the opportunity to go back and leave a legacy there as a businessman.

Sports plays a part in this legacy that I'm now embarking on as a businessman. When you receive a scholarship to a university, whether it's athletic or academic, it opens doors beyond your wildest imagination, doors that the average young person can't see at the time. If you do the right thing, play your cards right, work diligently, surround yourself with people who are trustworthy and who have the same goals and aspirations that you have, then usually good things will happen. I'm a perfect example of that.

ROGER STAUBACH

I've always said you really need the "tea bags of life" in business—the people that are going to perform when the water is hot. Through the years, I've preached the old saying "Adversity reveals genius and prosperity conceals it." As an athlete, you find out the best in your teammates when times are tough.

Roger Staubach played quarterback for the Dallas Cowboys from 1969 to 1979 under Coach Tom Landry, won two Super Bowls, and was inducted in the Pro Football Hall of Fame in 1985. After beginning his real estate career with Henry S. Miller, Jr., in 1971 to supplement his football salary, he founded The Staubach Company in 1977. He served as its chairman and CEO until 2007, when he became its executive chairman. When the company merged with Jones Lang LaSalle in 2008, Staubach became the director and executive chairman of that firm's Americas Region. In 1986, he created Staubach Retail Services, which evolved into SRS Real Estate Partners in 2009. He was born in Cincinnati, grew up in Silverton, Ohio, and graduated from the United States Naval Academy with a B.S. degree in engineering.

Unspectacular Preparation Yields
Spectacular Results

I WAS AN ONLY CHILD. We had a great little family and we lived in a Catholic neighborhood that was middle class, at most. There were a lot of kids and we all loved sports. I was seven years old when I started playing baseball. Next came basketball, and then in the seventh grade I started playing football. My life was wrapped around football, basketball, baseball, staying out of trouble, and trying to make my parents proud of me.

My dad, Robert, was a traveling shoe and leather salesman. He traveled all over Ohio and Kentucky. He was gone during the week but was always home on the weekends, and he helped coach my baseball team when I was real little. If we had weekday games he would change his schedule and try to be there when he could. I really wanted to make my parents proud, so when they came to the game they could say, "Hey, that's my kid." I always felt that I did it for them, and, fortunately, I did have this ability to be a decent player at every age that I played. Sometimes kids level off at eighth grade or high school, but I continued to be able to compete at higher levels, especially in football.

In life you've got goals and ambitions. I knew sports were something that I could do pretty well, and that I was going to try to be the very best I could be. I was going to be a professional baseball player first. Then I was going to be a professional basketball player. And then I was going to be a professional football player because I wanted to please my parents. You've got to have that kind of motivation in your life, and then you've got to have that inner competitive spirit, and I think I really got that from my mother, Elizabeth. She played the piano and wasn't a great piano player, but, man, she worked at it all the time.

I've always believed that it takes a lot of unspectacular preparation to get spectacular results. I remember football in grade school, where we had these young coaches running us in the heat. A lot of kids didn't want to do it. But there was no way I was going to quit. It was something inside of me. I didn't want to go home and tell my parents I had quit.

When I was playing baseball, the catcher got hurt. My dad was the assistant coach, and I played third base or shortstop. They needed a catcher, so the head coach said, "Roger probably could adapt to catching." I didn't want to be a catcher and put all that equipment on. But my dad said to me, "We need you to be the catcher. The team needs you to be the best catcher you can be, and that's all I'm asking you to do. Just do the best you can and we'll see how it works." I caught for about the next eight years before finally moving to the outfield in high school.

That episode of being switched to catcher had the biggest impact on my life. When I was told that someone wanted me to do it, I was going to try to do it the best I could. That proved to be a big deal for me because I experienced something similar in football, and I was better prepared when my high school coach, Jim McCarthy, switched me to quarterback. I didn't want to be a quarterback. That move changed my life.

I went to a very large all-boys Catholic school, Purcell High

School, with about twelve hundred kids. Sometimes in high school football, boys play both offense and defense. But we had such a big program it wasn't necessary. I was a starting cornerback my junior year. When Coach McCarthy asked me to play quarterback, I told him I didn't want to. We had an experienced quarterback going into his senior year. I would have to learn to play quarterback in about six months and beat him out of the starting position. "Why do you want me to do it?" I asked my coach. Aware that I was captain of the basketball team, he responded, "Well, the other players listen to you."

I'm very thankful that Coach McCarthy used leadership as the reasoning for wanting to switch me to quarterback. But I didn't see it initially. I was very competitive, so I showed leadership through the example of working hard, not getting on people's backs or anything like that. I was elected the president of our student council. I never campaigned to lead anybody.

People saw something in me that was more than the athlete. It fell into place. I had a good arm, but it was strictly from baseball. He didn't even know if I could throw the ball. He just said, "Hey you, start working at quarterback." I got a friend of mine and we started taking snaps. When I started playing quarterback as a senior in high school, it was a whole new beginning for me.

I would have probably been a decent college football player on defense, but when I went to quarterback it made sense. I went to New Mexico Military Institute for a year and then to Naval Academy, where I played baseball, basketball, and football. Wayne Hardin at the Naval Academy was a heck of a coach. Dallas Cowboys coach Tom Landry was a phenomenal coach, and he kind of adapted to my running style. His influence as a person meant a lot to me, too. He was probably as good as it gets as far as walking his talk and living his life.

Before I joined the Cowboys I served four years in the Navy, and my wife, Marianne, and I had three kids. I had an engineering degree. When I was at the Naval Academy, everybody at that time got a B.S. in engineering—and that's what it was for me, a "B.S." I really wanted to get some business experience in case I got hurt. We had three kids. I wasn't a rookie with a lot of money and playing golf in the off-season. I started out making twenty-five thousand dollars a year. I interviewed with a couple of companies and with the Miller Company, a real estate firm, in 1971. But I only worked in the off-season. I worked out every day. Then I went down to the office. I learned a lot about real estate and worked on commission. I stayed with it, and Mr. Henry Miller, Jr.—he died in 2009, at the age of ninety-five—became my mentor. After we won the first Super Bowl, I was tempted to walk away from real estate. But the morning after the big win, I got a telegram at our hotel from Mr. Miller. He said, "Congratulations on winning the Super Bowl, and by the way you've been promoted to vice-president." I said to Marianne, "Oh, I can't let him down now." So I continued to work in the off-season. I didn't compromise football at all. Landry knew my approach to my work habits, so it was never a problem for him.

I made a commitment to everything I've done, and that helped me earn respect in real estate. But then you've got to show your stuff and your commitment to the business. It definitely took a number of years, but going to work in the off-season helped a lot. If all of a sudden at the good part of my career I was getting into real estate people might have asked is he really committed or is he just representing the company and opening the door? But because of the years I had with the Miller Company, my commitment showed and people commented, "Hey, listen, he's stayed with it."

One of the benefits of having earned respect in the industry was that at the Staubach Company I was able to hire the great people that came and believed in me. That's why we became a great company; indeed, one of the best parts of my whole life is that they wanted to work for me. If internally you have a bunch of slugs that say, hey, what's in it for me, and a bunch of "fee-and-me" brokers, you're not going to get a lot done. We didn't have that. Our internal trust was significant in how we built our business and how we were able to show the customer that we were a very safe choice to help them, because a lot of the real estate deals we're involved in are very significant.

You've got to keep competition, whether in business or in sports, in perspective. I'll never forget this. When I was playing basketball in high school, I had a chance to win the game against St. X at the Xavier University Field House. I had a one-and-one free throw with a few seconds left. We were behind by one point. If I had made the first one we'd have tied. I missed the first one, and it was a one-and-one so I didn't get a second shot. The game was over. I ran to the locker room and didn't shower. I just took off, went home, and sat up in my room for a couple of hours. I felt horrible. Then, all of a sudden I realized, "Hey, life is going to present these challenges again. I'm going to face these issues again. I have to do the best I can and I can't be afraid of those challenges." And that was really helpful. I've been in the middle of a lot of close games. We won some; we didn't win them all. And that's life. Life is the same thing. Every day there's something that can disappoint you, and you've got to just continue to do what you do and stick up for what you believe in and persevere. You just can't quit. Those are the things sports have taught me and they're totally apropos to business. I've always said you really need the "tea bags of life" in business—the people that are going to perform when the water is hot. Through the years, I've preached the old saying "Adversity reveals genius and prosperity conceals it." As an athlete you find out the best in your teammates when times are tough.

You win some and you lose some in real estate, too, and there have been big disappointments. When we made presentations to companies and then they'd hire somebody else, it would be a real downer. When I lost a game on a Sunday, I kept to myself. I'd just be quiet. It took me a day or two, and by Tuesday, man, I was pumped up for the next game. It's the same in business. You have disappointments. But if you continue to do the right things, you win. When I played baseball, my dad said something that was interesting. He said,

"When there's runners on second and third base and the score is 4–3 with two outs, I don't like to come to bat, but when I watch you play, you seem to really enjoy coming to bat in that situation." And I did. Even professionally we'd have some tight games. We'd win some, but no one is always going to win. Michael Jordan has probably missed a key shot here and there. That's not to say I'm in that category, but I still competed at that level. I had some really rough defeats, but also a lot of really great victories, and that's what life is about: being able to do the very best you can under the circumstances. And the way you do that is you have to pay a price to get there to have the opportunity to do it.

Just like in sports, in business there are going to be more good things than difficult things. We found out the other day that this company with which we had a great meeting struck a deal with another company, even though they liked us and what we did. Disappointing, yes, but the next day we won a big piece of business with somebody else. This is what has kept my adrenaline going.

Hard work and perseverance are two things you learn from sports that help later in business. That old saying "There's no traffic jams on the extra mile" has always been part of me. You've got to give that push to differentiate yourself. Even if you're not equal to somebody else talent-wise, if you give the extra, you can win, and you can make the difference. I always had that confidence. If you work real hard, you produce confidence. But it's hard to be confident when you haven't paid the price to be successful at something.

In our company people are tired of hearing my "no traffic jams on the extra mile" speech. I have a great story about our '71 Dallas Cowboys team. We were four and three in the middle of the year. We had the talent but we weren't playing together. Coach Tom Landry gave us a great game play, but he was frustrated with the attitude. All of a sudden the players turned it around. Mike Ditka said, "Hey, listen, let's put the personal agendas secondary to the team." It's always somebody else's fault. Well, we turned around a four-and-three season. We won ten straight football games, and it was strictly by changing the culture of the team, from all these personal agendas to a single *team* agenda. I use that story a lot in our company. And it's true. It just shows what you can do when you have the right people in the right places working together.

The biggest correlation between football and real estate is teamwork. I've seen it work. I've seen it as part of my life. Team players aren't people who just fall into step. A team player is someone who has that respect for someone other than themselves, someone you can trust. I learned so much about teamwork in sports. There's no way in the world that I would have accomplished what I did—and I wish I would have accomplished more; I'd like to have won about ten Super Bowls—without the support that I had. That's number one. I've preached it in our company. At the end of the day, when we sold our business, I controlled only twelve percent of it because through the years I had distributed ownership options and stock because this company was built by a lot of people and we benefited together. Now our job is to benefit Jones Lang LaSalle, which we're going to do.

Appreciating other people, appreciating the contribution of someone other than yourself, is what sports taught me, and it has helped me so much in life. It's showing appreciation to those who care about something other than just what's in it for them. No way would I have had a chance to do what I did without the coaches, teammates, my wife Marianne, and my family, who were part of my life, and I carry that thought into the running of our business.

DANIEL D. VILLANUEVA

There was an assistant coach in New Mexico who got very mad at me when I was the editor of the newspaper. I wrote in one of my editorials that sports were not ends in themselves; they're simply a means to an end. He called me an ingrate and was furious with me, because he said sports were everything. They aren't. It's how you use sports and what you do with them. Any success that comes as a result matters.

Daniel D. Villanueva is a partner at Rustic Canyon/Fontis Partners, LP, a California-based private equity firm that he co-founded. He previously was co-founder and managing director of Bastion Capital Corporation and Bastion Management Corporation, the first private equity fund to focus on the Hispanic market. He spent twenty-five years as a television executive. From 1960 to 1968 he played with the Los Angeles Rams and the Dallas Cowboys under Coach Tom Landry. He graduated from New Mexico State University. He was born in Tucumcari, New Mexico, and raised in Calexico, California.

Do It with Passion

WHEN I WAS YOUNG I had trouble with my legs. They kept collapsing when I was playing. At that time, the minute people saw somebody fall they'd think polio. The missionary ladies in Calexico took me to see a doctor in San Diego who changed my diet. I used to skip a lot of meals because I'd play outside and would play from when the sun came up until the missionaries turned out the lights. When you're one of twelve kids, either you're at home to eat or you starve. They're not going to wait for you. The doctor also put me on a running regimen. My mother would get me up in the morning and push me out the door. I would run to a canal a little over a mile away and then run back home, which was four blocks away from the Mexican border. My legs started building up, and my weak point became my strong point.

We used to play a little kicking game, and I would win all the time. It was obvious that my legs were getting very, very strong. The coach saw it and asked me to kick and punt when I was fifteen years old. I made all-Conference three years in football, four years in basketball—which was my best sport—and two years in baseball.

There were a bunch of us in my family, and we all competed in athletics. To keep us in line, my mother, Pilar, would threaten to cut out our sports. She was illiterate, never went to school, and didn't speak English. She married my father when she was fourteen or fifteen and he was a year older. Altogether she had sixteen children, though she counted twelve because they were the ones that survived. Two died in infancy and two were stillborn. Mom would listen to the radio, and while she didn't speak English, she knew numbers. At the end of the game, the radio announcer would say "Calexico 12, El Centro 27" and she'd know when we'd been whipped. I'd get home after a loss and the house would be dark. But if we won, the lights would be on and I'd have dinner waiting for me. That was her way of pushing us. If I lost, during the week she'd say, "Good morning, loser." She was always challenging me and asking, "Did you do everything you could. Did you play your hardest?" That was important to her, because sports were going to be my ticket out. She knew I could go to college and play. She would go to some games, and you could always hear her. She didn't know a fumble from an interception from a touchdown. But she'd just get all excited when she heard our name, Villanueva. When I played with the Rams, the *Los Angeles Times* ran a story on me and the title of the article was: "His Mother Was a Coach."

I was doing my student teaching at Las Cruces High School in New Mexico when I received a phone call inviting me to try out for the Rams. I was the only Mexican-American in the NFL. And I was reminded of it every day in L.A., because every time I went on the field, they'd play bullfight music, which drove me crazy. I'd look around and think, "Who's the idiot playing this?" Oh, I can hear it now. My team from '60 to '64 had some tough years; we just did not have a good offense. They used to call us the "tango offense"—one, two, three, kick, one, two, three, kick. I led the league in punts with eighty-seven in 1962. We didn't get a lot of field goals because we didn't get down there very often. But I got through by focusing on what I could do.

I never negotiated a contract. I used to sign them, leave them on the desk, and tell the team to fill it out and send me a copy. I didn't care what I made. My dad, Primitivo, used to say, "Don't give me a fish. Teach me to fish and put me where there are some." I was where the fish were. I was in the NFL. If I didn't make a success of that, shame on me. So I didn't want to make myself too expensive. I knew that it would work out and thought because of the exposure that I got and the role that I was given, I could make something out of it. The first year I made fifty-five hundred dollars. The next year I made seven thousand, then nine thousand then eleven thousand. I never made a lot of money. But I made the decision early on that I would try my hardest to do some good. So I passed up a lot of things to do what was sarcastically called "freebies," and that is visiting parents at parents' groups, going to award banquets and father-son dinners. I decided to do some good in my community, because I had a unique opportunity to do so. When I was with the Rams, I did over two hundred appearances a year. I'd speak to anybody who would have me and tell kids to stay in school and urge parents to get involved and find out what their kids were being taught, or if they *were* being taught.

When the Rams traded me to the Dallas Cowboys in 1965, it was as if somebody had punched me in the stomach. I felt like a cow that's been sold. It hurt. But suddenly I was with a team that people were fanatical about. They started calling us America's Team. Those were heady days. Every town that we went to there'd be this huge throng of Cowboy fans. Everywhere I went, Hispanics in Cleveland, Chicago, and New York, would come out. My final game was the legendary "Ice Bowl," which we lost, 21–17, to Green Bay in eighteen-below-zero temperature after Bart Starr's quarterback sneak in the final minute of the NFL championship game on December 31, 1967. I don't have a ring, and that's painful.

When we lost that game, in my heart I knew that was it for me. Even though I had two years left on my contract, I walked away and said, "I'm not playing anymore." My business partners at a television station in Los Angeles had asked me to stop playing the year before, but I said, "Give me one more year. I think we can win this thing." So they gave me another year, and that was very difficult because I commuted to L.A. after every game and prerecorded some shows. Then I'd take a red-eye back to practice. By the end of the year I was drained physically.

I started my career in television in earnest in 1968 but had been in journalism for many years before. I had been editor of the paper at New Mexico State University and worked part-time at the *Las Cruces Sun*. I learned early on, if you do things for people, it will come back to you in spades. One summer during the Rams' training camp, a man asked me to help his son, who wanted to be a kicker. I started to say, "I can't at this time, when I'm in training camp." But after seeing the look on this kid's face, I agreed to do it. We had two-a-day practices and I worked with him three times a day, before and after the morning practice and prior to the afternoon session. After the season, the man, Jerry Simmons, who was head of sales for Metromedia, now Fox, asked me to meet him. He took me to a brand-new little Mexican station called KMEX and told the manager, "This is Danny. He's the only Mexican-American in the NFL. I want you to put him on the air, and here's your sponsor. You're going to make money on him." He gave him Ford Dealers of Southern California as a sponsor, and later he brought over Coca-Cola.

Jerry had no way of knowing I had bought into the theory of "if you embrace English, you've got to forget Spanish." I went over big to the other side. My degree is in English literature. I had to go back and almost relearn Spanish. I'd sit there and read the Mexican sports newspapers in front of a mirror. I was awful and took some of the worst assaults from my own people. In Latin America you can't just go on the air like they do here. They give you a license to be an announcer. You've got to know history and geography and have perfect diction and grammar. They were so intolerant of me. But I looked at it as I did my legs when I was growing up in Calexico. My weakness is going to be my strength. I took it on as if it were football all over again. That was my challenge. I was going to work so hard and win them over. I worked at it, and there came a point where I became an example and the poster boy of somebody who came back and dominated in my native language. I set my eyes on management and started working long hours, six days a week. There was this bitter guy, Paco, who was very articulate and worked in the control room. "Why are you here all the time?" he asked me one day. "Why do you work so hard? Do you know they're abusing you and taking advantage of you?" I looked at it as if I were abusing them and taking advantage of them, because I was learning the business.

For two years I even worked seven days a week. I did Spanish-language television Monday through Friday, and I worked at KNBC Saturday and Sunday. It was not fun, but I wanted to prove that you don't have to give up English to speak Spanish, or give up Spanish to speak English. What I'd do was listen to the radio in the language I was going to do, and that way I could get myself thinking in that language. I compared it to the NFL. I was one of the last guys that did both punting and place kicking, which are totally different. It requires a little more concentration, just like switching between languages.

I was learning every aspect of the television business and wasn't going to be outworked. After I left football, I went full-time over at KMEX as a sports director, then became news director. In 1970 we won a Peabody, an award for excellence in radio and television broadcasting. I moved up to station manager, then general manager, then president, and then I became a partner in the network. I used to hearken back to when Paco told me that and I ended up asking myself, "Who's taking advantage of whom?" There was a guy doing the minimum, and he lived and died doing the same thing. He never moved up, and he was always bitter. That was a life lesson for me.

Along the way we bought stations in other cities. We merged New York City, L.A, and San Antonio into a company in Miami, and that became the forerunner of Univision. We called it Spanish International Communications Corporation, or SICC, and the name of the network was Spanish International Network, or SIN. Hallmark bought both of them in 1990 and called it Univision, which was a name that I came up with years before. Univision was the name of a segment we had on a variety show that aired on Sundays, *Siempre en Domingo*—always on Sunday—and it was meant to give the message "unite through television."

Another life lesson that I learned through sports was, whatever you do, you have to do it with passion. I had an offer to go into English-language television. I was told, "In a few years everybody will be speaking English. You're in a dead-end business." But something in my gut told me that I should stay in Spanish and forget English. We had trouble making payroll, and then we borrowed money and had to personally guarantee it. I put my house up. But we had an incredible passion and our gut told us that we were the hope of a community and that we needed to do this and that somehow we would survive. We took on almost a religious fervor in what we did.

We closed the deal with Hallmark in January of 1990 and I decided I would retire. I didn't know what I would do. My son Jim, who was an academic all-American kicker at Harvard, then went to Stanford Business School to get his M.B.A. He wanted to get into private equity and asked me to help him. So I had to put on my helmet again. I had to go into a whole new business, learn a whole new vocabulary, and create a whole new network of friends and associates. It was like starting again from scratch. But that's what he wanted to do. I joined up with a guy who had been working with Mike Milken and we formed Bastion Capital, the first Hispanic fund in the United States. We raised $112 million and started investing it. What's the first investment? Telemundo, which was in Chapter 11. I'm right back in television again. We bought it for three hundred million—we put in thirty million—and later, along with Sony, Liberty, and two Eskimo tribes, sold it to NBC for two billion dollars.

With Fontis we do deals from five to twelve million and have a particular emphasis on companies serving ethnic markets, such as Johnson Products, a hair products company we invested in last year. I will soon retire so I can concentrate more on philanthropic projects. I made a three-million-dollar commitment to New Mexico State that included one million dollars for a new school for early education called Myrna's Children's Village, named after my wife. It's a laboratory school run by the College of Education where we prepare teachers to teach pre-kindergarten kids. We take them from six weeks to five years old. Last September I concluded my scholarship fund for Hispanic students. I promised to raise half a million dollars, and we did that as an endowment so we only give away the interest. And we donated funds to create a club inside the university's Stan Fulton Athletic Center.

This has all become possible because of sports. What sports gave me is another view of the world. It gave me another view of our community and a chance to make a difference. There was an assistant coach in New Mexico who got very mad at me when I was the editor of the newspaper. I wrote in one of my editorials that sports were not an ends in themselves; they're simply a means to an end. He called me an ingrate and was furious with me, because he said sports were everything. They aren't. It's how you use sports and what you do with them. Any success that comes as a result matters. I also say it's not how much capital you can accumulate, but how much you give away that will determine your life. I just hope to leave the way I came in—bare naked.

PART 6

The Doctors and Scientists

DR. JAMES ANDREWS

If you're still talking about what you did yesterday, you're not doing much today. So don't take anything for granted; in other words, don't float on your past laurels! You better be on your A game or you'll fall on your face.

Dr. James Andrews is an orthopedic surgeon. He is a founding member of Andrews Sports Medicine & Orthopaedic Center in Birmingham, Alabama, a founder and the chairman and medical director of the American Sports Medicine Institute in Birmingham, and a founding partner and the medical director of the Andrews Institute in Gulf Breeze, Florida. He graduated from Louisiana State University, where he was Southeastern Conference indoor and outdoor pole-vault champion, and from LSU School of Medicine. He did his residency at Tulane University and has fellowships in sports medicine from the University of Virginia under Dr. Frank McCue and also from the University of Lyon (France) with Professor Albert Trillat.

The Only Results YOU Ever Remember

I WAS BORN IN NEW Orleans when my father, Rheuben Henry, was stationed there during World War II. When he left to go overseas we moved back up to north Louisiana, where we had family. My grandfather and grandmother were big landowners, and my mother, older sister, and I lived with them on a farm. When I was around three years old and my daddy came back from World War II, we moved twelve miles away, to a little town called Homer. It was a typical southern town with a parish seat in Louisiana and a square and stores built around the courthouse. Everything in that town revolved around family life. Social activities were sports at the local high school.

We were really a sports family. I got involved in pole-vaulting early on in my childhood. Don "Tarzan" Bragg was my pole-vaulting hero and the world record holder at that time. We lived on the outskirts of Homer, behind the schoolhouse. Behind my home was nothing but woods, and I spent most of my time playing Tarzan out in the forest, swinging on vines, jumping ditches, and building forts. When I was ten or eleven, I cut a bamboo pole out of a bamboo patch, built a little crossbar in the backyard and started pole-vaulting. When I was about thirteen years old I was an Eagle Scout, and one of my heroes, Bob Richards, came and spoke at my Eagle Scout ceremony. He was the second guy to ever vault fifteen feet, and he had won two Olympic gold medals, in 1952 and 1956, as well as a bronze medal in 1948. He made quite an impression on me, and in high school I won the state championship with a vault of thirteen feet. That vault was my best in high school and was pretty good back in those days.

In addition to pole-vaulting, I played all different sports in high school. We had to, because there weren't that many students. We had a really good football team called the Homer Ironmen. My daddy, who played football at Northwestern State University in Natchitoches and was a real sports nut, was at every practice of mine. He went around the town square, raising money to buy steaks and chicken, and after practice he and my high school principal cooked for us in the school cafeteria and fed us dinner. If he couldn't raise enough money, he'd pay for it himself. Then after dinner he'd take everybody home.

I was a receiver and later the quarterback, and he was the father on the sidelines who carried the chains at the football games. He'd get penalized every game for screaming and hollering. Our school was so small, we only had eighteen men on the football team, and the only time we could scrimmage eleven against eleven was in a game. I even played in the band at halftime. Twelve of the eighteen guys off that Homer Ironmen team ended up playing college football, and five or six of them played for the Louisiana State University Tigers. My first love was football, but I was never big enough to play college football. But at five-feet-eleven, 155 pounds, I was just the right size to be a pole-vaulter, so that's where I found my niche. I earned a scholarship to LSU as a pole-vaulter.

After I went to LSU, my daddy used to drive 250 miles from Homer down to Baton Rouge to watch football practice and to watch me vault. He'd show up for every meet. He was unbelievable. That was his big hobby. Man, he loved sports. He was my main motivating factor. He really wanted to be a coach so he helped me learn how to excel as a vaulter. As you might expect, I could never please my dad. I could win the state championship in pole vault and he'd say, "Why did you miss that last height?" Or if I'd make all A's and one B, he would say, "Well, you should have made all A's." He was always driving me to be the best I could be.

Like a lot of the veterans of World War II, he was a heavy smoker. Toward the end of my sophomore year in college he was diagnosed with lung cancer and died within a few weeks. Before I took my final exam in my sophomore year, I got a call and was told, "We don't think your daddy is going to live through the night." Fortunately, the state troopers came and got me so I could be home to see my daddy before he passed away. After that I decided I'd better get on with my life and education. I applied to medical school my junior year, the same year I became the Southeastern Conference pole-vault champion. I remember being in Birmingham for that event. I didn't even get to the bar on my first attempt at fourteen feet. Then I said, "I've got to make this jump," and on the second attempt, fortunately, I cleared the bar and won the championship. That was exciting. That summer as I was cutting the lawn I found out I was accepted to medical school. I thought, "Well, I got in, I better go." So after three years of college I went to medical school, believe it or not, without graduating, and gave up my last year of pole-vaulting.

The fortunate thing back in those days at LSU was if you were an LSU athlete and were admitted into medical school, you could get a legislative grant and that paid for your medical school. So I got a scholarship to go to medical school for four years, which was unbelievable and fortunate for this small-town country boy.

All the time I was growing up I wanted to be a doctor. I was stimulated because we would spend summers on my grandfather's farm, where I lived until my father came home from overseas. I can almost remember my granddaddy rocking me on the front porch of his home. He prided himself in being the healer in that countryside.

There were no doctors, so he was thought of as the country doctor, even though he didn't have that education. He made salves and ointments and would treat everybody. He "planted a seed" by telling me that I was going to be his little doctor when I grew up. I guess I was going to be a doctor from the word go. Even in high school I never thought of doing anything different. Also, our next-door neighbor was our local small-town family practitioner, Dr. Gladney. With those influences, plus my interest in sports, I wound up in sports medicine.

I still dream about pole-vaulting and getting up and over the bar. It's something that gets in your blood. The best vault I ever did was something like fifteen feet, one inch. Don Bragg had the world record at that time, and it was around fifteen feet, nine inches. Right after that the fiberglass pole was introduced into the sport and the record went sky high. When I look back at that time, I always wonder and perhaps regret giving up athletics, but I think I ultimately made the right decision.

I've learned a lot from by background as an athlete and from athletics in general that has helped me in my sports medicine career. That background gives you a step up in terms of understanding athletes' psychology and knowing how to relate to them, how they respond, what their goals are, and how ultimately to take care of them. I still treat a lot of pole-vaulters from all over the country who come to me, knowing that I was involved in their sport.

Obviously now, my playing field is the operating room. I am challenged every day there. Every patient is different and unique. Every operation is challenging and never routine. And of course I love challenges and competition.

The wins in sports pass through your mind pretty quickly and you're naturally on to the next challenge. But when you lose, it stays with you a long time. When I competed, I used to ask myself: What could I have done better? Did I get enough sleep the night before? Have I trained hard enough? Have I overtrained? And the same thing happens in sports medicine. There's a saying that is founded in competitive sports that says "the only results you ever remember are your bad ones." The same thing holds true in surgery. You can do twenty cases, and those twenty patients can do perfectly well. Then you come to the one patient who's not doing well. Those twenty who have done miraculously well, they're gone from your mind. But the ones who wake you up with what I call my worry list are the ones who aren't doing as well as they should be. And they're the ones who stay on your mind, as you try to figure out what you could have done differently. The same thing goes if you didn't have a good vault, or a good meet, or if you get beat in any sporting competition. For example, I remember my senior year in high school we got beat at the end of the football game by our local rival, Haynesville, the town twelve miles away. That was the big game of the year. It was like the Auburn-Alabama game in high school in north Louisiana. I threw a pass to our halfback and it landed at his feet in the dirt at the goal line. We should have scored to win the game; however, we lost as the buzzer sounded. I still remember that like it was yesterday.

My wife, Jenelle, is now one of my main motivators, and she has a little saying that goes as follows: "If you're still talking about what you did yesterday, you're not doing much today." So don't take anything for granted; in other words, don't float on your past laurels! You better be on your A game or you'll fall on your face. I learned a lot of that philosophy from my mentor Dr. Jack Hughston, whom I trained with in Columbus, Georgia. He was the father of sports medicine in the Southeast and nationally recognized as one of the leaders in the field. I spent a year with him during my residency, and then in 1973 I went back to practice with him for thirteen years, until I came to Birmingham in 1986.

Even though pole-vaulting is an individual sport, working together as a team was probably the most important thing I've ever learned and continue to live by. Teamwork in sports medicine encompasses our nurses, athletic trainers, therapists, fellows, and secretaries. It's a real team effort to take care of patients. In other words, it's certainly not an "I" thing. It's a "we" thing. In sports you learn how to set goals and how to get better and better and better. I wanted to be as good as I could be in orthopedics and be one of the best. It's pretty brazen to say I tried to be the best, but to be one of the best certainly has been my goal.

On a different subject, once I was asked during an interview if I've ever been nervous operating on celebrity patients. I answered, "When I operated on Jack Nicklaus's knee, just as I got ready to start the surgery, all of a sudden I said, 'Oh my God, I hope I've got the right knee. This is Jack Nicklaus!'"

In our family situation, Jenelle and I have six children, all with first names starting with an *A*—Andy, Amy, Archie, Ashley, Amber, and Abby. We now have five wonderful grandchildren. I have always encouraged all of my children's involvement in sports so they would learn the lessons that sports had to offer. Plus it kept them out of trouble, off the street, and busy. Even though sports takes up time, I think kids who are involved in sports work harder in their educational endeavors than kids who are not involved and have a lot of leisure time. To summarize, sports teaches valuable lessons that mold you and drive you to excel. I know for a fact that I wouldn't be where I am today without all the wonderful experiences that sports provided for me.

DR. KEITH L. BLACK

When I was a professor of neurosurgery at UCLA, I was also on the Admissions Committee at UCLA Medical School. When I'm in a position to select a resident, I'm looking for athletic achievers, because I know that, number one, they're disciplined; number two, they know how to be a member of a team. And if they are accomplished in a particular sport, they have the focus and the drive to excel.

Dr. Keith L. Black is chairman of the Department of Neurosurgery, director of the Maxine Dunitz Neurosurgical Institute, and director of the Johnnie L. Cochran, Jr. Brain Tumor Center at Cedars-Sinai Medical Center in Los Angeles, California. He graduated from the University of Michigan with a B.S. in Biomedical Science (with distinction) and a medical degree (with distinction). He was born in Tuskegee, Alabama, and raised in Auburn and Cleveland, Ohio.

Achieving Balance

MY FATHER, ROBERT BLACK, SR., was more focused on having my brother and me concentrate on books than on balls. He always said, "I don't want you to get your B's confused." He was overly worried about African-American boys in particular being exploited in sports. A lot of the conversation at the dinner table was, "They ought to have a book in their hand, not a basketball" and "As much time as they spend bouncing that basketball, if they spent that much time in their books, they'd be a lot further ahead." The conversation was not, "Did you see the Lakers beat the Celtics?" That put sports in perspective for me early on, which was a good thing.

As the high school principal at Boykin, the only black elementary school in Auburn, Alabama, where my mother was also a first-grade teacher, my father was a quiet radical. He was into teaching civil disobedience. Students would go out and protest in front of the mayor's office. He was very active in his underground Biracial Committee, which was made up of both blacks and whites working toward integration in the South at the time. The public swimming pools were segregated, and my father organized a couple of his students to jump into the all-white pool in the summer of 1964. He came home one evening and said, "My sons are not going to just ride the backs of the other students. You need to participate and jump into the all-white pool." I was not quite seven. One hot afternoon in August my father drove my brother, myself, and a couple of friends to the all-white pool. In an act of civil disobedience, we got out in our swim trunks, went through the gates, and jumped in.

It was great being in the water, very refreshing, but we weren't planning on a long afternoon swim. By the time we got through the gates and were in the water they were calling the police. We stayed a few minutes and got out. We made our statement. The police took down our names, but that was essentially it. We didn't get arrested. My father had floated the issue ahead of time to the Biracial Committee and knew it would find its way to the mayor and the chief of police. When no objections came back, he was aware that nothing would happen. He didn't just let his sons go jump into the all-white pool without any preparation. The experience taught me a couple of things. There comes a time when civil disobedience is a necessary form of protest against injustice. And that if you are going to protest, it's best to plan ahead.

We left Alabama and moved to Cleveland when I was ten and in the second half of the fifth grade. The main reason for the move was so that I could attend Shaker Heights High School, which was part of one of the best public school systems in the country. My brother attended a private boarding school in the North. There was still a lot of racism in the North but it was more covert. When we moved to Cleveland we had trouble renting a house in a predominantly white area because of the racial divide line. My parents ultimately had to get a white couple to pose as us so that we could get the house rented to us.

I patterned myself after my brother Robert, who is eight years older and played basketball and football. In junior high I played wide receiver on the football team and forward on the basketball team.

However, I tended to enjoy the water a lot more. Football is a contact sport, and a couple of pretty hard hits made me think about whether I wanted to continue. I stopped both sports in tenth grade and switched to swimming. I could naturally swim the backstroke very fast. I went out for the swim team at Shaker Heights High School to make a statement and to break racial barriers. The school was about seventy-five to eighty percent white at the time, and I was the only black student on the swim team. No one expected a black student to go out for swimming. Everyone held the stereotype that if you're black you're going to sink, your body isn't built for swimming. I swam all the way through my senior year and never encountered any overt racism. It was more that I was an oddity: *Look at the black kid. Can he really swim?* I always wanted to prove them wrong.

I would have to get up at five o'clock in the morning to swim for an hour before class five days a week. It was snowing and dark. Then I swam for another hour or two in the evening. It took discipline, but I wasn't thinking about that. I was just taking one stroke after another and getting the job done. Sometimes in life that's what you have to do. Putting in the work is key. The interesting thing about swimming is that you're sort of in your own little bubble in the swimming pool. It allowed me to focus and meditate and be methodical in building up my endurance and trying to shave another second off my time here and there. And, unlike football or basketball, you don't get a lot of glory in swimming. You learn to put in the work and time without expecting a lot of accolades in return. Not a lot of the student body turned out to the swim meets to cheer for your victories. I'd feel more of an internal victory than one that I could share with the rest of the school, where my friends and classmates might say, "Oh that was a great race yesterday."

When I was doing athletics I was able to think better, focus better, and get the rest of my work done better. I was living off those endorphins. Coming out of high school, I was accepted into Harvard and Stanford undergrad, which was great. But I was also accepted into a special accelerated program at the University of Michigan where you got admitted into both the medical school and the undergraduate school at the same time, and earned your M.D. in six years out of high school instead of the usual eight—four years of undergrad and four years of medical school. I was ecstatic. It was a dream come true to get into that program. It was a special program where I could treat patients after the first year of the program and take medical school classes, gross anatomy, and physiology in the second semester of the second year—who could beat that? My first brain operation on a brain tumor patient was in my second year of residency. It felt so natural, as if I belonged in that space at that time.

Once I was in my neurosurgical residency, I constantly drew upon my experiences from sports. Athletics prepared me for the physical demands of my studies: getting up at four o'clock in the morning, working late into the night, the studying constantly, and attending to patients. In a sense you have to be athletic but also keep your mind sharp and focused at the same time, which is what a good athlete does. The great athlete has to have a view of a court and a keen perception of the game that's in play. There's a lot of mental focus that goes into being a champion.

I'm chairman of the neurosurgery program at Cedars-Sinai Medical Center, and we select residents. When I was a professor of neurosurgery at UCLA, I was also on the Admissions Committee at UCLA Medical School. When I'm in a position to select a resident, I'm looking for athletic achievers because I know that, number one, they're disciplined; number two, they know how to be a member of a team. And if they are accomplished in a particular sport, they have the focus and the drive to excel. Those are very positive traits. Now, for someone looking at a field like neurosurgery, unless they've achieved in some area other than just their academic work, they will not be viewed in a highly positive light. We want to see the star athlete, the one that has excelled in some other area besides just academics.

I view myself now more as a coach than an athlete, but the same analogies apply. How do you get a group of ten neurosurgeons, all of whom are superstars in their own right, to work together as a team in order to make the Neurosurgical Institute better overall, versus them working toward their individual glory? How to give and take, and how to play support roles and key roles and push science and the clinical care forward?

My demeanor is pretty much the same in the hospital as it is in a competitive sports environment. I don't like to gloat, and I'm not loud when I win because I realize that you can lose the next game. I keep it fairly even and am more meditative. I tend to keep my emotions somewhat even when I lose in sports, and it's the same in medicine. I don't know of any doctor who is going to be able to keep every one of his patients alive, because all of your patients ultimately die. You can feel good for a short time about your victories when someone comes in with a brain tumor and you take it out and return to them their ability to walk, see, and speak. But you have to mitigate the way you feel when you lose as well; otherwise it's hard to keep going forward.

I encouraged my children to participate in sports so that they'll understand winning and losing and learn to be members of a team. To some extent I preached "Don't confuse your B's" like my father, but I felt my father grew up in a different generation and sort of went to the extreme. The obstacles and hurdles for his generation were so high that just to get on base was a huge achievement for them. He was first-generation college. My mother was the only one of her siblings who went to college. My parents were focused on making sure that their kids could succeed academically. In my generation we have a more multidimensional and broader perspective. It goes back to the Greeks, to the classical ideal of a strong body is a strong mind. Particularly with so many distractions for young people now, it's important for them to view their body as their temple, and I think athletes tend to do that more than nonathletes. Athletic students are much less likely to be into drugs and do things that are harmful to their body. It creates a better-rounded, healthier individual.

My daughter, Teal, who is twenty-two, is a very natural swimmer as well. She was very strong in the backstroke and freestyle and still holds two records at Marlborough School in Los Angeles. My son, Keith, was involved in a lot of club basketball early on. I watched the coaches say, particularly to African-American boy, "Basketball is your ticket out," which reminded me of my father's words. As my son was growing up, even though both of his parents were physicians and he grew up in Bel-Air, he, like ninety-five percent of the African-American boys that have any kind of athletic ability at all, felt he was going to be an NBA star. He was going to play basketball in college and then go on to the NBA. His dream was to be the next Kobe Bryant or LeBron James. And why not? He looked at his dad, who's working all of the time, and thought, "Yeah, he's a brain surgeon, but he doesn't get the same accolades as Kobe Bryant." In that scenario, do you want to be your dad or do you want to be Kobe Bryant? For a twelve-year-old kid it's a no-brainer. I would rather be Kobe, too, if I could. He has a lot of money and a lot of fame. The Kobes of the world get to play basketball. They're not stressing, trying to save somebody's life on the operating table. If they lose the game, nobody dies. But my approach as a father was, "Son, that's great. That's wonderful. Do the athletics." We got him outside basketball coaches to help him with his shot and ball-handling skills, but at the same time we stressed academics. That took a lot of parental courage. He eventually came around and thought, "Well, maybe I'm not going to be the next LeBron James, and even if I play in college, I don't have what it takes to go to the NBA. Gee, I better start getting my grades together and get into a good college."

Like everything in life, it's optimal to have a balance. You have a strong body, a strong mind. If you achieve a balance between athletics and academics, that's the best of all worlds because in society now there's not just one way to the top. The principles of success in life are very similar in both academics and sports. When you become too focused on one or the other, you lose your edge. You don't want that person who spends their whole life in books and with no athletics on your business team, nor do you want someone who doesn't get the academics done, someone who thinks they're going to be the next LeBron James. They may be, but that's quite a long shot. You have higher odds of being a brain surgeon.

LELAND MELVIN

Coach Shealy used to come into my hotel room the night before [a game] . . . and say, "Leland, close your eyes. You're lined up on the thirty-yard line. You're running a post corner into the end zone. . . ." Once I got on the field, I had already done it. Actually, visualizing a particular move was a really important part of my preparation for the game. I did the same thing when I operated a fifty-eight-foot robotic arm on space shuttle Atlantis. We practiced repeatedly on the ground and thought about it so much, that when it came time to do the actual installation of the Columbus module at the International Space Station, I had already done it; it felt like second nature.

Leland Melvin is a NASA astronaut. He completed his first spaceflight in 2008 and his second in 2009. He received a Bachelor of Science degree in chemistry from the University of Richmond, where he was named an NCAA Division I Academic All-American and still holds school records in career receiving yards and career receptions. He was drafted by the Detroit Lions in the 1986 NFL college draft. After his football career, he earned a Master of Science degree in materials science engineering from the University of Virginia. The Virginia native was born and raised in Lynchburg.

The Power of Visualization

I STARTED PLAYING SPORTS WHEN I was in the fourth grade. My father, Deems Melvin, was my coach, but even before that, he was teaching me to throw a football, a baseball, and shoot a basketball. He's retired now, after teaching language arts in middle school for more than thirty years. Both my parents exposed me to everything, whether it was the arts, academics, or athletics. I have very fond memories of my father's baseball games on Sunday afternoons; the weekly outings were a family affair. We would have a picnic lunch and watch my dad play ball, while my mom tried to keep my older sister and me out of trouble. That tradition continued, and when I went to college my parents and sister would come to all of my games to cheer me on, again, a family affair. Teamwork, perseverance, dedication, and hard work were qualities instilled in me by both of my parents, but especially my father. I saw all of those traits in him, when he played ball, so he was a good example, a great role model, and a wonderful mentor. Many athletes say, "I'm not a role model," but everyone *is* a role model. It's just whether you're a good one or a bad one, because children are always watching you. You're modeling behavior whether you mean to or not. From the very first pass I caught, my dad was there, instilling in me the right thing. In writing my essay to become an astronaut, I reflected on what my dad taught me over the years. Those reflections resulted in a phrase that I used on my application: "Work hard, have fun, and share the ball. There's plenty of glory to go around if you share." Those early lessons had a great impact on me.

At Heritage High School, I played on the football, basketball, and tennis teams. I was a subdued and quiet kid, who usually motivated my teammates by example. I wasn't a head-butter or cheerleader, but matter-of-factly said, "Hey, it's time to perform. It's time for us to do our jobs as team members."

A huge turning point occurred during my senior year of high school. I played both wide receiver and defensive back. At the time I didn't know it, but a recruiter from the University of Richmond was in the stands when I dropped a perfectly thrown touchdown pass at Lynchburg City Stadium. Fortunately, my coach, Jimmy Green, believed in me and called the same play on the next down.

The second time around I was praying the ball into my hands and caught it. But the recruiter, Morgan Hout, was walking out of the stadium. He heard the crowd screaming, turned around, looked back, and saw me in the end zone. If my coach had not called the same play, I wouldn't have gone to the University of Richmond on a football scholarship. This is a case in which he truly believed in me, even though I had horrifically failed and dropped a touchdown pass, in my hands, in the end zone. That kind of belief in a player means a lot to me, and I still remember it to this day. It was a good lesson. When you have tough times and when things don't work out, you always have to believe in yourself, because other people haven't given up on you. When I signed the letter of intent at the University of Richmond, Hout told me he left the stadium after I dropped the pass and quickly returned to see why the crowd was cheering. He was amazed to see me in the end zone with the winning touchdown. He said, "Maybe this guy can play for the university after all."

I never thought about playing college football, so everything I gained from the experience was a bonus. My freshman year in college we were zero and ten, so the last thing I had was visions of playing in the NFL. But things got better at Richmond, and we ended up going to the playoffs my junior and senior years. That gave me exposure to the NFL scouts, and in the eleventh round of the NFL draft in the spring of 1986, I received a phone call from the Lions notifying me that I had been drafted. There was silence and initial disbelief on my end of the phone. Yet still, I was raring to go. When I speak to students, I tell them, when you get the call it's imperative to be ready, so make sure that you've done everything in your power to be prepared. "Thoroughly prepared; academically, physically, mentally, emotionally, and even spiritually." When asked to perform, whether it's flying the space shuttle or assuming the starting position on the team, *you are ready!*

I had done everything to be ready. Two weeks into training camp with the Lions, I pulled a hamstring—a really bad pull. I played in three preseason games, caught a few passes, and then they cut me on the final cut. In twenty-twenty hindsight, I probably should have let my hamstring heal more before trying to get back on the field. I went from the Lions to the Toronto Argonauts in the Canadian Football League. I had a practice contract with Toronto but my agent called me and said, "Dallas wants to try you out for the next season." I signed as a free agent with the Cowboys. Two months before going to the Cowboys' mini-camp in January of 1987, I started working on my Master's degree in engineering. When the Cowboys cut me from the training camp, I went back to the University of Virginia full-time in the fall of 1987 to complete my graduate degree. Initially, I was disappointed it didn't work out with the NFL, but the fallback plan was to work as a materials science engineer. It was somewhat of a seamless transition from the NFL to an engineering job with NASA, because I had already set the groundwork by enrolling in grad school. I had something else that I could do that was just as exciting. Things happen for a reason, and now I'm flying in space.

The biggest lesson I learned from sports is to not give up. That goes back to that dropped touchdown pass my senior year in high school. That lesson continued on in my freshman year in college when we went 0–10. Some guys quit the team. People thought that we could not turn it around, but we did. It's crucial to realize that there will be some failures in your life. The space shuttle *Columbia* accident in 2003, for example, was a huge setback to the space program, and a lot of people lost faith. People asked, "Are we doing the right thing? Can we recover from this?" And we did. Having that "can-do" spirit and believing in yourself, even in the darkest and worst of times, is something that we as a civilization have called upon to overcome adversity. The lesson from my early experiences was to look forward.

Dal Shealy, my coach at Richmond, helped keep us motivated. He was a strong man of faith and said, "You got to keep at it. You got to keep at it." He came to my space shuttle *Atlantis* launch at Kennedy Space Center in 2008, as did a number of the guys from the football team. We stay connected and are supportive of each other in all different capacities of our lives.

My background in sports is invaluable to me as an astronaut. Before my college games on Saturdays, Coach Shealy used to come into my hotel room the night before. He would sit at the foot of the bed and say, "Leland, close your eyes. You're lined up on the thirty-yard line. You're running a post corner into the end zone. You are accelerating past the defender. You're now looking at the ball. The ball is coming into your hands. You tune out the crowd. You're now in the end zone. You caught the ball. You've won the game." Sleeping on that visual helped get me ready. Once I got on the field I had already done it. Actually, visualizing a particular move was a really important part of preparation for the game. I did the same thing when I operated a fifty-eight-foot robotic arm on space shuttle *Atlantis*. We practiced repeatedly on the ground and thought about it so much, that when it came time to do the actual installation of the *Columbus* research lab at the International Space Station (ISS), I had already done it; it felt like second nature. During that installation, ISS Commander Peggy Whitson, who was also an athlete in college, was standing right behind me. I had never flown the ISS robotic arm before, and she was there watching supportively. She was mostly silent. As commander she was responsible for every aspect of this multibillion-dollar international outpost, and one aberrant move by me could jeopardize the vehicle, or even our lives. When the lab was installed, she said, "Great job," and gave just a pat on the shoulder. It's that kind of leadership that lets someone work until they need help instead of jumping in and trying to show them how to do it before the task is done.

Having a background in sports helps whenever you face pressure-filled situations. Say, it's fourth-and-long and there are two minutes left, and you have to go ninety yards to make a touchdown. If you've done it successfully in practice, you have a feeling that you and your teammates can overcome this tough situation. Similar things happen in orbit when you're supporting a space walk. Space walkers only have so much oxygen in their suits, so the space walk has a very finite amount of time. So as a robotics operator supporting the space walker, I must be efficient to ensure timely execution to complete the tasks. Just like on the football with two minutes to go.

Athletic training, spaceflight, it's all the same. It's all about preparing yourself to be successful by visualizing the steps it takes to get there. We visualized getting to the moon, next maybe Mars, and beyond.

DR. ALFREDO
QUIÑONES-HINOJOSA

When the pressure is on, you've got to keep your composure. And I apply that to what I do today in brain surgery. Sometimes things don't go well and all you hear are the anesthesia machines beeping, or someone telling you "one minute" if you have a patient under and you are stopping their blood to the brain. . . . Time is ticking, and that pressure—having to be alone and not knowing what's going to happen—can be nerve-racking. But if you've played sports, you know about that pressure and can deal with those moments.

Dr. Alfredo Quiñones-Hinojosa is an associate professor of neurosurgery and oncology, neuroscience, and cellular and molecular medicine at the Johns Hopkins School of Medicine in Baltimore, Maryland. He serves as the director of the Brain Tumor Surgery Program at the Johns Hopkins Bayview Campus. He received his medical degree from Harvard University, where he graduated cum laude.

Maintaining Enthusiasm

I GREW UP IN A farming community outside of Mexicali, Mexico, near the border with the United States. When I was about fourteen years old I began to go to school to become an elementary school teacher. Back then, if you took a special exam and you got straight A's, you could take a national exam in order to attend a special school to become an elementary school teacher. I was just like any other kid, full of energy and mischief. I was blessed with a decent mind, and that's about it. I was younger than many of the other students by at least two years. I also developed a little bit later in life. Fortunately, or unfortunately, I was also usually the teacher's pet, and they all trusted me. I used to grade physics exams for one of the teachers. Some of the kids knew this and didn't like me. They picked on me and tried to get into fights. One day this kid picked a fight with me. I didn't want to fight him and ended up having to try to defend myself. I realized how inadequate I was in doing so and took up boxing.

When I first started, I wanted to learn how to defend myself. But I soon realized that this was a discipline that was going to teach me a lot of life lessons. I trained for a year and then I had a few very small, amateur fights in Mexicali. I was seventeen and the first two fights they put me against a fifteen-year-old and then an eighteen-year-old. Both opponents were out of shape and not very good. I sort of moved around them. As I won those first two fights, I thought to myself, "I'm the man. I'm ready to rock and roll." My trainer was trying to build my confidence and once she felt I was getting a little too cocky, she put me against someone good. Talk about learning a lesson. Never, never underestimate your opponent. It's better if people underestimate you, and you overestimate your opponent.

In the last fight that I had, I underestimated my opponent, who was good, and for the first two rounds he was wiping the floor with me. He was dancing around me, but I kept coming after him. Every time I came up to him, he kept landing jabs and uppercuts. In the last round he put me down on my knees. The guy is pounding and the trainer said, "Don't worry. Just don't get up." I had a choice of either staying down and not doing anything or getting up and finishing the round. I don't know what got into me. I got up and went back at it. This time I was jabbing more than just going after the guy with my guard open. I kept getting beaten, but I didn't give up and finished the fight. That was a decision that I made in a split second and it is a lesson that I've carried throughout my life; never give up and finish with all your heart. It doesn't matter how good or bad you are. What matters is the passion that you have for what you do and the dedication.

As a kid, once I realized I had gotten what I needed out of the boxing, which was the discipline, the ability to work hard, the concentration, and learning how to move around the ring, I never wanted to pick a fight anymore, and when the kids picked fights with me it never bothered me like it did before. I learned that bullying is a period that a lot of kids go through. At peace with that, I began to assist other kids who were really in trouble in school by helping them do better on tests.

It's the little lessons that you learn through life that have a great impact and translate into everything else you do subsequently. I was a kid, going on nineteen, when I hopped the fence at the border to come to the United States. I got caught and was sent back to Mexico. I had to make a decision. I can either hop the fence again or give up. What do I do? I hopped the fence again, the same day. It was like in boxing. Even though I went back and took a beating, I changed my tactic and put up a fight. I knew what I needed to do to succeed. That was a lesson learned. It's not like I wanted to leave my country. We had a wonderful life. Yes, we were poor, but we had an extended family. We didn't have anything to eat at times, and I saw what poverty does. I, like a lot of poor and uneducated people, had a dream that I was going to come to the United States, make a lot of money, and go back to my country. I never saw myself being where I am today as a brain surgeon. I'm an actor in this play. The script has been given to me at every turn I take.

When I arrived in the United States, I worked the fields as a farmworker in California's San Joaquin Valley. There was a lot of uncertainty and a lot of pain. I couldn't speak the language. Imagine what it's like to work at a place where you don't have a voice, you're almost invisible. Because you don't speak the language, you sometimes get treated like less than a human being. My hands were bloodied with pulling weeds. But things that might have bothered other people, I saw as challenges. I turned that negative energy into a positive energy and said, "I can't pull weeds for the rest of my life. I better teach myself how to drive tractors on the farm." Within a year I was doing that.

I saw everything as an opportunity to learn and to challenge myself. It's the same principle today with brain cancer. I know people say, "There's no possible way that you're going to find a cure for brain cancer," and I say, "I'll give it my best." Muhammad Ali was one of my heroes, and I remember how he was the underdog to George Foreman in 1974. He worked his magic and tenacity, used his brain, and turned everything around. I remember when Michael Jordan did the same against Utah in the 1997 NBA Finals. He was sick with stomach flu. His eyes were sunken. Everybody said there's no possible way he could be effective. He came back and the Chicago Bulls won that game and the series. That defines success; not giving up, and finding that fight, that fire in your belly. I did that in the field. Sure, it was hard. But it made me who I am today.

I made three dollars and thirty-five cents an hour working in the fields seven days a week and saved seven thousand dollars. I used to eat the corn from the fields, along with cantaloupes and watermelon. I spent probably a dollar buying a burrito from the burrito lady and then sometimes I wouldn't even catch her because I'd be in the middle of the field, driving a big cotton picker. I wore the same pair of jeans for a whole year, and I paid three hundred dollars for a trailer that had holes in the roof. I worked in the Valley for fourteen or fifteen months, then went to Stockton and shoveled sulfur. My next job was cleaning railroad tanks that carried fish oil. I began to learn how to weld and within a year I ascended the ladder and became a foreman on one of the night shifts. I enrolled in morning classes to learn English at San Joaquin Delta College, a community college in Stockton, where a couple of professors took me under their wings. They saw something in me and asked me where I was going to go to college. I didn't know the difference between a two-year and a four-year college because I didn't know the American system. I said, "Wait a minute, is there something beyond this?" I ended up at the University of California, Berkeley, by 1991, then went to Harvard Medical School.

I'm not a genius, but perhaps I do have something that may be a little bit of a distinguished characteristic, and it goes back to the lesson of boxing. When most people are down, they stay down, because it's tough to go back and take another beating. I don't do that. If I am down, I get up. I don't care if I'm going to get beaten again. I get back and take some more. And I keep going back until I succeed. Success, as Winston Churchill once said, is going from failure to failure with no loss of enthusiasm. I feel very strongly about that, and it applies to everything I do.

Every Friday I go into the operating room and usually operate on two very large brain tumors. Each operation is about six hours long, so there's about twelve hours in the operating room and a high level of stress. I have had patients that have not done well. They're comatose. They're not waking up. They're struggling for their life. That evening, I have a big meeting with my laboratory. I have about thirty scientists working under me. I support their salaries and their endeavors. And I have to make a decision. Should I just call it quits today and tell the lab, "I'm sorry, we're not going to have a lab meeting today because I'm really beaten, I'm tired, I just can't handle it"? Or should I get up and go do it. In every single one of those occasions I go back to that moment when I was down on my knees in the boxing ring and made the decision not to give up and come back and fight. I say, "Let's rock and roll." I go to my lab meeting, often around seven-thirty, and I have dinner with my lab together as we have our meeting. We leave around eleven p.m., after which I go back to the hospital and see my patients. I make it home between midnight and one a.m., but I'm reinvigorated because I can look back and know I left it all behind. It's the same deal as in sports.

When I was boxing, I trained by running three to five miles a day. Running allowed me to think and relax. I used to go for long endurance runs alone in the middle of nowhere, outside of Mexicali. There's no one there to push you other than yourself. I ran for my school track team and competed in local races. I ran a ten-kilometer race in Mexicali when I was seventeen. Half of the race was in Mexicali and half was in the United States. There were thousands of competitors. I came in ninety-nine. As I was running, I didn't know how good the person ahead of me was or how good the person behind me was, but I could hear the person behind me literally breathing down my neck. That was the biggest challenge; when the pressure is on, you've got to keep your composure. And I apply that to what I do today in brain surgery. Sometimes things don't go well and all you hear are the anesthesia machines beeping, or someone telling you "one minute" if you have a patient under and you are stopping their blood to the brain. Time is ticking, and that pressure—having to be alone and not knowing what's going to happen—can be nerve-racking. But if you've played sports, you know about that pressure and can deal with those moments.

I didn't play very much sports because I always had to work and help my family work. But my wife, who swam competitively at the University of the Pacific, and I feel very strongly that we want our children, who swim, play soccer and baseball, to know that sports is not about winning. When they come out of the swimming pool, I want to see them breathing hard. I want to see that determination on their face, and I want them to look back on the lane where they were swimming and make sure that they left it all behind. That was the same thing I did in boxing, and what I do in my life, in the operating room, whether my patient is alive or not doing well, as things happen sometimes. I always look back and say, "I left it all in there in the operating room, my passion, all my energy, my knowledge was right there to take care of this patient." It's no different in sports. You never want to look back and regret.

When I was at Harvard in 1997 and about to take my citizenship oath—I took advantage of President Ronald Reagan's 1986 amnesty—the speaker, a very wealthy person, talked about the story of four generations of immigrants who came from Italy. He came from a family of poor people who slowly but steadily began to climb the ladder until he went to Harvard Business School and became a very successful businessperson. His father was a teacher, his grandfather a policeman, and his great grandfather a baker. I sat there and thought, "Holy guacamole! Ten years ago I was working in the fields. I just hopped the fence as an illegal immigrant. I bypassed all these generations and I'm sitting here at Harvard Medical School." I was a migrant farm worker, and it is interesting that what appeared to have been a bad situation ended up being a blessing for me. It hits me from time to time, but I try not to think too much about that because I still believe that I have a lot to do and haven't done anything. I like to keep it that way because, once again, the moment that you overestimate yourself and you underestimate your opponent is when you fail. It's the lesson from sports.

PART 7

The Former Politicians

BILL CLINTON

Golf is also a lot like life. You get breaks you don't deserve, both ways. You have to learn to make the most of the good breaks and shake off the bad ones.

Bill Clinton is the forty-second president of the United States and served from 1993 to 2001. He also served as governor of Arkansas and as Arkansas's attorney general. He graduated from Georgetown University and in 1968 won a Rhodes scholarship to Oxford University. He received a law degree from Yale University. He was born in Hope, Arkansas, and raised in Hot Springs, Arkansas.

The Fairest of All Games

I'VE ALWAYS BEEN A SPORTS nut, though not much of an athlete. My biggest achievement was getting on the cover of *Sports Illustrated* holding a basketball, to celebrate Arkansas' 1994 NCAA Championship run. I have been a fanatic football fan from the time I was old enough to know what was going on. Growing up in Hot Springs, Arkansas, we were always playing some kind of sports, mostly softball, basketball, and football. Because I was in the band, I couldn't play football in school. That was something I always regretted, but I liked music a lot, and by the time I got to high school, a rule was passed stating that if you were in the band you couldn't play football, basketball, or any other varsity sport, because my school was thought to have too many kids in too many different kinds of activities. I did play on a church league basketball team in high school, but besides that, I never played competitive team sports until I went off to England to study.

At Oxford, the university is organized into separate colleges, all of which have their own sports teams. I was interested in rugby, but I had never played before, so I couldn't have made the university team.

I did get to play one season for my college team, probably because I was the biggest guy on my squad. Interestingly enough, I also got recruited to play on the university-wide second basketball team, just because I was over six feet tall, knew the rules, and could get up and down the court. That's how undeveloped the sport was then. Today European basketball is much more advanced.

I never did master the rules and subtleties of rugby, but I just loved it. I'll never forget the first time I scored—it's called a "try" in rugby. There were people hanging all over me. I had no skill but I was big. Back then there were no substitutes, so if you got hurt and you had to leave the game, your team played with one fewer person. So you tried to stay in. When we played one of the colleges at Cambridge, I got kicked in the head. Really dizzy, I went over to the sidelines and asked the coach what I should do. He said, "Get back in there. You're the biggest guy on the squad." I said, "But what do I do? I'm dizzy." He said, "Just get in somebody's way." So I went out and got in somebody's way.

In all competition, whether in athletics, music, academics, or student politics, I followed one rule: Never quit. Even if you know you're going to get beat, play the game as hard as you can until it's over. My mother drilled that lesson into me, and it has stood me in good stead. I've pulled a lot of victories from the jaws of defeat just because I never quit. And I've found defeat easier to live with and learn from if you give it your all. I couldn't have been prouder of Hillary for seeing her presidential campaign through to the end, and winning the last three months of the campaign after losing badly in February's caucus contests. Her parents and her involvement in sports also ingrained the "never quit" ethos into her. It's an important lesson to teach young people.

Athletics prepares people for life. Venus is one of the greatest tennis players ever, but she doesn't win every match. You can't win every time. But you can play hard every time. When you play a tennis match, if you lose, there's another one next week. Even if the whole season is over and you don't win a Grand Slam tournament, you get to play next year. Political defeats last longer. In politics, if you lose, you have to wait two or four years to run again. Some people have to wait ten to get another chance. But if they don't give up on their dreams and they keep playing, even if they don't achieve exactly what they set out to do, they wind up in a better place than they would have if they hadn't tried at all.

When I was twelve, my uncle gave me an old set of golf clubs, and I started playing on a local course. I never had any lessons, but I played whenever I could until I was sixteen. After I met Hillary, I starting playing again with her brothers, and have been hacking away ever since. One reason I like golf is because the ball stands still. It's also the fairest of all games in a way because of the handicap system—as long as you tell the truth about your handicap. If I play against a six-handicap and I play at a fourteen, that person gives me a stroke on each of the eight hardest holes. Golf is also a lot like life. You get breaks you don't deserve, both ways. You have to learn to make the most of the good breaks and shake off the bad ones. You play by PGA rules, unless all the competitors agree to a modification. Often you end up having to call a penalty on yourself. I like that, too.

I'm not a very good golfer, but I love to play. My lowest handicap was a ten, the first year I got out of the White House. After that, it rose again because I started traveling so much, stopped and wrote *My Life*, then had my heart surgery, then went back to work as soon as I could. I'm probably a fourteen or fifteen now, and I'll probably never get to single digits. But I still enjoy the competition and I almost always try to win. One exception was when I golfed with President [George H. W.] Bush, President Ford, Bob Hope, and Scott Hoch, who is now on the Senior Tour, at the 1995 Bob Hope Chrysler Classic. I flew to California from the White House, arriving late and getting very little sleep. The next day, I played poorly but I was having such a good time, I didn't care. I was just happy being out there.

At least I finished the round without hitting any spectators with my wild shots.

None of the presidents had a very good round that day; Hoch had the best shots from tee to green I'd seen in years, but he couldn't make a putt. By contrast, Hope was amazing. Already in his nineties, he still had a long, fluid swing, and he sang the whole time. Two years later he came to Washington, called me, and said he wanted to play golf. So I took him to the old Army-Navy course for nine holes. Because he couldn't see five feet in front of him, he had a young aide help line up his putts. He parred an uphill par-three hole that wasn't easy, missing my twenty-foot birdie putt by just a few inches. At the time of our last golf outing, Hope was ninety-five years old.

I got to know and like Gerry Ford in the last few years of his life. He was an avid golfer, and we shared two great golf days together with Jack Nicklaus in Vail, Colorado. I outdrove Nicklaus only once, by a yard. It was one of the happiest moments of my golfing life. We were playing a par-5 hole, which we both reached in two. I was just eight feet from the cup with a genuine shot at an eagle. When I missed the putt badly, Nicklaus smiled and said, "You didn't think you were worthy of an eagle. You need to get over that." Then President Ford chimed in, "Or you can just wait a few years, and an eagle won't be an option anymore."

Since I left the White House, I've played a lot of golf with President Bush, usually near his home in Maine in the summer. Often sportscaster Jim Nantz and New England Patriots quarterback Tom Brady join us. It's no contest—Nantz is good and Brady is a terrific golfer. Even with my handicap, I've never beaten him. One problem is that when you're not in the White House anymore, they don't give you as many short putts. At least George didn't get them either, though he's such a good man, I couldn't have complained if he had.

When I was in the White House, sports often helped me connect with citizens. Gang violence had been a concern of mine since the early '80s, and there was a lot of it in Los Angeles in 1993 when I went there with Ron Brown, the Secretary of Commerce who was also the first African-American chairman of the Democratic Party. We had read about a sporting goods store owner who had built a basketball court in the lot behind his store for neighborhood kids, to keep them off the streets and out of trouble. To show our support, Ron and I went to the store and joined a game, on opposite sides. The kids were laughing at us because we arrived in our suits. We took off our suit coats, pulled our shirts out, removed our ties, and got after it.

Ron was one of my closest friends and favorite golf partners. He was also a pretty good basketball player. We were really trying to beat each other. The kids thought it was very funny that these two middle-aged guys were trying to kill each other on the basketball court in street shoes and suit pants. At least we knew enough to rely on our teammates, always trying to pass the ball to a kid who could score. Of course, our main purpose was to let the kids know we cared about them and identified with them. I also wanted to get as much publicity as possible for the man who ran the store and the young people who were supporting him so that more kids would come to play and more adults would support those kinds of activities. However, once we started playing basketball, I sort of forgot the social message; I was trying to win the game. I don't remember if I did.

Through 1995, I was also an avid jogger. I started when I was about twenty, and Hillary got me into a daily routine when we started dating in 1971. For twenty-four years, I ran twenty miles a week. It made me sunnier, happier, and more clear-headed. When I was in law school at Yale, I had a total of six different jobs when I was working my way through law school, sometimes as many as three part-time jobs at once. I didn't get a lot of sleep, but I found that if I made my daily run, I needed less sleep. One of the most memorable runs in my life occurred at five in the morning on June 25, 1967—forty-three years later, I still remember the date. The night before I had gone to a Ray Charles concert in Washington's Constitution Hall. I loved Ray Charles; he gave a terrific performance and I was revved up. I literally couldn't go to sleep. So at five in the morning, I put on my running shoes and went out and ran three miles. Afterward, I finally fell asleep.

The first summer I came home to Arkansas, in June 1973, I ran every afternoon. It was a really hot summer, and I loved to run in the heat. I was young and could do it then. The pounds just fell off of me. I weighed 185 pounds for the first (and last) time since I was thirteen.

In 1995 a man came from Colorado to Washington on a mission. Standing on Pennsylvania Avenue, he pulled out an assault weapon and opened fire on the White House. There was a white-haired guy who looked sort of like me walking in the front door at the time. Thankfully neither he nor anyone else was hit. The shooter was mad at me, saying I had taken his Constitutional rights away by banning assault weapons (I think his behavior validated my position). Afterward, the Secret Service came to me and said, "We can put fifty people on you, but if you keep running on the Mall, we can't guard you." From then on, I had to drive to Fort McNair or Haines Point to run, which I continued to do with some frequency for a couple more years. Finally, it just petered out, and I wound up working more in the gym, especially after I tore my quadriceps muscle when I fell off Greg Norman's step in 1997.

I started running again after I left the White House. That's when I should have known I had heart blockage. No matter how hard I worked or how much weight I lost, I had to stop every three-quarters of a mile or so and walk a hundred yards to catch my breath. Since then, my jogging has been mostly on the treadmill. I take vigorous walks in Westchester County where I live, do light weights, and a lot of stretch and balance work. Once you get older, keeping your balance and flexibility is really important, particularly in New York, where we have pretty harsh winters, and you can slip on the ice. I miss the long runs. I've always wanted to run at least one marathon in my life; maybe I still will.

After I had my heart problems, I wanted to do something to help other people avoid them. In 2005 my foundation and the American Heart Association created the Alliance for a Healthier Generation, designed to combat the wave of childhood obesity we're facing. It's the biggest public health problem in America today. Kids are consuming too many calories and not exercising enough. I have done a lot of work to change the food and beverage practices in school vending machines and cafeterias, and to increase health insurance coverage for overweight kids to see doctors and dietitians. I've also worked with Rachael Ray to help parents who don't have a lot of money or time figure out how to feed their kids better. One of the things that makes it very hard is that so many of our schools around the country have stopped their physical-education programs, for budgetary reasons. I think that's a huge mistake. Every Boys' and Girls' Club tennis program, every First Tee program for golf, every community soccer program—all these things are more important than ever, not only because of the lessons you learn through athletics but because we've got to save our kids from the consequences of obesity—including diabetes, heart attacks, and strokes. There's some evidence that we have at least stopped the rise in childhood obesity, but we've got a long way to go to reverse it and give all our kids a healthy future. I don't want to see any kids either die or become incapacitated before they have a chance to do what I did: live their dreams. I'm convinced sports help people learn how to live their dreams, beginning with lesson one—never quit.

WILLIAM S. COHEN

The mental toughness I acquired through the course of my sports career certainly helped me in the practice of law, where you have to be very disciplined in terms of mentally preparing to go into combat with the opposing counsel, and frequently with the court itself, the judge. It just comes back to tough discipline, determination, competitive desire. Understand you're going to lose some cases, you're going to lose some basketball games, but the desire to continue to go out there and compete is what drives you.

William S. Cohen served as U.S. Secretary of Defense from 1997 to 2001 under President Bill Clinton. Before that he spent eighteen years as a U.S. senator, and six years as a congressman before that. An author, he is now chairman and CEO of The Cohen Group. He graduated cum laude with a major in Latin from Bowdoin College and cum laude from the Boston University School of Law. He was born and raised in Bangor, Maine.

Playing Through the Pain

I WAS VERY CLOSE TO my father, Reuben. He was called Ruby. He was quite a character and was loved by a lot of people because of his work ethic. There were very few people who would work eighteen hours a day, six days a week. For over sixty years he produced rolls and bread at the Bangor Rye Bread Company. It was his shop with his dad, who started it back in the '20s. It was a very small family operation with my mother, uncle, and aunt, and they made everything by hand. I'd go down to his bakery just to be with him.

My dad would try to involve me in many sports. He was a boxing fan. He'd take me to the club fights and I would sit on his knee, watching matches. He used to take me to all of the Bangor High School basketball games. He was fairly daring. If he didn't have a ticket for me, which was required, he would put me under these big tweed coats he used to wear and then walk in, with me hiding in the coat. I would simply be in this cocoon, terrified that we were going to be exposed, that someone was going to lift the coat up and see me underneath. But then he would rush to the seat, put me on his knee, and watch the game.

My father was quite a good basketball player and used to gather with friends several times in the course of a week following work and go to the YMCA. When I was four, following one of the games, I decided to show my prowess in dribbling, which I thought was quite extraordinary. I started at one end of the court and dribbled all the way to the other, except at the very end I bounced the ball off my foot and it went out of bounds, which provoked laughter among all of those who were witnessing my stellar performance. I took the laughter as criticism and vowed at that point that I would begin my practice routines and would not display my prowess again until I was satisfied that I was an accomplished basketball player. That did not occur until some eight years later, when I was twelve years old and was playing in an organized, new league called the Pee-Wee League, for kids twelve and under. I had asked my father to come to the game. He was not inclined to do so since he worked eighteen hours a day, six days a week. Yet he could see it was important enough for me to ask him to break away from that, and he came. I scored either twenty-four or twenty-six points that evening, and from that point forward he never missed a game of mine, be it from the Pee-Wee or church league or high school. He was at all of them, encouraging me and instructing me along the way.

He hoped that I would have fun with sports, but it was the competitiveness that I enjoyed. I think I had been born with that competitive spirit and the desire to go up against my peers, but also against older people. When I joined the Y, I was supposed to have been nine but got in when I was eight. I started competing against kids who were eleven and twelve, which I knew was going to make me a better player. I also grew up, initially, on the third floor of a tenement building in a fairly rough neighborhood for a small city, which was very ethnic. On Hancock Street you had virtually every ethnic minority you could think of: Polish, Irish, Greek, Syrian, Lebanese, Jewish, and Italian. It was sort of a Lower East Side of New York kind of street. We had our little gang fights, and you had to prove how tough you were. It was a very competitive environment, and you had to be tough enough to hold your own out on the street.

By the time I was twelve I was about five-foot-eight. I didn't grow much beyond that. I'm five-eleven and three-quarters now. But at the age of twelve I was bigger than the others. I started to play organized baseball. I pitched the first no-hit Little League game in the state but that was due to my speed and wildness. Very few people ever got close to the plate.

Honestly speaking, I wasn't a natural in basketball, but it was the competitive desire to be as good as I could be, and the constant practice that helped me excel. I went to the Y almost every day. I'd go on Saturdays, spend the entire day there, and play back-to-back games with different teams. We moved up from the lower economic level to low middle class when I was eight. There were two backboards on the street. There was one near me, and another down the street at the O'Learys', where I'd always find bigger, older boys playing basketball. Even during the winter months, when there was snow on the ground, I would go down there. They'd have a light on the side of the house and I'd focus only on the backboard, shooting for an hour or two, even when the temperatures were below freezing. I would stay out as long as I could, until I couldn't take it anymore, with my eyes tearing up and my ears aching, I'd finally go home.

I don't think the pros, at that point, were on my mind. I wanted to play for Bangor High School. That was a dream at a very early age. And in Bangor there's not a lot going on on Friday night. They would always pack people into the "old auditorium," as they called it. It was really quite thrilling as a young boy to be there. You'd have the band playing, the cheerleaders coming out, the ballplayers who were pretty much idolized as in any small town. I remember sitting on my father's lap, saying that one day I'd be out there playing for the Bangor Rams. As I was playing and developing, I also had the experience of interacting with the black community, and when I say "black community," there was virtually no black community in Maine. We had five or six black families who lived on the other side of town, so to speak, and the general attitude was they were fine as long as they "stayed in their place." You had the racial or racist component even in small-city Maine. But I became friends with a black ballplayer named Bobby Nelson. He was ten years older than me. I admired his athletic ability, so I struck up a friendship with him. More importantly in terms of my development, I was invited out to Dow Air Force Base when I was thirteen, fourteen, and then fifteen to play in the games. I think I was the only white person they asked to play. They were servicemen and so it was a great experience for me to play at a different level with men who were very, very athletic. My dad or mother would drop me off and I would go there for a couple of hours, three or four times a week, and play with them.

High school basketball in Bangor was a very big thing. I started as a sophomore and think I was the second ballplayer in the history of the school to be named to the first team my first year. There were three radio stations and two television stations covering the games, and the sports pages were filled with print the size of World War III declarations. I was a co-captain and it was my senior year that I was named to the all-State team.

The Bangor Auditorium had wings that went up on both sides at dramatic angles, and my parents had special seats reserved for them. I knew exactly where they were. I never had to look at them. I just knew they were up there.

My dad was always an inspiration. My mother, Clara, was a great supporter, too. She didn't miss any games at the high school level. As a young boy you want to please your mother, but you always want to please your father. When I was in high school, he would go to the bakery at three in the morning, make the dough, bake the bread, and, during the day, deliver all the bread. One of his routes took him past the old auditorium where we practiced. He would come into the sessions and sit on the sidelines while we were going through practice and would yell at me, "Pass the ball. You missed that pick." He was there all the time. Finally, the other players came to me and said, "Bill, our dads don't have a chance to come and watch us practice and it's a little bit awkward for us." So I went to him one day and said, "You know, Dad, it would be best if you didn't come by the practice because it's unsettling to the other players to have you there when their fathers can't be there." He said, "Ah, no problem." He just dismissed it as not a big thing.

One time during the winter, I felt his presence when I was dribbling down the court at practice. I looked out in the window and I saw a silhouette. It was my father standing on a railing and cupping his hands around his face to peer into the window through the auditorium. He had a hat on and snow was piled two or three inches above his head. He had been standing out there during one of these storms, watching me play but not wanting to embarrass me. It was one of those moments that you don't forget. I never let on that I knew he was out there. But it was always a comfort for me to know that it mattered such that he would stand out there in the cold and watch me. Wherever we played in the state he would be there. He was quite proud of me, and I was pretty proud of the fact that he cared that much.

Sometimes I was frustrated with him because he demanded so much. One time I scored forty-three points in a church league game. I walked off the court and was pretty proud of myself because they had running time at that point where the clock ran even during foul shots, so you had limited time. We had 113 or 115 points on the board. I went over to see him and I said, "Well, what did you think?" I expected him to give me a pat on the back and say, "Outstanding." He said, "If you hadn't missed those two foul shots you would have had forty-five." I was momentarily deflated. And he didn't say it cruelly. It was just an observation. You can do better—it was always that standard—and you've got to put forth your very best. Don't ever accept what you've done as being your very best, and don't rest on any laurels. You've got to go out there every day and prove it over and over again. He was a great inspiration and such an example of hard work.

My dad wanted me to go to the University of Maine in Orono, about eight miles from my house, so he could continue to watch the games on Friday night after he finished work. He was disappointed when I went to Bowdoin College because he couldn't see me play all the time. But we would play the University of Maine and, obviously, he would come to those games.

I knew at that time that I wasn't going to be big or strong enough to play in the professionals, even though I was hoping otherwise. I decided that education would be the most important thing for me. I went from playing in front of 6,500 a game to fifty people at Bowdoin College. It's a small liberal arts school not known for its outstanding basketball teams, though it did have great hockey teams.

I played for the freshman team, and it went very well in terms of scoring. I had such a good year as a freshman that there was a press account one time in the *Portland Press Herald* that said I could score forty on a good night and twenty on a bad. Well, that really got every other team's competitive spirit up and they said, "Like hell!" And so I was double-teamed much of my career in college. Even though I would have good nights from time to time, my accuracy went down because I had to shoot faster, and so I wasn't quite as good as I was as a freshman. As a freshman I was in the thirties frequently and sometimes in the forties, but I probably averaged, I think, through college probably somewhere between sixteen and seventeen points. I'd have some high games and some low ones. Our team was not particularly strong or deep. A double-team never works if you're up against five good players.

I started as a sophomore and was all-State two years in a row, and then named to the New England All Star Hall of Fame team. I was very combative in college. I either got fouled out or kicked out of eleven games my junior year. As a result of being double-teamed, any time I tried to get loose I was shoved and hit. I suffered a broken jaw in high school, and a second one in college. I learned that there were limits to where I wanted to go on the court. But the competitive spirit—the determination to succeed, to discipline myself, to constantly go back out and shoot and shoot and shoot and shoot, to want to play against better teams and go up against better players—was what stayed with me from the very beginning.

I majored in Latin at Bowdoin because I was playing so much basketball and Latin was easy for me. I could go out and travel, come back from a road trip and be able to go in and take an exam and not have any trouble. It wasn't as if I had this deep love of Latin. I said to myself, "Well, I can be a Latin professor or I can be a professional basketball player." In my senior year I decided it was going to be neither and a friend of mine said, "Well, why don't you go to law school?" And that is what I did.

I was married at the end of my senior year of college, so I had responsibilities. My oldest son was born the following February, and I wasn't so sure I was going to make it in law school. It's very competitive. The first day of law school was classic. The professor said, "Look to your left and look to your right, because next year one of you is not going to be here," and statistically that's true in every first year of law school. It's very stressful, in the sense that you have no exams until the final exams, unlike in college, where you have quizzes and little tests to build up a record before you get to that final exam. So pressure is built up during the course of every semester. The pressure gets to some, and they simply drop out. Only by virtue of the discipline of my sports training and my determination to avoid becoming part of that one-third who were not going to be there by the end, did I make it through some tough times in law school. I translated that same kind of drive that I had as an athlete into my studies and did well. I made the Law Review and was the editor on the Law Review Board. It was the same drive that kept me out there during the winter months shooting foul shots, the same desire I had in law school, and would display as a congressman.

My athleticism came into play when I was running for Congress in 1972. I walked all the way from New Hampshire to Canada. That was the trademark that I established. It was almost 650 miles. I tried to average twenty-two miles a day and shake every hand that I encountered in every town, in every small business, at every newsstand. To average twenty-two miles a day and then meet people was quite a task. I started at six in the morning and finished usually eight at night, and it took me seven weeks. I stayed with a different family, picked at random, each night. I just asked if I could sleep in their house. It was quite an endurance test, and some of it went through very difficult terrain called the Haynesville Woods, where the only thing I encountered were monster logging trucks and angry black flies. Virtually no people. It was a great experience—the work ethic and the ability to walk that far every day. I did a foolish thing, too, because when I first started out I didn't know anything about hiking. You couldn't walk on I-95. It had to be a secondary road. These were narrow roads with soft shoulders, lots of rocks and uneven terrain. I decided to wear construction boots, thinking I needed something with really solid support. Big mistake. I developed huge blisters and ended up going to the hospital twice to have them cut. The blisters were so big I couldn't get my shoes on. I would go in and they would cut the blisters and then wrap my feet up. I would put my shoes back on and keep walking. That also became legendary, in terms of playing through pain.

The mental toughness I acquired through the course of my sports career certainly helped me in the practice of law, where you have to be very disciplined, in terms of mentally preparing to go into combat with the opposing counsel, and frequently with the court itself, the judge. It just comes back to tough discipline, determination, competitive desire. Understand you're going to lose some cases, you're going to lose some basketball games, but the desire to continue to go out there and compete is what drives you.

One of the few mementos I've got left, interestingly enough, is a little basketball medallion from the Down East Classic that I keep in my drawer at the office. It turns out that Admiral James Loy, who is part of my firm and was the commandant of the Coast Guard and number two at the Department of Homeland Security, played against me in the Down East Classic back in '62 in the Bangor Auditorium. I have the ring that I received from the National Association of Basketball Coaches for being named to the Silver Anniversary All-Star Team in 1987, and I also have the Teddy Roosevelt Award I got from the NCAA in 2001. It's a carved plaque that's in my office. The ring I wear from time to time if I'm trying to impress somebody. This is not often. I think I bring it out maybe once every five years, or show it to my grandkids.

The greatest lessons I learned from sports were the need for discipline, hard work, practice, following the rules, and the importance of teamwork. One person doesn't do it all by himself. If you're playing with a team, everybody has got to participate, and you don't win unless they do. You don't win it all by yourself. Ever.

CONDOLEEZZA RICE

I liked skating—there's nothing freer than being on the ice . . . I also loved that I had to work very hard and be very disciplined to even get mediocre results. It was difficult for me, but from an early age I liked things that were challenging.

Condoleezza Rice served as U.S. Secretary of State under President George W. Bush from 2005 to 2009 and as National Security Advisor from 2001 to 2005. The former Stanford University Provost (1993–1999) is currently back on campus as a professor of political science at the school and a Senior Fellow at the Hoover Institution. She was born and raised in Birmingham, Alabama.

Motivation

ILOVED TO PLAY SPORTS from the time I was really little. I was kind of a tomboy. From the time my father took me to my first football game when I was three, I was fascinated, though I didn't understand very much. I watched the football players from Ullman High School in Birmingham, Alabama, rush across the field in their green uniforms. From then on I asked my father, "How are the green boys doing?" I just loved them. After that, every weekend I would ask, "Am I going to football? Am I going to football?" I fell in love with the game from the very beginning, and by the time I was five or so, I actually knew a lot about it.

In addition to being a high school guidance counselor, my father was also a Presbyterian minister, so on Sundays, after he would finish preaching, we would go home and watch the NFL game. That was what we did together—that and watch the "green boys." My father played football, basketball, and tennis, and was a really good athlete. My mother, however, hated sports and didn't play anything, but I think it was generational. Women didn't have that many opportunities to play sports during that time, and my mother was more the artist and musician.

In Birmingham there were no professional teams, and blacks couldn't go to the University of Alabama football games, as those were segregated. I didn't actually go to a college or professional game until I was about eleven years old, after the 1964 Civil Rights Act passed. I still remember traveling to go to our first big college football game: we were living in Tuscaloosa, Alabama, where my dad was dean of students at Stillman College, and he told me we were going to see the University of Alabama play Tennessee. I was excited for weeks leading up to the game.

In addition to football, I loved watching figure skating on television, and when I was younger, I decided I wanted to learn to ice skate. People thought of it as a feminine sport because skaters went out dressed in pretty costumes and performed to music, so it was acceptable for girls from my generation to do it. But it's actually a very difficult sport, so it was good training for me to learn how to work hard at something that didn't come easy to me.

When I was four or five years old I was a little butterball, a chubby little thing, and kind of clumsy. When I started skating it really did give me a better sense of my body, and I became more graceful. But at eleven, I suddenly hit a growth spurt, so that by the time I was twelve I was five-foot-seven with really long legs, which made it harder to skate. But I kept at it.

I liked skating—there's nothing freer than being on the ice. Skating and jumping is like being weightless. It's a wonderful feeling—that is, until you fall; then it's not much fun. But I loved being on the ice. I also loved that I had to work very hard and be very disciplined to even get mediocre results. It was difficult for me, but from an early age I liked things that were challenging.

My parents were going to graduate school in Denver and working as teachers in Alabama. We would go back to Alabama for the school year and spend the summers in Denver so my parents could attend their graduate courses. During the day in Denver they would drop me off at the ice rink—in what served as a kind of high-priced child care—and I would skate all day. When we moved to Denver permanently I started skating competitively. Although I wasn't very good, I worked really, really hard at it. Since my dad had been a high school football coach he was really supportive of my sports and kind of demanding. I'd fall and he'd say, "Oh, you'll be all right." My mother, on the other hand, never watched me jump. She couldn't stand the thought of my jumping or falling.

I had various coaches in figure skating but none that was quite as influential as Wally Sahlin. He could be very demanding, but when things weren't going right for his skaters, he knew how to keep their spirits up. Things didn't go right for me a lot in skating—perhaps because of my height—but he could always make me feel better about a mistake and motivate me to keep working at it. My coach taught me that even if you failed on that day, you had to get up the next day and keep trying. Those were really important lessons. He would always say, "Well, you know, you'll get 'em next time." And I would think, "Get *who* next time?" It really annoyed me when I was younger, but now I understand. "You'll get 'em next time." I can hear him saying it now.

I did sports with my father and music with my mother, and those are still my two great interests today. I'm lucky I got to do both. Unlike with skating, I was actually very good at piano, and when I would perform it almost always went well. I was never nervous, whereas in skating I was always nervous. I never did particularly well and yet I'd get up the next day and go back to skating. I always thought I learned more from that experience in skating than I did from piano. When times get tough, even for me now, I draw on the fact that you can always get up the next day and things will get better, or you'll go back to work and try to make it work again the next day.

The other thing I learned from figure skating is discipline. When I was Secretary of State, people commented all the time that I got up at four thirty in the morning pretty much no matter where I was in the world. This discipline had been a carry-over from skating: I would get up at four forty-five in the morning to practice in the rink, so it was a familiar ritual.

But what really sticks in my mind as the time when I drew on my skating experience was in preparation for my first address before the Republican National Convention in the Houston Astrodome in 1992. I had been told there were going to be thirty thousand people in attendance. "Don't they play football in the Astrodome?" I thought to myself. "Why am I speaking in the Astrodome?" I was really nervous the night before and then realized that, unlike in skating, at least I couldn't slip and fall. That really helped.

When I skated in Denver, we had sectionals and regionals. I never made it out of sectionals but I skated really well once in 1969—it was a summer competition and I skated the best I ever had. I think it was the happiest moment of my life up to that point. I remember it like it was yesterday, and I still have my one skating trophy. Even better, I have my club tennis championship trophy. I finally realized that I wasn't going to be able to skate the rest of my life, so, I picked up a tennis racquet. I played a couple times and I really liked it, and then it became my sport. I didn't actually know anybody who played very much, so I used to go out and serve. My serve is still the strength of my game.

My latest passion is golf. For the last three years I've been learning golf, which really teaches you a lot, because you have to be incredibly patient to play. You have to get used to the fact that that little ball is sitting there and it's very hard to hit it the same way every time. The other thing about golf is you can hit a really good shot and have it go bad because it hit something. And you can hit a really bad shot and have it go well, which doesn't seem fair.

Like skating, golf is a sport I have to stick with and work hard at. But I enjoy it—I learn more about myself through the challenges I face in sports.

PART 8

The Business Executives (Part III)

GLEN SENK

There's a part of me that loves perfection . . . but you can't be perfect all of the time. The pursuit of perfection can have a truly paralyzing effect. People become so worried and consumed about doing something perfectly, they do nothing at all.

Glen Senk was named CEO of Urban Outfitters, Inc., in May 2007. He joined the Company in April 1994 as president of Anthropologie, became Executive Vice President of Urban Outfitters Inc. in May 2002, and was elected to the company's board of directors in June 2004. He previously held executive positions at Williams-Sonoma Inc., the London-based Habitat Group, and Bloomingdale's. He holds a B.A. degree, magna cum laude, in psychology, computer science, and mathematics from New York University, and an M.B.A. degree in marketing and finance from the University of Chicago Graduate School of Business. He grew up in Brookville, on Long Island, New York.

Consistently Good or Inconsistently Great?

My OLDER SISTER, PAM, HAD an interest in horses. My parents got her a horse, Uncle B, and a week or two after she got the horse she got a boyfriend. Uncle B sat in the stall, unattended. One day I visited him, the first visitor he had in weeks, and I immediately bonded. Until then, I had no prior interest in or exposure to horses. The next thing I knew I was taking lessons, instantly enamored with the sport, fully hooked.

There was just one problem: I was the most unnatural, pathetic rider in the history of the sport. It's ironic that my sister, who abandoned horseback riding as soon as she took it up, was a total natural, so beautiful on a horse. It took me at least six months to master the basic fundamentals. But for some reason I just loved it and worked with a fierce resolve to improve.

Uncle B and I were an odd match—I was just a young boy, nine at the time, and Uncle B literally had three legs in the grave. As my interest and skill level deepened and Uncle B's years advanced, we eventually had to upgrade to another horse. But I still remember Uncle B in my mind's eye as majestic and regal. Old as he actually was, Uncle B was the best horse to learn on. Because he was so kind and put up with my complete lack of balance and skills, I don't think I ever fell off him. That's the kind of horse on which you want to learn.

And learn I did. I remember practicing how to trot on an English saddle—when you do, it's called posting, which means you bob up and down with your body. It took me several months to learn how to do this correctly and trust me, posting incorrectly as a male is a bad thing. I still remember the whole experience, all the little successes and the failures that left me hopeful, discouraged, sore, ready to quit, and I'll never forget when suddenly a light bulb went off, and I realized, "Oh my God, that's the feeling. That's what posting should feel like. Now I get it."

That was the beginning of my transition from an absolute disaster to being reasonably good. Once I was in my early teens and showing real promise, I switched instructors to one of the top trainers in the world, George Morris. This was not a casual undertaking. Like competing at the highest level in any other sport, working with George required that I train to the exclusion of everything else. Life was practice and I think this kind of commitment would have been overwhelming if not for my parents' support. My mother, Arlene, who has since passed away, believed that the will to do something is as important, if not more important, than the ability. She wasn't afraid to strive for the best, despite odds or challenges, and she made me believe that I could accomplish anything. Does it take luck and talent, too? Sure. But my mother taught me that life is self-fulfilling: what you believe tends to become true.

She and my father, Hank, also held a deep commitment to excellence—excellence in any area in life, whether that be academic, artistic, or competitive sport. True to their commitment, they agreed to support my effort to become a champion equestrian, so as long as my talent continued to hold promise and, more important, my determination remained focused.

So began my training with George Morris, who is now the chef d'équipe, or the manager, for the United States Equestrian Federation's Show Jumping Team. Armed with a larger-than-life persona, George has led the U.S. show jumping team to gold medals in both the 2004 and 2008 Olympics. It's probably fair to say he has trained a good portion, maybe even the majority, of the best riders in America.

George had a profound influence on my life. What he taught me extended well beyond just riding. His lessons, fundamentally, were about discipline and focusing intently and intensely on details. George is a force of nature, an exacting tactician who believes that the strength and authenticity of one's convictions determines the likelihood of success.

I can't say that training with him was easy or even always pleasant. If a lesson started at three, you were there at five to three. You were not there at three, and God forbid if you were there a minute late. If you came to the lesson and your tack was not spit-polished, if a hair on your horse was not in place, George asked you to leave. For George there was but one perfect way to do something and he didn't accept a single excuse for anything that fell short. Don't get me wrong, George is a kind person, and only pushed because he cared, but what a disciplinarian. To succeed under that kind of scrutiny, you have to be very definite, very confident, and always deliberate. A horse, believe it or not, picks up on your self-assurance, your poise, and ultimately matches your drive and will to win.

The rigor was amazing. In addition to George's demands, keeping a horse is a twenty-four-hour-a-day, seven-day-a-week responsibility. I don't think I slept past six a.m. until I got to college. Horses rise early and have virtually no appreciation or respect for Christmas, New Year's, or Prom Night. They require a care and a level of attention that exceeds what most kids and young adults are able to provide. The deal I struck with my parents, who were well aware of the commitment involved, was that caring for my horse was as critical, if not more important, than competing. So in a sport where most of my counterparts had everything handed to them, I was up at three in the morning braiding my horse's mane, spit-polishing his tack, and cleaning his trailer. Between my German father and George, believe me, every last inch was inspected.

It took time and patience, but eventually I grew to deeply appreciate George's eye for detail. Nothing escaped his attention, and I learned from his teaching style and personality the idea of fine-tuning the minutia with continuous focus, in order to gain mastery of larger, more complicated skills.

Since then, I've learned to scale back George's intensity. Especially in the last ten years, I've seen that reaching for perfection can be a debilitating, even destructive thing. Consistency, I've found, is more important—it's more important because it's often more attainable. It's better to be consistently good than inconsistently great or terrible. Sure, there's a part of me that loves perfection, and in no way am I about settling, but you can't be perfect all of the time and shouldn't set such an unforgiving bar for yourself. The pursuit of perfection can have a truly paralyzing effect. I see it happen all the time. People become so worried and consumed about doing something perfectly, they do nothing at all.

These days, I see George once or twice a year at the shows. I smile and tell him how much of an influence he had on me. He gets so much recognition, I doubt he needs the validation from me, but I think it's important for him to understand how much he affected my life outside of riding.

I had various other instructors and remember things from each one. Gloria, an instructor I had early on, always said that it doesn't matter what you decide, just decide and stick with your decision. That's absolutely true in business. There's often never an absolute wrong or right and best is something measured in degrees. What makes you successful is having a clear point of view and the will to act. You can't get anywhere standing still, and often that's what people do while they're trying to figure out the perfect approach.

Another instructor, Victor Hugo-Vidal, had this great expression, "Look it." It was his way of saying "Look where you're going." When you're on a horse and you look in a certain direction, the horse can feel your balance. Your head weighs a lot, and a horse can feel your weight transfer as your head pivots. It's subtle but horses are remarkably attuned to these shifts, and as a result they tend to go where you're looking. In business, "look it" is having a vision. As a leader, your organization is so sensitized to how you're leaning on an issue or problem; you don't want to waver too much. You have to be extremely deliberate or you run the risk of guiding people in multiple, sometimes conflicting directions.

Despite all the work and effort I put into riding, I graduated from high school a year early and then rode full-time for the next year. After that I went to college, hated it, and dropped out, then rode professionally for a few more years. This was not exactly what my parents, who value education highly, had in mind. I wouldn't say they were unsupportive when I rode professionally, but I know that deep down they probably would have been happier if I went to college. Though I found success as a professional equestrian during that time, I couldn't shake the thought that "If I don't go to school now, I'm never going to go." So I returned to college and then enrolled in graduate school.

As a college student, I stopped riding. No one was going to finance my horseback training as a mere hobby, so I made the difficult and, at the time, very painful decision to quit horses entirely. I think that's just my personality, though. I'm all or nothing. If I couldn't train every day and compete at the highest level, then the alternative was nothing at all. Even after graduate school, as I entered a career in retail, I don't think I went near a horse. Not for the next eighteen years.

Starting out in retail, I worked very, very hard. When I was with Williams-Sonoma and the frenetic pace cooled down, I decided to start riding again. I got a serious horse and did pretty well. When I came to Pennsylvania to run Anthropologie, the pace hastened again, and I was busy six and a half days a week trying to build the business from our one store, and never had the time to even think about riding. Then about five years ago, I went to visit a friend who had bought his girlfriend a horse as a gift. At the stable I petted the horse on the nose, and I turned to Keith, my partner, and said, "I have to get a horse." Today I own five horses and compete roughly fifteen times a year. I only practice on the weekends, and I'm not nearly as good as I used to be.

Looking back, it's amazing how much riding taught me. Without a doubt, I learned more from horses than I did at New York University or the University of Chicago Graduate School of Business. When I'm confronted with strategic issues or problems with real complexity, I often draw parallels to how I approached challenges as a rider, both in a competition and as someone trying to make it on the professional circuit. There were so many lessons from that time. I don't think I fully appreciated what an education riding was.

Collaboration, for example, was something I had to master early on. Horses are much smarter than most people think, and much more responsive to cooperation than control. If you're too controlling, you lose agility and the ability to respond to and adopt their strengths and weaknesses. Sometimes, for example, I'm not feeling great and the horse steps in to compensate, while other times the horse isn't at peak performance and I've got to take the lead. It's a relationship where you have to give and take, learn from and trust the other. Without the spirit of collaboration, you can't have that level of trust and ultimately your performance suffers.

Patience is also imperative. You have to remember that horses are living beings, not machines. Like us they're subject to misfortune, foul moods, and the random events of life. Just when you think everything is aligned, after you've trained for months, the horse steps on a rock and he's lame, and you can't compete that week. In life, and particularly in business, you have to remain nimble, open to variation, and embrace change. That, in effect, is horseback riding.

Now, as the CEO of Urban Outfitters Inc., I see even more similarities between my job and my experiences riding. There's the need to punctuate a larger-scale, long-term vision with successes every day just like a young rider needs encouragement and small wins before performing well at a competition. You want to have balance and symmetry in your strengths, to build muscle in every facet of your company so that the entire organization works. You need to be a showman and have presence. Two people, and I've seen it, can show the same horse but yield completely different results. It's really how *you* position, how you sell. It's about creating a desire in someone else to buy something you have, and that's as true in retail as it is standing before a contest judge.

The real key is recognizing and building talent. Watching someone who shows real promise is a tremendously exciting thing. I remember when I saw True, one my horses, several years ago and thought, "Here is a horse that's going to be remarkable. Here's star quality." The fun is watching the potential become realized.

I attribute a great deal of my success in business to what I've learned from sports. Vision, planning, teamwork, patience, discipline, communication—these are all concepts that I learned early in life through my association with competitive riding, and I am so thankful for the people who instructed me, for those first horses who showed great patience and kindness, for my parents' support, and to my sister, Pam, for caring more about boys than she did Uncle B.

ISADORE SHARP

Leadership is the ability to influence because people trust and respect you. The important part is not your position of power but the power of your input due to the respect you generate. When you're given a promotion, it's like you've inherited a job.

Isadore Sharp is the founder, chairman, and CEO of Four Seasons Hotels, Inc. The company now operates more than eighty luxury hotels and resorts around the world, with more than forty additional properties under development. He was born in Toronto and graduated from Ryerson Polytechnical School, now a university.

Generating Respect

GROWING UP IN TORONTO'S JEWISH ghetto, I played hockey on frozen ponds, using magazines for shin pads and rocks for goalposts, before I made the Pee-Wee team. I also played basketball and football and ran track. It didn't matter what sports I would play, I could always make the first team, and in some cases be one of the better players on the team. My life revolved around sports because I enjoyed it so much. School to me was a playground. Because I was a good athlete, I was popular. A terrible student, I looked forward to going to school every day because I enjoyed the camaraderie that is developed in team sports, the bus rides, and singing songs at pep rallies. When I played junior football in high school, I even became a cheerleader when the senior team was playing.

My immigrant parents had no curiosity in my sports. They didn't have the time or the interest. They came to watch me play only once, a hockey play-off game that I had to coax them to attend. It wasn't then like it is today, where parents go out to watch their kids play hockey at six in the morning. Unknowingly, my parents gave me athletic coordination. I never trained in track. I just went into it. I felt bad one day because one of the brightest kids in the school, who was not an athlete in any way, went out and trained to run the half-mile event. One afternoon he was practicing and practicing. I went out and said, "Okay, I'll run the half-mile," and beat him. He said, "That's not fair. I worked hard at that and you didn't." I said, "Dave, I could study every day all year and would never be able to write an exam as well as you did if you went in and didn't study. We all have different skills." That's the way it works. But I remember how bad he felt, and I felt bad because it wasn't that important to me. It was just another race.

As a freshman, I was honored and surprised when I was voted Athlete of the Year at Ryerson Polytechnical School, where I went to study architecture. It wasn't until my senior year that I started focusing on education. After graduating, I went to work for my father, who worked in construction and built houses. There were just the two of us at Max Sharp & Son, and my father stepped back to let me take over the company. When I became a full-time builder, I hired a carpenter and laborer and we moved into the apartment-building business. I still continued to play basketball and hockey after work. A friend asked me to build him a little motel near the southern Toronto lakefront, for him and his wife to run, which I did. His motel was such a success that I thought a larger one could work downtown. I solicited opinions of current and previous financial backers, some of whom expressed skepticism because I didn't know anything about the hotel business. It took a few years before I arranged the financing. Doubters reacted by saying people would think the property was a flophouse because the location, once grand, had gone downhill and become a hangout for gangsters and hookers. But I believed in the concept and didn't think land in a fast-growing city like Toronto would remain cheap. The Four Seasons Motor Hotel opened in 1961. I had been checking out hotels for years and knew what was lacking. For example, we put in bigger bath towels and thicker hand towels. When my three sisters traveled, they took a small bottle of shampoo with them because they didn't like to wash their hair with soap. We put shampoo in all our rooms—a first.

When I got started in the luxury hotel business, I wanted to be the best, not biggest. Ethics probably plays a major role in how you can best achieve that, because you need a lot of people to join with you. And I think people appreciate it when you're honest and straightforward with them. It encourages them to do the same. One of the things sports taught me was good sportsmanship and to play by the rules. I'm not sure I was very competitive. If you're super-competitive you tend to win at any cost, and I never felt that way. I only wanted to win if we won the right way. That ethic—the one that drove me to be a good sport—is still with me today, and in business I play by the rules. I liked to win, but I didn't dwell on it. I accepted the fact that there are other people who are better, and that's not bad. That's the way life is. There's nothing wrong with not winning as long as you did your best.

In business I apply the Peter Principle, the idea that people tend to get promoted up past their top level of competence. Not everybody who is going to try to move up the ladder can move up the ladder. They can't take on that next level of responsibility. In my early years in the business, when I was hiring, we had employees who couldn't take it the next step. In the early days, I couldn't attract people who were good enough to continue with the company. So the first employees I worked with weren't necessarily the ones who would be able to carry on as the company grew. Everybody can't be a champion. Not everybody can keep moving up in their career. We all have our limitations, and sports helped me understand that's not wrong.

Through a helicopter skiing experience in the mid-seventies, I gained insight into the power of leadership. Hans Gmoser, the best-known guide and mountain climber of his time, pioneered helicopter skiing and used to fly groups of experienced skiers to the top of the highest mountain ranges in the Canadian Rockies. I recalled the incident in my book, *Four Seasons: The Story of a Business Philosophy.* Once, skiing across the top of a mountain in a remote, steep, and rugged range with endless rows of trees below, Hans told us to halt. "Pick a line and a buddy," he said. "We're going down, and you should be with someone if you fall. Some trees have big wells around their roots. Fall into them, and you could be lost forever." What line? I thought, as I looked down a hill so thick with tree trunks that there was little space between them. If I'd been alone, I wouldn't have thought this area skiable. But we all believed in Hans and although we had no way of knowing which trees had openings, we immediately followed him unquestioningly.

I knew this man wouldn't tell us to do something if he thought we didn't have the capacity to do it. But none of us sitting at the top of that mountain would have ever thought of skiing down it. But we all did and ended up with that thrill of doing something that was beyond what we thought our abilities were. The experience didn't change me, but it allowed me to talk about leadership in a way that encouraged others. Leadership is the ability to influence because they trust and respect you. The important part is not your position of power but the power of your input due to the respect you generate. When you're given a promotion, it's like you've inherited a job. Your superior has seen that you've done well, but now you're in charge of people who may not have seen how well you performed. In order to be an effective boss, you have to earn their respect and their trust. Once you get to that position, you're not just a manager; you become a leader. Therefore, having the skiing experience gave me a way to get that message across in a profound way that people buy into. And they know that once they're promoted, that's just the beginning of earning that job. They must now earn the respect and trust of the people for whom they're responsible.

Sports also taught me to always try, regardless of the opponent. If the other team is bigger and faster, it doesn't stop you from trying. You just do your best. It's a sense of self-confidence and belief, not arrogance, in what you're attempting to do.

I had that attitude when I set out to build a 230-room luxury hotel in London at a time when that city already had five five-star hotels. I had only two hotels in Toronto. The people providing the financing wanted a moderately priced hotel with 320 rooms. It took numerous meetings over several years to seal the deal. Very powerful and wealthy men, including the Duke of Westminster and his advisers, attended one of the meetings. On another occasion, there was a formal dinner with a dozen very proper British businessmen, and I had not yet become exposed to formal dining. A while back, somebody asked about this experience. "When you went to London and dealt with people who were in a different social class, a different financial class and are very Old World, very wealthy, powerful people, didn't you feel out of place and intimidated?" he wanted to know. I told him, "No, I didn't feel that at all. They welcomed me. I didn't understand all the etiquette and protocol, but you learn as you go along. I wasn't scared." He said, "You must have been scared. You were so outclassed, a thirty-something-year-old kid dealing with people who are so far above you in every way." This person couldn't believe that I wasn't nervous, but I wasn't. Through sports, I gained the attitude of "I'm here; I'm going to do my best and we'll see what the outcome is." It was a belief in what I'm attempting to do. I was prepared to suffer the consequences. Although I might have lost, I didn't mind trying my hardest. We got the London deal done with the number of rooms and price point I wanted, although I agreed to pay the rent they wanted for ninety more rooms. The first year the property opened, it was named Europe's Hotel of the Year. It won that title twice in its first ten years, something no other hotel had done before, plus additional awards.

A long time ago somebody said to me, "When you're looking to do something, know what you want, ask for it, and then make sure you get it." Knowing what you want is the key. Sports give you a positive attitude.

MAX SIEGEL

The most important thing I picked up from team sports is appreciating that everybody on the team has a role and none of them is more or less important than the other because without everybody contributing it's impossible to achieve a common goal. You learn how to get along with people and how to earn people's respect.

Max Siegel is CEO of the 909 Group LLC, a sports, entertainment, and lifestyle marketing firm, CEO of Revolution Racing, a motorsports racing team, and counsel at Baker & Daniels LLP, where he leads the sports and entertainment industry team. He previously served as president of global operations at Dale Earnhardt, Inc. Prior to that he held dual positions as senior vice president of Zomba Label and president of Zomba Gospel at Sony BMG. He earned a B.A. from the University of Notre Dame and is a cum laude graduate from Notre Dame Law School, the first African-American to graduate with honors from that law school. He was born in Indianapolis.

Pushing Beyond Your Limits

MY PARENTS SPLIT UP WHEN I was about five. My little sister and I went to visit my father for a weekend and he kept us for about seven years. During that time he convinced us our mother was dead and took us from Indianapolis to California and Las Vegas. As a music executive, he traveled frequently, which left us with my stepmother, who had substance-abuse problems. I've always been in search of some sort of stability, consistency, and structure in my life, so early on I played T-ball. By the time I was eight or nine I started to get heavily involved in organized sports, specifically baseball. When I look back on it, it was the one consistent thing that I could participate in; it gave me a lot of the discipline and emotional feedback that I didn't get at home.

As I excelled in baseball I started playing for a traveling team in Las Vegas that competed throughout Nevada, Southern California, and Arizona. And I was on a Little League All-Star team that reached the level right before the Little League World Series in Williamsport, Pennsylvania. I enjoyed the friendships that I developed with my teammates, coaches, and other families. It was nice to be a part of a team and an extended family as well as do something from which you could get immediate feedback.

When I was eleven or twelve, my father was diagnosed with cancer and he passed when I was twelve. I returned to Indianapolis to live with my mother (who was in fact alive), a singer, in an extremely volatile and dysfunctional household. My mother and stepfather were functioning alcoholics. I've pretty much been on my own since I was fourteen. I created my own stability. I say now that I was an overachiever for the wrong reasons: I participated in sports and held down jobs to literally keep from going home. I was a four-year varsity letterman in wrestling and three-year varsity letterman in baseball. I played football my first couple of years but was way too small to excel in that sport. I would go to class and try to finish my homework in study hall before practice began. I practiced from three o'clock to five o'clock and worked at Long John Silver's from seven o'clock to ten o'clock.

Even with the success that I had, my parents never showed up to my sporting events. The success was kind of empty because oftentimes there was nobody there to celebrate it with me. The losses at times were a little bit harder to take, but they were also a motivating factor to try to come back and win and get that positive reinforcement. What I picked up through sports was really how to connect with people in an emotional way and figure out what motivated them and what motivated me. It was great to have a common goal with my teammates; I felt as if I were part of something. The fact that nobody showed up became less important, once I felt I was contributing to the success of the team.

Ron Reichel, my wrestling coach and history teacher, had a huge impact in my life. I went to Crispus Attucks High School but transferred with him to Northwest High School. Coach Reichel was a former Marine and had a very military, strict, no-nonsense approach to both sports and the classroom. He was a strong male figure who would not tolerate anything that wasn't structured and disciplined.

But at the same time he was incredibly compassionate. He could figure out a way to push everyone on our team and the students in the classroom beyond what they felt they were capable of doing. I was drawn to him because he didn't accept mediocrity or excuses out of any of us, gave us great feedback, pushed us hard, but was also consistently compassionate. There was a level of trust that I felt even when he pushed me to do things I didn't particularly understand. I always felt he had my best interest at heart.

Midway through the season we had a wrestling tournament in Connersville, Indiana, and my opponent killed me. I'm forty-four years old and I still remember this like it was yesterday. I was incredibly intimidated by the guy that I wrestled because he was a year ahead of me and had a winning record. Later in the year we trained extremely hard going into sectionals and I practiced a move called the Japanese wizard because my coach thought my opponent, who was either undefeated or had only lost one match all year, would be vulnerable to it. Coach Reichel passed out cards to each of us and on each one he had written something that your opponent would say about you. Mine was something like my opponent noticed that when I lacked confidence I was easy to beat. But when I believed in myself I was hard to beat and that I didn't push myself beyond the limit. Near the end of the match I was dead tired. I thought I was going to die. At the end of regulation I had an escape and we went into overtime. With fifteen seconds left in overtime we were tied. I threw the Japanese wizard move on him, defeated him, and went on to the regional tournament. It was then I realized I was capable of pushing myself beyond what I thought the limit was for me.

I've drawn upon tough situations like that when I have encountered obstacles in business. For example, when I was president of global operations for Dale Earnhardt, Inc., Dale Jr. announced in May 2007 that he was leaving at the end of the NASCAR season. Everyone said DEI would not survive. It was difficult for most people to see the company without Dale Jr. And there was a time when we were sitting there, thinking, "It's all over right now. There's nothing we can do." We had to huddle up and figure out what the situation was going to be with him gone. We put our heads together and found a strategic acquisition. We bought Ginn Racing and were able to bring on Mark Martin. Dale Jr. was the most popular driver, but Mark was one of the most popular and well-respected drivers, and one that the fan base would accept driving the number 8 car, the number that personified Dale Jr. We were able to achieve a number of operational efficiencies, and as result of that, we renewed a significant number of our sponsor-ships and went into the next year pretty healthy. Drawing upon my past, where I have to push through setbacks, failures, and obstacles has been helpful for me throughout my life.

Baseball was the sport I loved and was really good at. From play-ing in summer leagues, I started getting attention from development scouts from teams and colleges. During the recruitment process, I became enthralled with Notre Dame. I decided that going to college and playing baseball there was the best decision for me.

During my senior year in high school I had a freak injury. I broke my hip during the sectional playoffs for state championship. I was sprinting around third base when the muscle connected to the hip pulled the bone off. Apparently, when you're still growing, your muscle is stronger than your bone. Because I was eighteen and still growing, the doctor didn't want to operate, fearing that if he hit the growth plate, then one of my legs could grow longer than the other. I spent about five weeks in the hospital. They fused the bone back together and I went through rehab. I worked out the whole summer and went out for fall baseball at Notre Dame. But I just did not have it at all. It was a huge emotional setback and something I had to make an adjustment to pretty early on. Emotionally, I had to go back to a lot of the things I had learned, especially from my wrestling coach, and that was learning how to deal with failure, how to focus, how to make myself a better person. My wrestling coach pushed us in the classroom as much as he did on the field. He was trying to instill in us, as varsity athletes, the idea that there was life beyond our athletic careers. I think that being focused, setting goals, accepting sacrifice, and valuing discipline, all of the things I learned in athletics, helped me push myself academically. When you're competitive and used to excelling at something, you want to be the best at whatever you set out to accomplish. So I worked hard academically.

I also did rehab during my freshman year in college and tried to come back by sophomore year. I still didn't have it. The experience helped shape my vision for the future. I knew I wanted to have a career in the sports industry, and stayed heavily involved in athletics at Notre Dame by working in the athletic department as an academic adviser for student athletes. During my senior year I decided to go to law school because a lot of my friends whom I had met when I was a freshman and sophomore were having a difficult time making that transition from college to either the pros or the workforce if they didn't make the pros. Some of them had been hugely successful in sports and played one, two, or three years in the NFL or NBA. All of a sudden they had to go from making $300,000 or $400,000 a year, which back then was a lot of money, to selling insurance for $20,000 a year. And, off campus, nobody knew who they were.

Through sports I learned that setting goals is really critical. In an individual sport you're competing against yourself. The only way to know that you're getting better is to set individual goals. Being captain of my wrestling and baseball teams taught me how to understand leadership and how to rally people around a common goal. The most important thing I picked up from team sports is appreciating that everybody on the team has a role and none of them is more or less important than the other because without everybody contributing it's impossible to achieve a common goal. You learn how to get along with people and how to earn people's respect. When you're in a team setting and it's competitive, people are pretty transparent and open. You know if the chemistry is not there. Accepting failure, losing, acknowledging that there are times when somebody else is better than you, and knowing the importance of really having to work hard to get something is what sports teaches you.

I'm having this discussion about self-esteem and life skills now with my wife, who, as a pediatric dentist, spends a lot of time around children. I've spent my entire career in sports and entertainment representing the Tony Gwynns and Reggie Whites of the world, and I've worked a lot with Evander Holyfield. Our ten-year-old son is in his first year in tackle football. We're discussing how serious a role sports should play in his life, the discipline it takes, and how his self-esteem will be affected by whether he plays. I said to my wife, if he doesn't go to practice or he doesn't work hard, then he shouldn't play, because my son needs to understand that he's going to have to invest the time and the effort to get the opportunity to prove himself. And once he gets on the field he's going to have to invest in his own improvement, if that's ultimately what he wants to do. He must understand that everybody has to pull their weight. I don't want my son to be burned out, but some of my biggest lessons in terms of what propelled me and what's giving me the resilience and strength to compete in the business workplace were the failures more than the successes. You want to succeed, but it's what you do when you fail that counts.

Through sports I've been able to bring people who probably never would talk to each other together around something they were passionate about—music and sports—and achieve some business objectives. Through the course of it, we all grew and learned as people. I was on Sony/BMG's global management team, had the most profitable division in the company with Zomba, but I was just bored to tears. Reggie White got me involved in NASCAR, and I became fascinated with the industry. It had everything—entertainment, sports, competition, marketing, the whole thing—and they were trying to grow the sport. The least likely friendship I would ever develop was with Dale Earnhardt, Jr., and that's something he and I have talked about. It was built around sports, competition, and our upbringing. Dale and his sister were sent to live with their stepmother and father, who was often away racing, after a fire destroyed their mother's home. We connected. The Earnhardts felt I was genuine and wanted to win. Being president of global operations at DEI, one of the top motor sports franchises in NASCAR, was probably the most challenging and stressful two years of my entire life, but the most rewarding on a number of different levels. I was the first African-American franchise president to exist in a sport which historically doesn't have a whole lot of African-Americans in it. Now I have my own NASCAR team, Revolution Racing, that's going to compete in 2010, and my company, the 909 Group, is helping manage NASCAR's diversity program, called Drive for Diversity.

Probably seventy-five to eighty percent of who I am and what I've been able to do I can attribute to sports. Apart from the skills I've learned, I've also met some really great people, people who've invested in me. I do believe that everything is divinely ordered but I'd say sports has allowed me to develop as a businessperson, to follow my passion, take care of my family, and do something professionally that I love, something that impacts people.

SARAH SLUSSER

Squash taught me how to be strategic. It's about where you place the ball, and then where the competitor is going to be, because you have to respond to where he's likely to hit. You're always thinking a couple of shots ahead. And that's relevant to business, where you always have to be thinking five moves down the line.

Sarah Slusser is a managing partner in the role of executive vice president at GeoGlobal Energy LLC. She joined the geothermal investment and development company in 2009 after twenty-one years at the AES Corporation, a global power company, where she served as senior vice president and a member of the AES Development Company's Steering Committee. She graduated cum laude from Harvard and earned a master's degree in public and private management from the Yale University School of Organization and Management. She was born and raised in New York City.

Five Moves Down the Line

I GREW UP IN MANHATTAN so every sport I played was indoors. I competed in volleyball, basketball, gymnastics, indoor track, and squash. When I was young I started playing squash at the Harvard Club with my dad. My dad started me and my three sisters and brother running around the reservoir before there were even running shoes. I was about ten years old. Everyone thought my father was crazy when he was running down the streets in New York with all these little girls tagging along behind him.

I did pretty well in gymnastics, then I got too tall for it. I'm five-foot-ten now. At the time, New York wasn't as sports-oriented as it probably is now, but our volleyball, basketball, indoor track, and squash teams at the Spence School did well. My senior year I won the White Jacket, an athletic award that goes to one senior. I felt honored and still have the white wool jacket with the Spence emblem on the breast pocket. Generally, I was the captain of the teams. Being a captain, I learned a life lesson at an early age. I tended to try to be a little different, so when we'd practice I'd wear something distinctive, such as colored socks. Finally my volleyball coach said, "Sarah, you are the captain of the team and you do need to model good behavior, so that means coming in uniform." That's been a strong business lesson for me. When you are the leader of a business, or leader of a team, what you do and how you act really matters because it's symbolic. That was the first time it occurred to me that when you're in a position of leadership, you have responsibility. That resonates with me to this day. I think about it a lot as a parent. My modeling as a parent is so much more important than what I say, and that's the same thing at work.

I'll never forget something else from my senior year at Spence. The head of my high school, Agnes Underwood, was this inspiring woman whom we would see running. She was working on her M.B.A. at Columbia at night, head of the high school, pregnant, and trying to stay in shape. Seeing her eight months pregnant and running around the track that we would train on made me think to myself, "Oh my God. She does everything." I remember thinking of all of the multiple things that she was doing with her life and how amazing that was. I envisioned myself like her someday.

When I arrived at Harvard, I played freshman squash and JV soccer for two years. I went out for lacrosse, and then decided to act in a play instead midway through the season. Water polo wasn't a sport yet and in order to make it one, it had to be a club sport for two years, so I played club water polo for two years. At Harvard, there are houses, and I played house volleyball and rowed house crew every year because house sports were not as demanding. I competed on the cross-country ski team one winter and played JV basketball my senior year.

I enjoyed the team aspects of sports and liked meeting all the new people in each sport. I loved trying something different and working on a whole new set of skills. In squash I didn't make it past freshman year because Jack Barnaby, a famous coach who'd been overseeing the men's team forever and was also coaching the women's, said to me, "You play a real nice game of cocktail squash." I was humiliated by that. That was very hard to hear. I decided not to continue. I probably should not have been discouraged by that, but found so many other sports that I liked. It's important to find a coach that's going to work with you, and that you're going to work well under, too. You want to be inspired.

For me that coach was my JV soccer coach, Reid Whitlock. He took it seriously and worked extremely hard with us. He saw that I wasn't the fastest on the field, but he saw I had long arms and legs, so he switched me to the goalie position, which I loved because it was more like volleyball in a way. I got to jump around and dive. He was a positive force for me and the team. The women's varsity team was good, and we were pretty competitive, too. It wasn't about excelling in any single sport for me. It was more about how active a role sports played in my life, in the sense of introducing me to new experiences, even the outdoors. Growing up in New York City, going to Harvard, and being able to play field sports was such an incredible luxury, which some other people took for granted. It was heaven. One of the reasons I did cross-country skiing was because I wanted to get outside and see the mountains. As a geology major, I did a lot of outdoor activities as well.

After Harvard and graduate school at Yale, I joined AES, a power company, in 1988. Back then, it was a small private company and only in the United States. I helped build that company. During my twenty-one-year stint I ran a division, was head of mergers and acquisitions, was part of the large development company, and led asset sales. Initially, I was a project director, which meant leading just one project. I became president of a division that included operations, construction, and development for Central America, Mexico, and the Caribbean. One of the biggest jobs I've ever done was developing and then building large-scale power projects. We built a large clean-coal plant in Puerto Rico that was a billion-dollar investment. We had a specialist in each area on the team, including a finance person, an environmental-permitting person, a community-relations person, and an engineer. I was the project director in charge of the whole project, making sure that all the pieces fit together. If we were in need of finance, I'd have to quickly work in that area to make sure that we were fully equipped to deal with all the pressures and issues on that side. And then, similarly, if the environmental-permitting person needed backup from the engineer, then the engineer could step in. A project like that takes five or six years to develop, and on that project we managed to keep the same people for that whole time period, no turnover. And that's because it was an exciting project, we all got along so well, and worked well together, very much the way a sports team works toward an end goal. It was a very defined goal, which was to get the project financed and start construction. When you're working with other people, it is helpful to have done team sports.

Now I'm at a start-up and we have twenty-five people. We are building a global geothermal business. It was a risky move for me after twenty-one years at one company. But I think that it hearkens back to being willing to try a lot of sports; and even within AES, I had so many different positions. Having joined new teams through-out my college years gave me lots of practice at getting to know new people over and over again. So, it's not just the new situations and environments that I learned to navigate, but getting to know the new people also.

My work is tangible, as are sports. When you're playing sports, you're constantly being tested and challenged in real time. The results are there in real time; the measurement is there. That's very helpful for business because it's about measuring your progress and having goals—and mini-goals within those goals—and then being able to accomplish them. Both sports and business put you in situations that are constantly competitive, and in both you need to remember that people are constantly getting better than you. If you don't keep up, they're going to pass you by.

Some people are practice players, but I always liked the moment of competition. It's exhilarating for me. It's similar to preparing for negotiations and then being in the negotiations. I find the actual negotiation, as long as I'm prepared, much more exciting and exhilarating. I like to rise to these occasions. It doesn't scare me. In my job, I'm constantly out negotiating deals and getting government agencies to approve projects, which can be more like cajoling than negotiating, or buying companies and negotiating the prices. The more prepared I am, the better I feel in that negotiation. So the more I've thought through, ahead of time, all the various permutations of the other side's reactions and what moves they may make and how I might then react to them, the better. Squash taught me how to be strategic. It's about where you place the ball, and then where the competitor is going to be, because you have to respond to where he's likely to hit. You're always thinking a couple of shots ahead. And that's relevant to business, where you always have to be thinking five moves down the line.

Playing so many sports helped me learn there's a lot of fish in the sea, and that's helped me in business. You don't have to just do one thing. There isn't just one company you want to buy. There have been businesses I've tried to acquire that somebody else has come in and swept out from under me. I move on immediately. It doesn't get me down.

In sports you learn how to play fair, a lesson I learned from my mother and one that I want to pass on to my two sons, who are twelve and fourteen and play football and lacrosse. In water polo, for example, there's a lot of dirty stuff that happens under the water that the refs can't see. Some of it is just because you're fighting over the ball, but some of it is dirty on purpose. There's scratching with the toes and wrapping your feet around other players. I know that a lot of people say, "Well, that's just the way it is," but in fact it's not fair to do that. It's dirty. If you win, you want to win fair and square, not because you cheated. Playing fair is a critical element to real success, since not playing fair negates any win. I think being a woman in a man's world has, ironically, given me more latitude than men have, allowing me to write some of my own rules which allow me to play fair regardless of what the rules are for men.

JACK WELCH

I learned a lot on the playgrounds. I learned that the team that fields the best players wins, and that has stayed with me all my life. Throughout my career, I'd get the highest-quality players, get the best team, build it, make them excited about winning, and rally them around a cause. That's what managing is all about.

Jack Welch is head of Jack Welch LLC, where he serves as special partner with the private equity firm Clayton, Dubilier & Rice. He served as chairman and CEO of General Electric Company from 1981 to 2001. He received his B.S. degree in engineering from the University of Massachusetts and an M.S. and Ph.D. in chemical engineering from the University of Illinois.

Facing Reality

I GIVE MY MOM MOST of the credit for teaching me how to compete, how to win, lose, and be a leader. I was a lucky guy to have a mom like Grace Welch. She wasn't active in sports. She was active in competition. When I was in the first grade, I started playing gin rummy with her. She'd beat me most of the time. I took it very badly, but I would rush home to play again the next day. She instilled competitiveness in me, because she would rub it in when she won. The games meant a lot to me. Even back then, winning felt good. Competing felt good, whether it was on the baseball diamond, the hockey rink, the golf course, or later, in business.

Salem, Massachusetts, where I grew up, was scrappy and competitive. All of my friends were jocks and we organized our own neighborhood baseball, basketball, football, and hockey games. Beginning as early as primary school, we had intense rivalries in every sport with schools from various neighborhoods in the city. I was the quarterback on Pickering Grammar School football team, and we won the championship. Although I was pathetically slow, I had a pretty good arm and a couple of quick teammates. I also pitched on the baseball team.

Once I got to Salem High School, I was too slow for football, and my pitching skills didn't improve. I went from being a starting pitcher as a freshman to the bench as a senior. But I was an okay hockey player. I captained the team and was the leading scorer. And I learned to take defeat in stride my senior year, thanks to my mother. We started off the season with three straight wins, but then lost the next six straight, five by just one goal. We really wanted to win our last game against our archrival, Beverly High. I scored two goals and the game went into overtime at 2–2. Almost immediately, Beverly scored the winning goal. I was frustrated and threw my hockey stick across the ice. I skated after it, then skated into the locker room. My teammates were already there, taking off their skates and uniform. Suddenly the door flew open and in strode my mother, wearing a floral dress. No one said anything. Every eye was focused on this middle-aged woman. She marched toward me and grabbed me by the top of my uniform. "You punk!" she shouted in my face. "If you don't know how to lose, you'll never know how to win. If you don't know this, you shouldn't be playing."

It was very embarrassing. But it taught me a good lesson. You've got to be a good loser. You got to want to win. You've got to be a killer winner but you've got to accept losing. Pretty much from that point on I was a fierce competitor all my life. But I never held grudges. I didn't keep revenge as a lasting goal. I was able to try and do better the next time without holding a grudge from the last time.

My mother taught me everything I needed to succeed. She would always stack me up against other people. "Look at them over there. They're not wimping out. They're studying hard. They're doing it." She would always have a paper tiger set up, a straw man, so I'd compete with myself. I guess I was like a trained seal. If I had to single out the one quality she taught me that mattered most, it's self-confidence. I played basketball, but I was short. I didn't recognize I was short until I saw a picture later in life. I was almost three-quarters the size of some of the other players, yet I never felt it. That's a testament to my mother, who convinced me that I could be anyone I wanted to be. It was really up to me. "You just have to go for it," she would say. I have a speech impediment, so giving speeches was always initially quite difficult. But it all went away with practice. When I was growing up, my mother told me I stuttered because I was so smart. She used to say, "Your brain works so fast, your tongue can't keep up with it." I tell kids that when I see them now. I have counseled kids of friends of mine who stutter, and I try to get them to think like that, or be comfortable in their own shoes. That's confidence, the quality I've looked for and tried to build in every executive who has ever worked with me.

When I was young, my dreams were clearly to be a Major League pitcher or a great hockey player. Besides being captain of the hockey team, I was also captain of the golf team. I pretty much taught myself the game of golf and had started playing at the age of nine with other older caddies at Kernwood Country Club in Salem. In those days we didn't think about how captains led. It was just a nice honor. I was a very good hockey player in my younger years. Not only was I captain of the hockey team, I was also an All-Star in the North Shore League. In college I played as a freshman and part-time as a sophomore, but I ran out of gas and never got good enough. I wasn't a natural. Nothing is worse than being pretty good. The game is over and you have got to get on with something else. But facing reality has always been a pretty good strength of mine, and it served me well when I took over as chairman and CEO of General Electric in 1981.

I've often used a story about the success of GE's nuclear division to pound home the need for a reality check. As I wrote in my book, *Jack: Straight from the Gut*, when I became CEO, I inherited a lot of great things, but facing reality was not one of the company's strong points. GE's nuclear business suffered a thirteen-million-dollar loss in 1980 and hadn't received a new order for a nuclear reactor following the Three Mile Island reactor accident in Pennsylvania in 1979. In the spring of 1981, I visited the division in San Jose, California, and was presented a rosy plan—which assumed three new orders for nuclear reactors a year—by the leadership team. I essentially threw a bucket of cold water on their dreams when I interrupted to say they'd never get another order for a nuclear reactor in the United States. I asked them to redo the plan on that assumption and to concentrate on selling fuel and nuclear services to the installed base. GE had seventy-two active reactors in service. By the summer, the team pleaded to put one or two more reactors in the plan instead of three, but I refused to budge. By the fall, there was a new plan ready to be implemented. Nuclear's overall net earnings grew from $14 million in 1981 to $78 million in 1982, and to $116 million in 1983. It's not easy getting people to see a situation for what it is and not for what it was or what they hoped it would be. "Don't kid yourself. It is the way it is," my mother used to say. And that's the way it was for me with sports growing up as well.

Despite not being a natural, I learned a lot on the playgrounds. I learned that the team that fields the best players wins, and that has stayed with me all my life. Throughout my career, I'd get the highest-quality players, get the best team, build it, make them excited about winning, and rally them around a cause. That's what managing is all about. And it's what it is on the playground. You toss the bat up. You put your hand on the bat, and you get the first pick and then the next guy gets the next pick and back and forth until you field the team. That's the purest form of differentiation, because everybody is betting on talent.

We started up a new business when I was at GE. I was the first employee. We hired the next employee and then the next employee. We built a team. We worked countless hours and we had this camaraderie. We built a business from the first dollar to a ten-billion-dollar success, and it was all about the same thing: hiring good people. When they weren't any good, we asked them to move on, the same way a team does. I see a good business so much like a great athletic team.

When I hired people, I didn't go after former athletes. If they played sports, if they liked sports, if they showed competitiveness that was always a big plus. But I wasn't particularly looking for great jocks or an applicant's credentials as a starting lineman or defensive end. How good they were didn't do anything for me. But how intense they were about doing it meant a lot. For example, I once hired a German mechanic, Horst W. Oberst, whom I met when the engine on my Volkswagen blew on the New Jersey Turnpike. I was towed to a local garage, where Horst impressed me with his gutsy determination to fix my car. I offered him a job at GE Plastics, he started a week later, and spent thirty-five years at the company, receiving several promotions along the way.

The greatest thing I learned from playing sports was differentiation in terms of picking teams, putting teams together, celebrating success, weeding out the good from the weak, taking care of your teammate, being candid with your teammate. Many times when I was playing, if a teammate didn't pass to me when I was free, I'd go up to him and say, "Open your eyes. I was clear." You have very direct conversations with teammates, particularly in hockey, because the game is fast. Somebody misses you when you're breaking away and clear and they're holding on to the puck. "Come on. Let it go!" you tell them. Just the speed in which you reflect how you feel is another part of this whole thing. Just like it helped to give and receive immediate feedback to my teammates, it's the same in business. At GE, I was known for my candor and never hid my thoughts or feelings during discussions. A couple of my favorite sayings were "My six-year-old kid could do better than that!" or "Don't Walter Cronkite me!" which everyone understood to mean: You report the bad news but you don't tell me how you're going to fix it.

Even when I was well into my thirties, I played hockey in a town pickup league in Pittsfield, Massachusetts. My friends and I had "life and death" golf and paddle-tennis games at the Pittsfield Country Club. I displayed that same competitiveness in the boardroom. Maybe some people thought I was too competitive. Did my competitiveness hurt me in the business world? You could probably find enough good people who think that. I hated to lose. I still don't like losing, though I know how to lose. And that's a big difference.

SUE WELLINGTON

The biggest thing I learned from sports that helped me in business was how to imagine a goal that wasn't a direct line from where I was starting out. In any sport you have to say, "Eventually I'm going to operate so much more differently and better, I can't even imagine how I'm going to get there." But it's essential to have the kind of imagination and perseverance so you can imagine yourself or your company as a much better athlete or a much better business and then march toward that goal, rather than say, "Well, we're just going to get a little better every year."

Sue Wellington served as president of Gatorade from 1998 to 2002, after rising through the corporate ranks at Quaker Oats, then the parent company. The former all-American swimmer and team captain at Yale grew up in Hampden, Massachusetts.

Imagination and Perseverance

WHEN I WAS GROWING UP, my mom and dad always had little games going on all the time. Memorial Day at my house was very competitive. Whether it was an egg toss or a three-legged race, you would pretty much dive over the finish line to win. My dad totally encouraged it. I have seen him, well past sixty, dive across the finish line in a three-legged race and come up with mud in his glasses. He's this little guy, five-foot-nine, and not particularly athletically endowed. But play him in a game of hearts and he's going to beat you. My mom, too. We even ate competitively. My parents are more competitive than athletic. My mom didn't have many opportunities, either. But she played basketball in high school, and she was the state archery champion in the state of New Hampshire. I think if gymnastics presented itself, my dad would have done it. But he was a college cheerleader.

I'm sure I started playing sports right out of the womb, and I started playing *organized* sports as soon as I could. This was before Title IX, a gender-equity law passed in 1972, so there wasn't much organized opportunity to play. Everybody I knew took swimming lessons from the time they were four. I swam my first race at seven and a half or eight at a small meet at the Hampden Recreational Pool in Massachusetts. I won a trophy, which was really exciting. I remember holding the trophy. At seven, I was already competitive. After I got a little taste of what it was like to have a trophy in my hand, I went at it. By the time I was eleven I was swimming twice a day, and pretty much kept doing it until I graduated from Yale, where I also played softball on the side. But I was a swimmer.

I wanted to swim for Coach Frank Keefe at Yale because he was accomplished. He coached eleven Olympic swimmers before he went to Yale. You can't have sent that many kids to Nationals and international competition without knowing what you're doing. He coached the men's team at Yale and I stayed a summer in New Haven, Connecticut, and swam in his AAU (Amateur Athletic Union) program. I made an argument to the university's administration to combine the men's and women's programs so we could swim for one great coach. It was political and difficult, and it took courage and leadership on my part and his part. But that didn't stop me. I was his captain for the women's team.

Once he was coaching both teams, men and women were together in the same lanes, which was tricky. I had several males in front of me in the breaststroke lane, or if I was in the individual medley lane I had several male swimmers in front of me. Practice was geared around the top twentieth percentile. I was an accomplished female swimmer but it was grueling in the back of the pack. But it always makes you a better swimmer to have somebody faster in front of you, because it pushes someone as competitive as me.

Coach Keefe was grumpy if you didn't achieve what he knew you could achieve; and when he got grumpy you got out of the way. He's big and gruff. When you're exhausted and come off a flip turn, you reach over and pull on a lane line. If he saw that, he'd throw a kickboard at me from forty yards away. He had great aim. Wendy Boglioli, our assistant coach my sophomore and junior year in college, was a national record holder. She was much more carrot than stick. She had a little two-year-old on the pool deck all the time. She wasn't much older than I was. I watched how she balanced and integrated work and life together.

Coach Keefe, who was an assistant on the U.S. team at the 1984 Olympics, is the one I stay in contact with. I was honored with the NCAA Silver Anniversary Award in 2006, and he's the one I wanted to give it to me. I would be there for him, too. In 2002 I handed him the trophy that is now in his name for the women's Ivy League swimming championship. He's meant a great deal to me, but more in terms of leadership and how I think than necessarily swimming. He's retiring at the end of the 2010 season. We're not in daily contact, but when we are in contact we laugh our heads off. Once I got into a position at Gatorade where I could do some things, I invited him to a Super Bowl and a Chicago Bulls championship game. We had a lot of fun interacting as adults instead of a kid and a coach.

My parents were into my swimming. They religiously attended all of my meets. I found it very comforting to have them there. I saw a lot of parents really drive their kids crazy, and drive their kids out of the sport. What I loved about having my parents there is they knew what was going on, so they didn't say, "Oh, good race," when I knew it wasn't. We were in it together.

While I swam, as long as I was consistently improving my time, I was pleased. When I went through a long period of time—it might be six months, it might be a year and a half—where I couldn't knock any time off, I didn't feel very good. But if I was improving my time, even if that meant coming in second and third, that was fine. I wanted to win, but I also wanted to keep improving.

There were two times that I considered quitting swimming. I wasn't motivated, because I wasn't improving. When I was a sophomore at Minnechaug Regional High School in Wilbraham, Massachusetts, I was trying, as I recall, to get under 1:10 in the 100 breaststroke and it was a long time in the making. And then in college

I wasn't getting better, I was even falling back a little bit for a while even though I was putting in the effort. But my parents always had this rule, and I've never figured out whether or not it's a good one or a bad one, which is: if you start a season in a sport you have to end the season. Or if you start a commitment you have to end that commitment. And then after that season, if you want to get out of it you can. Yet swimming seasons were very long, and one rolled right into the next one. I stuck with it through that season in college when my time wasn't improving. It was a hard thing to walk away from, and in the end I'm glad I didn't, because I ended up swimming faster in my senior year in college than I did my whole life and had a lot of fun doing it.

With swimming you're in the pool an outrageous number of hours, twenty-four a week, and you've got to want to be there. At Yale we started practice at six-thirty in the morning. I missed out on a lot, especially over Thanksgiving, Christmas, and spring breaks. That's when you reflect and say, "Wait a minute. My friends are doing something fun and I've got to train." But all the benefits were worth it. I don't know if I thought they were worth it at that moment, but at the end of the season they were, and certainly they were long term.

The sports connection is how I ended up at Gatorade. I was a math-econ major my senior year and started to think about what the heck was I going to do. Procter & Gamble wrote to the captains of teams and explained this thing called "brand management." I thought it sounded great. You could get your hands in a little bit of everything and be creative but analytical. Marketing sounded like it was right up my alley. I was kind of an extroverted geek. I didn't want to be some mathematician somewhere. I wanted to make some fun, big things happen. Brand management at Quaker Oats, which came to campus, seemed to be a perfect match for me.

I started marketing Celeste Pizza. What a great opportunity—to sell frozen pizza to the masses. I learned a lot about how you make, market, sell, price, promote, create, and lead a business, even though

I was twenty-two. I went from there to our snacks business, granola bars. And then at twenty-five I was given the greatest opportunity in the world. We owned Gatorade for a short period of time after buying it for $120 million in 1983, and I had worked for the guy who integrated the Gatorade business into Quaker. He asked me if I'd come be the marketing manager. I was twenty-five and said "Yes!" I thought I had just died and gone to heaven.

I remember putting together my first marketing plan for Gatorade. I went in to explain how much we were going to grow the next year so I could build a budget. I said we were going to grow by twenty percent. The business had grown by approximately three percent the year before, and Sandy Posa, the marketing head, laughed at me, while encouraging and challenging me. We grew by fifty-four percent that year and then just kept growing. When I got the keys to the car, we were probably quarter of a billion in sales revenue. I had the great opportunity to lead it to over two and a half billion dollars. "Grow, baby, grow" was one of our mantras. We just had a blast. It was really a great group of very driven people who knew about teams.

Swimming is an individual sport. Later in business I had to figure out how different individuals were motivated in order to establish a team goal. It was about understanding where everybody was coming from, that they weren't all equal, they weren't all motivated in the same way. I think people who worked with me on the Gatorade account would say that I set the bar really high and when they got anywhere near it I moved it—and that we set goals that were kind of hard to imagine at the time.

There was a lot of mutual respect. There was a lot of pushing each other. There was a lot of encouraged invention and there was a lot of respect for who we were marketing to. We always talked of "the athlete," and if anybody tried to bring an idea forward that wasn't about being an athlete, then we were going to reject it because we had this idea that if you really, really knew who you were marketing to, it would become a pretty big club. It wouldn't just include athletes, but you better understand who was right at the bull's eye.

I worked with a lot of different folks across the business who, like me, had come from sports backgrounds, and then others for whom if a bead of sweat dripped onto them, they'd wipe it off and go "eeew," a couple of real girly-girls. But by studying who we were going after, they got it. I remember that every Wednesday morning we had a big group meeting to talk about how we were going to pound our competition, and before we got started, we had a sports quiz. Somebody wrote it each week and tried to stump the group. I had ladies who while getting their hair and nails done would read the sports page and the box scores. We had a culture that was certainly athletic, even though everyone there hadn't been an athlete. We had fun at the off sites, where we all were competitive. There was always a little contest of some sort going on, and that continues with my kids. I can put a friendly wager on anything.

The biggest thing I learned from sports that helped me in business was how to imagine a goal that wasn't a direct line from where I was starting out. In any sport you have to say, *"Eventually* I'm going to operate so much more differently and better, I can't even imagine how I'm going to get there." But it's essential to have the kind of imagination and perseverance so you can imagine yourself or your company as a much better athlete, or a much better business, and then march toward that goal, rather than say, "Well, we're just going to get a little better every year." At Gatorade, we were imagining very big things and then achieving them, and then imagining even bigger things. It's about big, bold, goal-setting perseverance. And the spirit of teamwork—if you're not all pulling the oar in the same direction, you just can't get there. And that's pretty complicated stuff in business. In a sport the idea of a team is complicated, but in business it's incredibly complicated to try to figure out how to get everybody headed in the same direction.

One of the similarities between business and sports is it ain't all about you. I was in an incredibly individual sport, but if we didn't achieve as a team we couldn't put a relay in at Nationals. We couldn't put points on the board. I came into business thinking that I wanted to work with others to make something crank. I didn't want to be a mathematician who did something individually. In swimming in particular it's tricky because you're in the pool alone and everybody has different personalities and there's not as much time and opportunity to create a team. But I think we did it beautifully at Gatorade.

Hell, no, I didn't achieve everything in business I wanted to. That's totally contrary to the idea that you can imagine getting better. We could have done a lot more with Gatorade. I could have been a better swimmer. I could have been a better leader, a better team member. I don't feel especially accomplished. I think most athletes think that way.

Without sports I don't think I would have been a leader in business. I don't think I necessarily would have even been in business. I don't think I would have met my husband. I don't think I would have gone to college where I went. Almost every lesson I can think of comes from my sports background. You're a lot of things. You're a mom. You're a sister. You're a daughter. You're a leader. You're a businesswoman. I'm those things, but I was an athlete, and that's the one that stays with me even at fifty.

MEG WHITMAN

No individual is as important as the team, which was a valuable lesson later on in business. It's not about the individuals. It's about the team play. It's about the nature of the team you construct. The other thing I learned is this: on teams it matters that you play your position. If you are defense, you need to play defense. If you are right wing, you need to play right wing. And in business the same thing is true. If you assemble the right team and everyone plays their position, then things work a whole lot better. . . . And then— here's the key—you have to trust that the other people are going to play their position or, said another way, do their job.

Meg Whitman is a candidate for governor of California in the 2010 gubernatorial election. She retired as president and CEO of eBay, Inc., in March 2008 after a decade with the company. She served as Massachusetts governor Mitt Romney's national finance co-chair during the 2008 presidential primary campaign season, then national co-chair for the John McCain–Sarah Palin ticket in 2008. She was born and raised on Long Island, New York.

Play Your Position

WHEN IT COMES TO BEING competitive, I would say I'm in the top one percent. I think I was born that way. A lot of personality traits are in your DNA. I swam competitively from age five on. At school I played field hockey, basketball, softball, soccer, lacrosse, and tennis. Whatever sport they offered at school, I played it. I learned how to figure skate, too. I loved every minute of playing sports. It was a huge part of my growing up.

I loved competing and the camaraderie of the team. I loved traveling to the swim meets and the social interaction before and after the meets. And I loved the training. I liked going to swim practice. For many years I had swim practice from six to eight in the morning before school, and then again from four to six in the afternoon.

My middle school and high school swim coach at Cold Spring Harbor High School was Frank Ranhofer. He was a prince of a guy. He was also the math teacher and he used to help us with our math homework as we were traveling around to the meets. He was low key and very soft-spoken, but we all respected him tremendously. I think we liked him so much because he took the time to explain why in the world we were doing what we were doing. He'd say, "You're now going to do ten sets of fifty-yard sprints. We've got a sprint meet coming up in three weeks and this is going to help you."

The other swim coach who had a big effect on me was Danny Kong. He was my AAU, or Amateur Athletic Union, coach, so I knew him very well from seventh grade to twelfth grade. He was very motivational and drove us hard. "Okay, kids, I know you're about to keel over here, but you are now going to do another eight hundred yards," he'd say, and we appreciated him for that.

By the time I got to Princeton I wasn't good enough to make the varsity tennis team. I didn't make the JV tennis team. So, I asked myself, "What's the closest thing to tennis? Ah, squash!" If you played tennis you could pick up squash a lot easier than if you'd never played any racquet sport. I played first on JV, then on the varsity squash team. We played all over New England, and it was a ball. The coach was a woman named Betty Howe, who was terrific with the girls and smart and fun. Then I played lacrosse, which I had played and liked in high school. My mother, Margaret Whitman, also played lacrosse. She went to an all-girls private school in Boston named Winsor School, and Winsor, way back in the '30s and '40s, was encouraging all the girls who played basketball to play lacrosse. My mother swam, played tennis, played lacrosse, and played basketball, and in the 1930s there weren't a lot of women playing sports.

My mother and father were very clear that you needed to do your very best, whatever you were going to do. And that was true not only of sports but of academics as well. There was a very high expectation in my house that you would work up to your potential. The outcome was not as important as giving it your all.

My mother had a special bookcase built for my ribbons and trophies, the biggest number of which were probably from my swimming career. It was smart of my mother to create this little trophy case, because it was in my room and every day I could look at the different medals and ribbons. On some subtle level it was quite motivational. I don't remember going in there every day and ogling them, but I do remember thinking that the display was really nice and I drew strength from it.

From playing team sports I learned a lot of lessons. Probably the first lesson is this: no individual is as important as the team, which was a valuable lesson later on in business. It's not about individuals. It's about the team play. It's about the nature of the team you construct.

The other thing I learned is: on teams it matters that you play your position. If you are defense, you need to play defense. If you are right wing, you need to play right wing. And in business the same thing is true. If you assemble the right team and everyone plays their position, then things work a whole lot better. You not only have to know what your position is, but you also have to know what everyone else's position is. And then—here's the key—you have to trust that the other people are going to play their position, or said another way, do their job. I learned that in team sports. Because if you were playing defense and you didn't trust that your right wing was going to take the ball when you kicked it to them in soccer, or threw it to them in lacrosse, then you might try to run too far with it. So trusting your teammate to do what they are supposed to do was a very, very good lesson that has served me incredibly well in business. All those years in team sports I assumed that my teammates were actually going to do what they said they were going to do, and that they were going to do it well. Giving others the benefit of the doubt is built into how I think about things. I trust that my colleagues are going to do their job and do it to the best of their ability.

One other thing I learned that has stood me in really good stead is time management. A lot of people say, "Well, I don't have a block of an hour. I can't actually get started." But when you're playing sports you have to be really efficient. You have a lot of homework to get done and you've got to go to practice and you've got to sleep. Particularly when I was doing two-a-day swim practices, I had to get to bed by ten o'clock so I could get up at five or six to get to swim practice. I got very good at making use of ten minutes here and twenty minutes here. This is such a good thing to learn—how to use fifteen minutes to move the ball down the field, if you will—to get something done. I learned that lesson growing up, playing all these sports, because if I didn't use the fifteen minutes between activity A and activity B, four times a day, then I had wasted an hour.

I think sports can give little girls confidence. When you're five to eight years old, you don't know whether you're swimming in a little summer club or you're swimming in the Olympics. It's all the same. Even though I was a big fish in a tiny pond, the confidence competing instilled in me—that I could win, that hard work did pay off, that effort had a pretty direct correlation to results—was a very important lesson for me. And so as a little girl I gained a lot of confidence through sports. I think it's very important for everyone, but it's particularly important for women, because I draw on that inner strength and that confidence that I learned early on playing sports in everything I've done since.

If I'm giving a speech or I'm about to do something that seems pretty risky, like going to eBay, I have a certain sense of "I can probably figure this out." That was learned early on and it was learned on the playing field and in the swimming pool. Before eBay, I was the head of Hasbro's Playskool division, which had $600 million in revenue and about 600 employees. At eBay, which had thirty employees and a little over $4 million in revenue, I saw a very rapidly growing company that had tremendous potential. I said to my husband, "I think we should move back to California." He said, "You know what? Why not? This will be really interesting, so let's move and work it out. If the company doesn't make it and you have to go get another job it will be okay." I have always been a little bit of a maverick. Even in the big companies, I liked working on the test-market products or the new things.

I think keeping the harmony of the team in mind is something else I learned from sports. I've applied that to almost all of the teams I worked on, whether it was being a case team manager at Bain & Company, head of marketing at Disney, or the CEO of eBay. High-functioning teams actually get along and have fun together. It doesn't mean that you don't have debates about substantive issues, but the very best teams work well together, and there's a lot of trust, a lot of camaraderie; all for one, one for all. I learned that in sports.

As I've transitioned into politics, I see that campaign teams are sometimes dysfunctional. It is amazing. So one of the things I'm trying to do with my campaign team for governor of California is to build a really cohesive, one for all, all for one team, where we have role clarity. You have to know what position you're supposed to play and that we're going to trust each other to play those positions. We're going to have a strategy and we're going to execute against that strategy regardless of what's happening. That all comes right back to being on successful, winning teams as a high schooler and a college student.

The other thing that is important, when talking about business, is that in my entire career there have always been more men than women in the workplace. When I started at Procter & Gamble there were one hundred of us who entered the entering class as brand assistants, and just a few were women. If you are required to survive and thrive and lead in a largely male environment, having played sports is extremely helpful, because virtually everyone has played sports. So there is a common language, a common understanding. The male locker room is pretty different from the female locker room, but at least there is a basic, shared experience.

I saw this born out in China. I lived there for a summer when I was trying to sort out eBay China. What I was trying to do was to get the Chinese team to work together, which is very challenging because you've got Hong Kong Chinese, Taiwanese, mainland Chinese who've never left, and mainland Chinese who've been educated abroad at places like USC, UCLA, Harvard, Yale, and Princeton. And then you've got Chinese managers who were born in the U.S. and are returning to China. So you've got all these people who are Chinese, but below the surface they are as different as the French and the Americans. I mean, it was a remarkably disparate group.

I was trying to blend all these different perspectives into a cohesive team for eBay China, and the first place I went was to sports analogies. I said to them, "Okay, now listen. Here's the thing we've got to do. We've all got to play our position." And I will never forget this as long as I live—silence. Most of these Chinese managers had never played sports, and they were looking at me quizzically, "Play your position? What are you talking about?" They had never played on teams. That's because most of the Chinese who end up working for big companies in China have been the academic elite. They've been very strong academically, but they rarely played team sports. So it was extremely challenging to get them working as a team when they had no concept of a team.

When I speak to groups of women I'm often asked, "What factors have contributed to your successful career?" I always go right to sports, where I learned so much: camaraderie, fun, the joy of winning and contributing to a cause that is bigger than your own self-interest. I always say to young people: Go play sports. Figure out what you're good at, find out what you have a passion for. Everyone, even little children, can benefit from learning how to kick the soccer ball, hit the baseball, swing a tennis racquet. Even if you're not very good at it, your self-confidence builds as you improve.

Without sports, almost certainly I would not have been the same person I am today. I'm sure there are other venues where one could learn some of these lessons that I learned as an athlete. Music, perhaps. I'm not sure. But I do know sports are a remarkably effective preparation for life!

Acknowledgments

I would like to thank my God Jehovah for the blessing of life and all his undeserved kindness. I would not have achieved anything without His constant direction in my life. I feel so grateful to be able to know you.

To my mom and dad, thank you for giving me your character and helping me mold that into a strong character of my own. You both have helped me to love myself, to have confidence in myself, and to love my life. You showed me how to think for myself and outside of the box. For as long as I can remember, you've showered me with your unwavering belief in me, constant support, and unconditional love. All my dreams have come true because of you two.

To my sister Lynn, you are the best big sister. Your positive nature never ceases to amaze me. Your laugh always brings cheer to my day. Your encouragement after tough losses has fueled me over the years. It means so much that you believe in me. You're one of my favorites—and can borrow my phone anytime.

Isha, you have been a tireless supporter of my career. I don't know how you find the energy to support our family the way you do. You are the most giving person I know. Not only are you my big sister, but you're like a second mom. Thanks for making being a little sister so fun.

Serena, my best friend and doubles partner, I could not have achieved anything great in my career without your inspiration. You showed me how to have heart on the court, and because of you, my heart grew larger during matches. When I'm around you, life is the best.

My auntie Ruth Alexander, receiving your e-mails following a win or loss always brings brightness to my day. Thank you for the support and love.

I thank my agent, Carlos Fleming, who really brought this idea to life and found the perfect publisher and writer for this project. This collection of inspirational experiences would never have existed without you. Dawn Davis, the vice president and editorial director at Amistad, you have worked so hard on this project and believed in the concept from the start. I have enjoyed this journey. Thank you for making all possible. Kelly E. Carter, my co-author, you really brought the words to life. Thank you for all the help in preparing for the interviews and brainstorming a varied list of contributors with me. You are the best writer, and I am so grateful that you accepted working with me on this book.

To all my contributors, I have been so inspired by your stories. I wasted no time incorporating your beliefs and sayings into the fabric of my life on the court and with each new endeavor upon which I embark. I have learned so much from your life experiences and am forever grateful for your participation.

Keven Davis, I am not amiss when I say that you are the most exceptional lawyer, period. Thank you for your contributions on this project and helping making it a go.

Larry Bailey, my accountant, you are like my second dad. Thank you for all the advice over the years. It's great working with you and having you in my life as my friend.

A big thank-you to my fans and supporters. Though I will never meet many of you, I want you to know how much I have cherished your support throughout the years. It is my hope you get to know me better by the values represented in this book. The principles and lessons in this book are my gift back to you. May they make your life better, as they have mine.

Index of Sports and Contributors

VENUS WILLIAMS became a professional tennis player at age fourteen, beating the player ranked number fifty in the world in her first match. The first African American to reach number one as a professional in either the men's or women's game, Williams continues to appear at the very top of the professional rankings. In addition, she graduated cum laude with a degree in fashion design from the Art Institute of Fort Lauderdale and went on to partner with national retail chain Steve & Barry's to launch her athletic and casual clothing line. A multiple Grand Slam singles champion and a three-time Olympic gold medalist, Williams resides in Palm Beach Gardens, Florida.

Co-author KELLY E. CARTER is a former sportswriter at *USA Today*, the *Dallas Morning News*, *Orange County Register*, and other newspapers. She segued into entertainment reporting with a correspondent position at *People* before adding travel and food writing to her repertoire. A contributing editor at *Elite Traveler* and a freelance writer, she currently writes about lifestyles, celebrities, and business, and appears regularly on the Travel Channel. She lives in her native Los Angeles.